VOICES FROM THE FOREST

The True Story of
Abram and Julia Bobrow

By

Stephen Paper

ISBN: 1-4033-5559-2 (e-book)
ISBN: 1-4033-5560-6 (Paperback)
ISBN: 1-4033-5561-4 (Dust Jacket)

This book is printed on acid free paper.

1stBooks - rev. 8/12/03

I dedicate this book to Julia and Abram, whose experiences in this dark period of human history cannot begin to be fathomed by those of us who did not live through those times. This book is also dedicated to those many partisans who fell in unmarked graves and to those few who survived.

First, I would like to thank Leon and Shirley Markus for their outstanding work in translating the original tapes made by Abram Bobrow from Yiddish to English. I would also like to give special thanks to my brothers, Richard and Thomas and four friends who served as fine editors and sounding boards: Ann Fisher, Dahlia Greer, Gerald Paul Lewis, and Lisa Winter; Scott Pitters for his expert drawing of the map and Hedy Kamienowicz and Samy's Camera for their invaluable help with the pictures.

And finally, I would like to thank my parents, Bernice and Charles for their many years of encouragement.

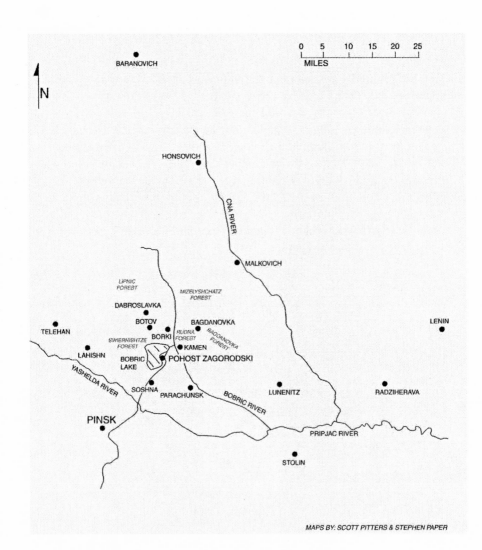

MAPS BY: SCOTT PITTERS & STEPHEN PAPER

MAPS BY: SCOTT PITTERS & STEPHEN PAPER

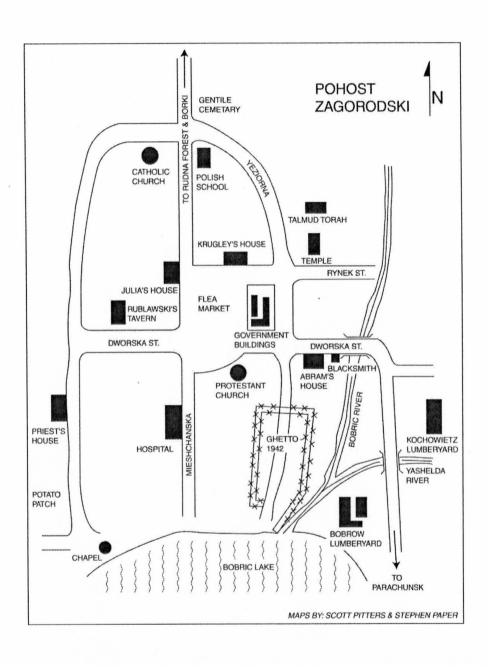

PROLOGUE

I remember it was a very hot sultry day, and humid, rare for a desert area of Southern California. The kind of sticky day when you shower, towel off, and in five minutes you want to shower again. When your most fervent wish is for a large oak tree near the local swimming hole, and a rope dangling from an outer limb that you can use to swing out into the water like a character out of an Edgar Rice Burroughs' novel. That day my shirt clung to my skin until I tore it off and went bare-chested. After being ridiculed by my brother for being so scrawny, I begged my father to hold a hose up so we could run through it back and forth on the grass in the front yard. He turned on the water and showed us how he held his fingers just so over the nozzle to create a wide spray of water. We jumped and did cartwheels and somersaults through the cooling fountain until he had to go back to work and then Bill and I took turns spraying each other. Kids from the neighborhood drifted into our yard and were soon laughing and playing in our sprinkler. It was a nice break from our chores on the chicken farm. Or perhaps I should say it was a nice break for my brother. Papa always maintained that he didn't get a lot of work out of me.

Papa went into the backyard. On a day like today, he had to make sure the chickens got plenty of water.

Later, Papa came back, took off his shirt and laughed and said it was about time we did some work and now it was his turn to run through the water. Getting up a head of steam, he ran and slid so gracefully on the wet grass, he was like a professional skater. I was so proud of him at that moment.

I remember sleeping with my door open that night and only using a single sheet pulled up to my waist. Still it was hard to fall asleep, and finally dozing off, hard to stay there.

A boy of ten, an innocent, I was soon to leave that innocence forever.

I guess that was the first time I kept my door open at night. I had never been one to be afraid of the dark and I liked my privacy, and usually slept with the door closed, but it was just too hot. For what seemed like long stretches I lay awake that night. Even with the door open, the air hung so heavy over my face, I wished I could shove it away with my hands. There was nothing to do but change positions to find a cooler part of the bed, and this done, to stare at the ceiling and pray that this weather would change soon. Then I fell asleep, woke and repeated the search for a cool place all over again.

It was after one of these moves that I heard it. It was unsettling. At first it sounded as though someone was weeping. Very quietly weeping. Then something went thud on the ground. Now I was concentrating, trying to hear. Next came a scream and I started, sitting up. I was scared. What could this be? Slowly, I got up out of bed and tiptoed to the doorway.

I could hear my father's voice, at least the half-crying, half-strained, sounds were somewhat close to the timber of his familiar voice. But these sounds were so anguished, so hopeless and forlorn that I was not entirely sure.

"If only we'd got there sooner," he cried. "Only a few hours sooner!"

I edged toward the living room. I could see him. I thought he must be awake. He turned over and pounded the couch with his fists until his hands were red. Then he started crying. Again, in a voice that was tormented beyond my ability to understand, he yelled, "Why? Only a few hours. Was that so much to ask?" Some of his words were in English, some in Yiddish, which I understood, and some in a language that was foreign to me. He turned over on his back and I could see that he was not awake. His eyes were closed, tears running down his cheeks. With a violent motion his right arm struck the backrest of the couch, causing a pillow to fly up and come down on the carpeted floor. I noticed a red streak across his forehead and wondered if he had hit himself.

"If we'd only got there sooner. Oh God, what have they done?" he said softly.

I realized he was having a nightmare, but I was very confused. How could he be having a nightmare? Kids have nightmares, not adults. Adults know things. They are not afraid. They are big and strong, especially my father. How many times I've seen him in the backyard with his homemade gym doing exercises on the parallel bars, swinging up and over a high bar, or doing pushups and pull-ups. I often tried to rub my arms to make the veins appear the same way they did on his arms. Mama said he played professional soccer in Europe and was an expert ice skater. He was the strongest man I'd ever seen. And wise. He always had an answer for me no matter what the problem, and he would always answer with a sort of mischievous twinkle in his eye as if he knew he could always make it all right. One other thing struck me as I watched him twist and turn and his arms flail out as if to hit someone or something—I had never seen him lift his hand in anger. I had never seen him mad. Or frightened? What a joke. Nothing ever frightened him. And if something did, like now in his dream, where did that leave me, and Mama and Bill?

I suppose all children see their fathers as heroes and I was certainly no different. I couldn't bear to see him like this. I had to wake him, to help him, to reassure myself that he was still powerful and unafraid, but what was I to say?

I moved closer, to the head of the couch. Now I was trembling, perhaps afraid of what I would find.

He turned over again.

"Papa," I said, but the word was too quiet and hard to get out, my mouth was so dry. Clearing my throat I tried again. "Papa. Wake up. Are you all right?" Now louder, "Papa."

He stopped moving. His eyes opened. His shirt was soaked in sweat. He looked confused. I am certain that for a moment he did not know where he was.

Then he reached out and put a hand on my shoulder.

"Jerry," he said in that soothing voice of his, as though it was me having the nightmare. "What are you doing up so late? What time is it?"

"I heard you, Papa. I couldn't sleep and I heard you and I was scared."

"It's all right, Jerry. Come here."

He sat up and hugged me. "Just a little bad dream. Nothing to worry about."

"Why are you on the couch? Why aren't you with Mama? Is anything wrong?"

"No, my boy. Nothing." The silence that then ensued is something I will remember all my life. He was staring at me with this kindness in his eyes, but it was mixed with a sadness that seemed to reach down so far, it must have emanated from his very soul. I could see he was thinking about me and trying hard to decide whether I was ready to hear, old enough even. Somehow it seemed as though he wanted to protect me from whatever it was that haunted him.

What was so hard to tell? Was he a thief? A criminal? Worse, was he not strong, not a hero? I confess that in those moments I suddenly was afraid he would tell me, and what he would tell me. I was ten. What was he worried about? What could I possibly not be old enough to comprehend?

He started to speak, very slowly and softly. "Jerry. I'm out here because I don't want to hurt your mother." I could see that he knew that I was now even more confused.

"I have these dreams, son, and sometimes they are so terrible that I hit things with my fists and my arms go flying all over. If I stay in the bedroom with your mother, I might accidentally hit her." He smiled and brushed my hair back. "Now we wouldn't want that would we? Mama's too sweet for that."

I laughed, but stopped quickly. I still had to know.

"Why are the dreams so bad, Papa. What are they? Does Bill know?"

"A little. He's older, you know."

"Ah, Papa."

He became very serious once more. "Don't be in such a hurry to grow up, Jerry. The story behind the dreams is not an easy story." He paused for a moment to look at me.

"Your mother and I have already discussed when the time would be right to tell you and Bill," he said, looking all the while as if he was weighing it right then and there. "Maybe it's finally time. You're ten now. That's pretty old." He paused again and looked into my eyes so long that I involuntarily lowered my head. Then he gently raised my chin with his hand and spoke softly. "I'll tell you what. I'll speak to your mother tomorrow. If it's okay with her, we'll set up a time, and I'll tell you and Bill the whole story. It will take more than one sitting, perhaps a week, possibly more. But you have to make me a promise first."

"Of course, Papa," I said.

"You have to understand, your mother does not like talking about this, and she has not talked about it for twelve years. She is an amazingly strong woman, and God, what she went through...So there are rules."

I nodded my understanding.

Any questions, you bring to me. If your mother wants to tell you something, she will, but you are never to ask her. Okay?"

"Okay."

"And this story you are about to hear...it will not be easy for you. Do you understand?"

"Yes."

"Not easy at all. You will have to be brave. You must promise me that if it is too frightening, you will ask me to stop. I'm serious, Jerry."

"I understand, Papa."

"Remember. There is one more thing. And this is so you don't get worried about me. This will seem strange to you, but I want you to know. I have had these dreams every night for those same twelve years. Every night."

He looked at me with those kind, blue eyes. I don't think he has ever looked at me with such kind eyes or tired eyes as he did that night. "I'll talk to your mother tomorrow. Now go to bed."

Not able to help myself, now that curiosity had taken hold, I blurted out, "Why did you have to get there sooner? And where? Was it during the war?" I immediately felt guilty for having said anything, but he just calmly asked, "You know about the war?"

"Uh-huh. With the Germans and the Japanese."

"All right. I'll give you an answer tomorrow. Now go to bed."

***

The heat did not abate the next day, but Papa stopped work early and came in for lunch with my mother, and every time Mama made a meal, it was a real feast. Bill and I waited outside until they finished, and then Papa came out to take us for a walk. We meandered toward the back of our three-acre farm through the orange trees up to a line of eucalyptus that marked the border of our property. We walked for a good ten minutes without him saying a word. Then, with a sort of tightening up of his mouth, an expression that often appeared when he was considering a tough problem, and a great exhalation of breath, my father began to speak.

"There have been two moments in my life when I was frightened...more like terrified. That is not to say that I am very brave, it is probably more a testament to my being either stupid, or shortsighted. You both know about the war, so I'm not going to give you a history lesson, and I know you've heard things from your friends at Hebrew school—so many of the farmers around here seem to be survivors. What I'm going to do is tell you about two of the lesser known aspects of the war, at least here in this country; aspects that are no less important for being little known.

"Everything I'm going to tell happened either to me, your mother, or your uncles and grandparents, but everything happened. If I talk about something that I wasn't directly involved in, I'll try to describe it as closely as possible to how someone, your mother for instance, related it to me. Okay? I'm going to start with the first of those moments that took such a terrible toll on me, that almost literally made me sick."

He took another deep breath and it looked as though he was carried back to those troubled times, and he could see everything once more as if it was unfolding before his eyes.

"Remember, if you want me to stop, if you feel frightened or even uncomfortable, it's all right. I don't expect you to feel comfortable. If you don't want to hear anymore, just say so. You boys should know, your mother and I are very proud of you. We won't think any less of you, if you want me to stop the story. Are you ready?"

Bill and I nodded. I was no longer dreading this story and my curiosity was up, but what about it could make a man like my father have nightmares? It was about the war, so I was certain it would be exciting. Nevertheless, something inside me was still apprehensive.

THE FIRST DAY

CHAPTER 1

ABRAM

Bill and I were up early the next morning, and most of the chores were done almost before the sun was up. Papa laughed and said he'd never seen us work so hard. Of course, he was really talking about me—Bill always worked hard. He sent us in for breakfast and we stuffed our mouths and ran back out to him. Then, he started his story.

***

I wouldn't say that we had an idyllic life, but it was good enough. We had a roof over our heads and food on the table. Now this might sound boring or you might think what's the big deal? But later, as you will see, it became very important to us. We had wonderful friends and a big family. And we were all very close. Your mother had over a hundred uncles, aunts, grandparents and cousins in our little village—it was called a *shtetl*.

We lived in the Pale, a part of Russia that was set aside by the Czar for the Jews. Our village, Pohost Zagorodski was under Polish control in 1939, although the area and people were considered Byelorussian or White Russian. If you walked about, you would see that it was small, with only 4500 people, eighty percent of whom were Jewish. There were many wooden buildings and houses, some thatched huts, dirt streets, a busy marketplace and horse and ox-drawn carts.

According to your mother, I was a rather mischievous boy, always getting into trouble or playing like a tough guy, but I only remember the important things: how close I was with my family, how all I wanted to do was follow my father Samuel into the lumber business. I was certain that marriage and children would follow because I always loved the idea of family.

Even at that young age, your mother Julia and I liked each other. In fact, my brother Shlomo and his wife kept teasing us about when we were going to get married. Shlomo was married to your mother's sister, Esther, and boy, did they give it to us. Now that I look back at it, I guess it seems that our lives were laid out for us at an early stage.

When I was young, maybe about your age Bill, I took these things for granted, but all of that changed one day in 1941. For me, that date, July 13th, 1941, will always be the death knell for our people in Europe.

I want to tell you a little about the forests, they were such a large part of my life, even as a child. They were magical—at dawn, with the mist rising up from the ground, they looked like some forbidding netherworld. And they were frightening. There were wolves in those forests, and quicksand.

You could walk for miles without seeing anything but forests of birch, oak and pine trees, so thick in places you could not even squeeze between them, like a jungle. They seemed to go on and on and on forever. When I climbed a tree, wherever I looked, my field of vision consisted of different shades of green, with maybe a small gap here and there for a river or lake.

There were gently slopping fields, also of green and dense forested marshes. And in the fall, when the leaves started to change colors, it was glorious. The pines stayed green, but the others went from bright red to orange to yellow. It was almost as though a rainbow descended on the forests. At that time of year, my brother Shlomo and I loved to run barefoot through the woods and hear the dead leaves crackle under our feet.

In the winter, it was a completely different world. We would skate and play hockey on the frozen rivers and lakes. Everything turned white, from the pines bleached with frost, to the frozen swamps and forests, to the wooden houses in the village with shiny white drifts of snow piling against their walls and clinging to their roofs. To these marshes and swamps and forests, your mother and I owe our lives.

The night of July 12th, 1941, a group of us left our village a few hours after dusk, moving cautiously. A few days earlier, my father called my brothers and I together. He told us to make plans, just in case the worst rumors about the Nazis were true. It was simple—we would meet in the forest and hide out there. I left that night, my father and brothers were supposed to leave early the next morning.

My mother and sister were safe—the Nazis were only taking men over the age of ten. Whether they were going to put the men in a work camp, a ghetto or shoot them, nobody knew.

You have to understand, *we had no idea of the horror of what was going to follow.*

Skirting south of the marketplace to avoid any German patrols, we cut across Yeziorna Street to the immaculately-kept grounds of the Protestant Church.

At nineteen, I was a wiry and athletic boy and the youngest of the five. Ruven Sosnick, one of my best friends, and I led the way, with Ruven's father lagging slightly behind. Two of my cousins, Berel and Hershel Denenberg, closely followed the older man.

"I hope it's not going to get cold tonight," Ruven said. We had taken no food with us and only light jackets to go with our normal summer clothes. We were on the run and we did not have time. It had been a hotter than usual July, but the nights could still be cool.

Staying in the shadows, I peered down Mieshchanska Street across the marketplace into the darkness. It had never seemed so empty.

One by one we crossed the dirt road and gathered behind the brick walls of the hospital. Joseph Sosnick was breathing heavily. A great sadness had settled over his features.

Slowly, I raised my head above the wall. It was still clear. I motioned for the others to follow. We crept between the low wooden cottages of the *shtetl*, some bearing thatched roofs and others with well-kept, wooden tiles. Lights were noticeable in most of the windows, but I could see no one stirring.

The area we had to cover was not great—the village was small with many of the houses crowded in close to the marketplace—but to me, my mind racing with an endless succession of questions and misgivings, it was taking too long. I just wanted it done, over with. I had never felt so unsure of myself.

If we could cross this last street, Dworska, without being noticed, it was clear sailing through the dirt field behind Rublawski's tavern. Then, it was not far to the Gentile cemetery and the vast Rudna Forest beyond, and safety.

The field was utterly dark. We moved silently though the mud, knowing that each one of us was tormented by our individual thoughts. At one point I stopped abruptly.

"This is ridiculous. We're running away. We should go back."

"What do you want to do?" the older Sosnick whispered angrily, cutting me off. "Fight with your hands? I had a rifle. The Russians took it."

I knew Sosnick wasn't angry with me. Sosnick just felt helpless. Like the rest of us. I looked in the old man's eyes. Sosnick's lips were visibly trembling. His normally ruddy cheeks had gone ashen.

I shrugged my shoulders, turned and started walking again. In my whole life I had never run from a fight.

The decision to leave Pohost Zagorodski had not come easily to me. When it was finally made, I had few thoughts of warmth, hunger or anything else. My thoughts were limited to my family, the loved ones still at home. Why didn't they act? Did they not understand the immediacy of the danger? Would they make the decision to escape? I was uncertain whether my brother Shlomo would leave in time or my father would leave at all. It was difficult to think of much else.

4

What of Shlomo? Always happy, always joking, full of the joy of life—and always unhurried Shlomo. How many family members were there? My three brothers, my sister Esther, my parents, grandparents, aunts and uncles. My nieces and nephews. I could not even count how many cousins. And Julia, your mother. Did we warn everybody? I just wanted to stop thinking!

There were two German guards standing beyond the intersection of Mieshchanska and Yeziorna Streets close to the cemetery. Perhaps two hundred yards away. I held up my hand to stop the other men. Then I silently directed them to the Catholic Church where we could hunker down behind the white wooden fence and wait it out. There was a curfew. We had no choice. If we were found outside, we could be shot by the Germans.

The soldiers started walking toward the intersection.

I watched through the slats of the fence as the Germans stopped, lit cigarettes and headed east up Yeziorna Street. I found myself saying a silent prayer: *"Please God, let my brothers hurry Shlomo and Papa along."*

We waited a good ten minutes before we climbed back over the fence, and it took another ten minutes before we reached the outskirts of Pohost Zagorodski, near a collection area for corn and fodder, where the strong smell of old straw permeated the cool night air.

Josef Sosnick broke the silence. "I have to think this over." He walked into the field to a bundle of hay and resolutely sat down.

Before the Soviets overran the eastern half of Poland in 1939, the local peasants had either sold or traded their surplus goods to the townspeople. For the last two years, they were forced to collect their corn and straw for the Russians. The Germans had not been in power long enough to issue their instructions—only two weeks—so the fodder had been left in piles and stacks for that time, although some had been looted by bandits or starving peasants.

The rest of us stopped walking and watched the elder, redheaded man. Ruven, also redheaded and fair-skinned, went to his father's side.

No one said a word. My cousins and I soon followed and sat down in a circle amidst the rotting corn.

We all had the same thoughts. We had made this decision, but not one among us had wanted to leave his family.

***

We had all heard of the German *Einsatzgruppen*, but somehow, none of us had been able to actually grasp the concept of this Nazi killing machine. It just wasn't real yet.

Few of the inhabitants of the *shtetl* were unfamiliar with Nazi Germany's treatment of Jews. But, although refugees and rumors from western Poland had quickly made their way east across the Bug River into the Soviet zone, not all the stories had been believed. How could a sane, rational people believe such tales? At the time, many thought it was just more Soviet propaganda.

But by mid July, there had been warnings that two different *Einsatzgruppen,* killing squads—one from Pinsk that was killing only Jewish men, and another from the west that was killing everyone, men, women and children—were in the area.

It had been quite chilling for me, sitting with my family only the day before—to hear it put so matter-of-factly, as though it was a simple common-sense business proposition: you murder the men, we will murder the men, women and children. That's it. Let's get to work. It could not, by any stretch of the imagination, be true.

I can see you think I'm making this up. Cold blooded murder. I couldn't believe it either.

Early that morning, Ruven and I had gone to the forest to chop kindling for the night's cooking. This was the only way for us to get fuel for the fire in those days. Stripped to the waist, we worked hard, sweat dripping down our backs, as our axes felled four slim birch trees. Next, we hacked the branches from the trunks, and were starting to break them up when a grizzled, sun-baked old man walked up to us. The man was friendly, the sort of man that I had seen countless times doing business with my father at the lumberyard.

He was very excited, as if he could not wait to tell us some good news.

"Boys!" he crowed. "You won't believe this. It's finally happening."

"What?" I asked, leaning on my ax handle. Ruven stopped chopping and wiped his brow, flicking the sweat to the ground.

"The SS units went into Lahishn and Telehan yesterday and cleaned them of Jews."

"What do you mean 'cleaned them of Jews?'" I asked, but in my heart, I was trembling. I clenched the ax handle so hard that I'm sure my knuckles turned white.

The peasant was surprised. "You don't know? They killed a lot of people there. Those villages are *Judenfrei.* The Jews are all gone."

I looked at Ruven, as much in sadness as in anger. From the mouth of this ordinary old man. Somehow his gloating had, for me, distilled the thousands of swirling rumors into a more concrete form of truth. Yet the words *were still* just the mouthings of an uneducated peasant. I don't think you can even begin to understand the enormity of what he said. And though deep down inside there was still some hope, now I had an intuition of a desperate, tragic future. I was truly scared. But this man? I would make

6

certain he would pay for his satisfaction. This would be one person who would get no more pleasure from the destruction of a Jewish town.

I started moving toward the peasant, but Ruven quickly grabbed my arm. "No," he whispered. "We don't have time. There are more important things to worry about."

"What?" asked the man.

"We want to thank you for the information," Ruven said hastily. "You say this happened in Lahishn?"

"And Telehan."

"And they're heading this way?"

"No," the man said, mulling it over. "I think they headed in the opposite direction. Yes. I'm certain of it."

"Abram," Ruven said quietly. "We should return home with the kindling. We have much to do."

I nodded, never taking my eyes off the peasant.

I grabbed a pile of wood in one arm and shouldered my ax. *You will never know how close you came*, I thought as I turned and walked away. I can see that man's face as if he were standing before me right now.

Ruven stared for a second at the old man, then turned and ran to catch up with me.

After walking for a few minutes, I looked to see if the man was still there. He had disappeared down the dirt road.

"You know what this means," I said to Ruven. "The ones from Pinsk. Let's go." We both dropped our bundles of kindling and started running for the village to spread the alarm.

***

How long ago that seemed. Now we sat on the bundles of straw, some wondering if they should move on, others thinking the Rudna was too far away, and that it was better to hide among the piles of straw and corn in the collection area. I knew that we were just making excuses to stay.

Josef Sosnick, his red hair looking so disheveled, was the first to break the silence. He stood up, drawing a long, expansive breath. "This is not right of me. I can't see leaving my family behind and hiding here. Ruven, I just don't see it. You stay with your young friends. I'm going home."

"You can't go back," Ruven said, standing up and grabbing his father's arm. "Please. They'll certainly kill the men. We don't know about the rest."

"I'm sorry, Ruven. I have to go home."

I looked at Ruven. I knew what was coming.

"Then I should go with you," Ruven said, as tears formed in his eyes.

"We all should," I added, also standing up.

7

The Sosnicks had already been refugees for two years. When the Russians marched into eastern Poland, they quickly began to "Sovietize" the population and its institutions. Under the new Soviet regulations, all bourgeois had to move from the cities to the smaller villages. This was in order to keep better watch over them. Sosnick was a wealthy lumberman from Pinsk, thus a bourgeois. In 1941, the Russians sent some of the bourgeoisie to Siberia, ironically saving them from the German onslaught. Josef Sosnick was forced to move his family to Pohost Zagorodski.

"No. This is different," Sosnick said with a moral force that surprised even his son. "No. Ruven. You are already here, safe. And boys, you and your families made the decision for you to leave. I am going back to bring my wife and other children. I left them and that was wrong of me, trusting that the *Einsatzgruppen* would be the one that doesn't harm women and children. How can any one of us put our trust in these barbarians, or in the words of a peasant? What if it's the wrong *Einsatzgruppen*? But you, Ruven, you and your friends are soon to be out of danger. At least if you keep moving to the Rudna."

"But we have families too," I protested.

"Yes. You do. And they will follow you as soon as possible. Was not that the plan?" He looked knowingly into each of our faces. "Yes. If you young boys go back, you simply slow down your family's flight out of danger. Would that be wise?"

I shook my head. I knew that Sosnick was right.

"But Father," Ruven argued, "the chances are this *Einsatzgruppen* is only interested in the men. The other one was moving away from Pohost Zagorodski. You will only put yourself in danger. What if you're caught?"

"I will move quickly. You'll see. I'll bring everybody to the Rudna before morning, if I do not have to waste more time arguing with my son."

"I'm sorry, Father." Ruven sat down heavily.

We all knew he was right about us, but what if he was also right about trusting the *Einsatzgruppen* approaching the village?

"I've made up my mind, and I want you here, safe." Josef Sosnick put his hand on his son's shoulder and squeezed. "If I know you're safe, at least my mind can rest easily. "Do you understand?" Ruven stared at the ground and shook his head. Then Josef Sosnick turned and walked back toward the road to Pohost Zagorodski.

***

At your mother's house on Mieshchanska Street, everything was in turmoil after they received the warning. Only Jeruchim, your mother's

8

father, who you were named after, Jerry, and your mother herself, were able to maintain any semblance of composure.

I had always thought of your mother as a shy, bashful girl. She had light brown hair with a tint of red over her forehead and was very slender and attractive. Though I always admired her, I was quite unprepared for the strength of character she showed under the unimaginable gravity of the situation.

Julia told me how Leah Zipperstein, your grandmother, buried her head on her husband's shoulder that night, overwhelmed with guilt. I had known Julia's family for a long time. Our fathers were partners in the lumber business.

Leah felt guilty because her husband had wanted to get out of Europe in the early '30s. He had made a trip to Cuba and was ready to leave, but Leah couldn't bear the thought of leaving her relatives in Pohost Zagorodski. She had more than a hundred, including her mother and father. She kept saying over and over, "I'm so very sorry. You were right. I'm sorry."

Jeruchim held her tightly and would not have any of her apologies. "You couldn't have known. None of us did. There will be no blame in this family. Now we'll have to make the best of it."

Jeruchim gathered the twins, Sarah and Rachel, and Julia, Avremel, and Esther around the family table. Avremel was about your age, Bill. Twelve years old.

Jeruchim looked intently into the faces of his children, one after another, as if to lend an air of solemnity to his instructions, and told them they would work together.

He wanted them to each gather three or four dresses and a few coats. However much they could wear. They would have to wear the dresses one on top of the other and the coats on top of the dresses. Leah would do the same. He wanted Avremel to gather three pairs of pants and three shirts and two coats. Also sweaters. This done, everyone was to stitch up a bag to carry any other things they might need for a long journey. Only necessities. The bags must be small and most importantly, light.

Avremel protested when his father told Julia to help him make his bag.

Jeruchim shook his head and allowed himself the first smile he'd had since the German army arrived. He told his son to go ahead.

They couldn't carry much water, it was too heavy, and eggs or other perishables were out of the question.

Leah suggested slicing rye bread and drying it out in the oven. That would be easy to carry.

Avremel got excited and exclaimed, "Like Moses and matzo."

Jeruchim then told his wife to find all the *zlotys* she could. This was the name for Polish money. They would sew the *zlotys* into the shirts and dresses or jackets of everyone. Who knew if they might get separated? Everyone should have his or her own money.

Jeruchim wanted everyone to be ready to leave at dawn.

Avremel had no sooner left when he ran back up to his parents, holding a blue sweater with tan elbow patches.

"Can I take this? Julia made it for me," he asked.

"Of course, son," Jeruchim said, smiling. He patted his son on the back and told him to hurry.

Leah now sobbed hoarsely. She imagined the worst—her children in rags, huddled together in some wooden hut in the forest. What if they were caught? What if Avremel was separated? What if her baby was all alone? Her eyes burned with fear.

In a separate room that was a new addition attached to the main house, Esther sat on the bed holding up different articles of clothing as though it mattered which ones she chose. The addition had been built for her and my brother Shlomo, before their wedding. That morning Shlomo told her to stay with her mother. She would be safe there. He would leave at dawn to join his brothers in the forest. Now her father had made a different decision and she was confused. Would they all meet in the Rudna? When would she see Shlomo again? It was all too much for her. She kept staring at the same two dresses, as though paralyzed. Julia had finished quickly and then gone out to the annex. She matter-of-factly grabbed both dresses and a third, as though this was just an everyday occurrence, and soon, Esther was back to normal and getting ready. Julia then went to see 7

Julia told them to do as their father said and everything would be all right. They had to be able to leave by tomorrow. If they did their packing like big girls, everything would be fine.

An hour later, back in the living room, Jeruchim told them it would be very rough, but they would persevere and come through this dreadful time. He promised them.

Julia could not help thinking that she was lucky. Whatever would the people with young children do, or the older people?

***

While all over Pohost Zagorodski people were making their preparations, we four men sat silently, each in his own way mulling over Josef Sosnick's words.

Finally, I had had it. I knew I had to follow through with the plans no matter how painful. I stood up. "No more excuses," I said bitterly. I started moving in a direct line towards the Rudna, now a mile away, across the recently harvested lands of the peasants. The rest got up and followed. Our pace was not quite as brisk as earlier, and it was not long before our pants and shoes were wet from the heavy dew.

I had a sour taste in my mouth. I couldn't even spit. My throat was too dry. No one had thought to bring water. We continued through the muddy fields for an hour. Even though it was a pitch-dark night, I began to recognize the area. I could just make out a small cluster of beech with a few oak trees, beyond which was a farm owned by a man that my family had known for years.

I told the others that I knew this farmer and that he was a good honest man. Everybody's nerves were on edge by this time so I had to reassure them. I led them across a small pasture to a dirt road leading to the farmhouse and went up and knocked on the door.

A rough, gray-bearded man holding a lantern came to the door. He squinted through the dim light and recognized me. His face brightened as he grabbed my hand in both of his big, craggy hands.

"You got away," he said to me. "This is good." I'll never forget how he averted his eyes and spoke in a low voice as if embarrassed to know the reason for our sudden arrival. "I'll do anything I can to help you."

"We need a place to hide," I said, breathing deeply. "Just for the night. We don't want to put you in any danger."

"You can stay in my barn. There's plenty of straw. You can sleep there. The Germans will probably go to the villages first, but you shouldn't stay here long. Once they exterminate those in the villages, they'll come to the farms and the countryside."

So I was right. He was ashamed. Exterminate, I thought, almost reeling. Does everyone know this certainty except us? But I thanked him. Of course I was grateful.

The farmer motioned with his lantern. He lit the way down a dirt path to the barn, and inside he pointed to a ladder we could climb up to the loft. Bidding us goodnight, he walked out of the barn.

As our eyes slowly adjusted to the darkness, we looked around our meager sanctuary. The attic was barren save for three large piles of hay and various tools scattered over the floor. Quietly, we began clearing a space by moving the tools into a corner. Then we each picked up a bundle of hay and spread it over the rough, wooden boards of the attic to make tolerable bedding. Two to three bundles of the hay seemed to suffice for at least some degree of comfort. We were so exhausted, none of us bothered to go for more.

But lying down on the hay, I could not get comfortable. Every little sound startled me, whether it was the slightest creaking movement of a window shutter or the scurrying of a field mouse across the hay. I noticed the others shifting and moving about as well. No one could sleep.

"Abram," Berel Denenberg whispered. "Hershel, Ruven."

"What?" I asked, turning to face my cousin.

"I'm glad I'm not here alone."

"So am I," I said softly. Hershel and Ruven whispered the same.

I shifted around until I found a position that was bearable, lying on my back and staring at the ceiling of the loft. What would the morning bring I wondered? Is it a certainty that tomorrow, German soldiers are coming to kill me and my family? All the men in my village? How could this be? I still couldn't believe it.

***

I guess I drifted in and out of sleep, and it seemed I had hardly fallen asleep when the random sounds of gunfire jerked me awake. I crossed the floor of the hayloft to a small shutter facing the road to the farm. Edging it open, I saw ten to twelve riders on horseback. They were too far away for me to make out, but the gunfire was coming from their direction. I saw them ride toward the village of Borki, which was a bit closer and easily seen from the elevation of the barn loft. They were in dark uniforms. I quickly woke up the others and told them to look. Ruven went to the open shutter.

Suddenly, there were screams.

"They're Germans," Ruven said excitedly. "The riders are Germans. My God! Abram. They're pulling a whole family out of their house! Abram. We know them. Look."

I rushed back to the window. The Germans were dragging the whole family of my friend, Meyer, out of their grocery store: his mother, father, sister, and his two brothers' wives.

I stared in shock as the Germans roughly forced them down on their knees in a perfect line. While three soldiers held the sobbing and confused family in place at gunpoint, a sergeant ejected the magazine from his luger, then shoved it back in. He had a satisfied look on his face. I could see the mother put her hands together in a supplicating manner toward the lone officer and gesture to her children. Even as she begged him to spare their lives, the sergeant walked casually up behind each of the victims, and one by one, shot them in the back of the neck. They each fell, head first into the dirt and were left there. They were the aunt, uncle and cousins of your mother, and the only Jewish family in this outlying area. I learned later that White Russians had pointed them out to the Germans.

I moved away from the window and collapsed as if my legs could no longer find the strength to hold me upright. My back hit hard against the jagged wooden slats of the loft wall. All I could think was: it's true. The rumors were true.

I was startled as I heard footsteps coming up the ladder.

"Boys," the wife of the peasant who had harbored us whispered urgently. "Start running! The soldiers are headed in this direction!"

CHAPTER 2

INVASION

Three weeks earlier on June 22nd, 1941, a bright, cloudless Sunday morning, the German army crossed the Nieman River into Russia. It was the Soviet's turn this time, and, ironically, it happened on the same day Napoleon had crossed the Nieman in 1812 on his way to Moscow 130 years earlier.

Von Bock's Army Group Center began its assault on Brest-Litovsk and headed in the general direction of Pinsk. The Fourth Army moved to converge on Minsk from the south, while the Ninth Army formed a pincer driving on Minsk from the north. My village, Pohost Zagorodski lay directly in the path of the Ninth Army's right flank.

But this was not Pohost Zagorodski's first invasion. Two years earlier, Stalin made a non-aggression pact with Hitler. This allowed the Germans to invade Poland from the west while the Soviets invaded from the east. Since 1918, my village had been part of Poland; before that, we were part of Russia under the Czars.

The Jewish people were naturally worried about who would get to our *shtetl* first, the Nazis or the Communists. Of course we had heard rumors about the treatment of Jews under the Nazis, so we were very relieved when the Soviets took over Pohost Zagorodski.

In looking back, at least for myself, the Soviet invasion seemed almost benign, a lost paradise. Of course, there were those wealthy citizens who were rounded up and forcibly deported to the east, and there was the nationalization of many privately owned businesses. I probably thought it so because neither my family nor I were really hurt by them. The only major thing we suffered was the loss of the family business, and I'll tell you about that. But in comparison to what happened during the time of the Nazis, it almost seems petty to complain about it.

Pesach, your grandfather's older brother, came west from Russia to visit us now that we were again part of the Soviet Union. But he also came to advise Samuel to donate the lumberyard to the Soviets. If you do this, he told my father, they would take it, and most likely allow us to continue working. It might not provide what we considered a living wage, but there would be food on the table. If not, they would expropriate it anyway, and we would end up with nothing except a possible trip to Siberia. Your grandfather took the advice. He offered the lumberyard and they took it.

But that wasn't enough for them. Within a week, they called a meeting with all our employees from the lumberyard and invited them to speak out against the former owner. It was funny to see the faces of the Soviets when Papa's workers got up to speak and every employee, *to a man,* testified how well he had treated them. After a few of the workers had spoken, one of the commissars got up. I remember his name was Lilchuk.

"I will tell you a brief story," he said. "One day in the Soviet Union, not long after the revolution at a meeting similar to this, a worker named Smilov was asked to stand up and say something about his employer, the owner of a paint factory. Smilov rose in front of his fellow workers and the owner of the factory. Sweat was pouring down his face and all he could do was say over and over how wonderful was Lermantov the owner." Lilchuk paused as he looked condescendingly into the eyes of the workers. "What is wrong with this? I'll tell you. You should not be afraid to speak out against the owners, whether they are here or not. Why? Because you are now the owners."

I still remember the contempt on Lilchuk's face as he looked at my father.

Again some of the workers got up and spoke. You have to understand, there were some 300 men at the meeting, and not one of them got up to speak against your grandfather. I truly believe, one of the main reasons we survived is because of the way Samuel Bobrow treated people. His workers, his customers, the peasants, everyone. And he did not treat them well because he expected things in return or because he thought he might need their help in the future, he did it because he felt that you should always be fair and honest. And he was, to a fault. These same workers and farmers often gave us food and clothing and put their own lives in danger by helping us during the war, but we'll speak of this later. That night, the commissars decided to let us continue to work at the yard. Later, your grandfather said, "We've avoided the wolf that would devour us and let in the bear that would starve us."

Life for my family did not change that much under the Russians. I still worked at the lumberyard with Papa and Shlomo, while David and Label worked in the forest sorting the trees, which were then tied together and floated down the Yashelda River to the yard. Later, I joined Label and kept records of the different logs we sorted and sent down the river: oak, pine, walnut and beech.

One of the peasants who worked under me for almost a year was an eighteen-year-old orphan named Boychick. He was blond and fair-skinned and a very hard worker. A good-looking boy, he was also quite shrewd.

Besides work, we spent a lot of time together, eating lunch or drinking homemade whiskey or schnapps when we could find it. I remember laughing at his answer when I asked him how he was doing living under the Russians. He said, "I still eat well, I find a drink when I need it, and the occasional peasant girl to warm my bed. I'm happy enough."

But there were other dislocations under the Russians. Long lines for food and a black market became part of daily life. Search and seizure operations, where the Soviets looked for contraband and illegal foreign currency, were periodic occurrences.

Zionist activities, along with other political and public agencies, were banned. Prominent activists were interned or exiled. David Bobrow, my oldest brother, was arrested for being a Revisionist leader. The Revisionists were Jews who wanted to buy land in Palestine, but also wanted the right to protect it. Leftists, who wanted to buy land, but leave defense in the hands of the British, called them terrorists.

Religious affairs, whether Gentile or Jewish were frowned upon. The *shtetl* began to take on a whole new look. Many things typical of the *Shabat* and of the holidays changed, and *shtetl* life had always revolved around *Shabat*. Gone were the festive streets and closed shops, the candles in the windows and the sight of the Orthodox Jews in their black caftans and long beards hurrying to the synagogue. People dressed differently. Fur hats and coats, ties and fancy gowns disappeared, as did women wearing makeup. People wore short jackets and shabby clothes. High boots, which made one look more like a peasant, replaced fashionable shoes. People in the *shtetl* tried to look inconspicuous.

There were other reasons why the Soviets were welcome in eastern Poland. Under the Russians, anti-Semitism was officially condemned and recognized as a punishable crime.

Papa told me that Marshall Pilsudski, the leader of the Polish Republic was thought to have a fondness for the Jewish people. Because of him, we worked and socialized and played with our neighbors, Jew and Gentile alike. We had our own schools to supplement the education at the Polish schools, and anti-Semitism, if it existed, was beneath the surface.

As Papa explained, in 1920, five Soviet armies were approaching the outskirts of Warsaw. Cossacks from the Ukraine had already crossed the Vistula. The object was to destroy the infant Polish Republic.

There was a myth that Pilsudski, then a general, and leading a group of Hussars to scout Soviet positions, was surrounded by Cossacks. Pilsudski broke through their line and headed south to warn the defenders on the Vistula that the enemy had gotten behind them.

Chased by thirty Cossacks, he came upon a small farm near a Jewish *shtetl*. Taken in by the Jewish lady and her daughter at the risk of their own lives, he was disguised as a peasant lady milking cows. The Cossacks left them alone only on account of their urgent pursuit of the Polish general. Pilsudski escaped to lead the defense of the Vistula and successive victories over the Soviets.

This might be the reason for Pilsudski's honorable treatment of the Jewish people. And they, in turn, called him their protector. But other people say his reforms only amounted to lip service.

At least things did not get worse under Pilsudski.

After his death, the antagonism of the Poles toward our people started to intensify. *Pogroms* reappeared and generally, the police did nothing to stop them.

Aryans-only clauses were inserted into the statutes of Polish trade unions. Universities introduced separate seating for Jews in lecture halls and Polish students enforced the rules with their fists. Radicals encouraged the Jews to emigrate. The Catholic Church of Poland tolerated anti-Semitic sermons and anti-Semitic literature was produced right in the Church.

In Pohost Zagorodski, I then saw members of the Mloda Polska, a skinhead group of ruffians, stand in front of a Jewish store. They would not bother any of the Jews, aside from a few sneers and looks of contempt, but they barred non-Jews from entering. "Don't buy at Jewish stores," their leader said to any Gentiles approaching the shops. "Buy at your own people's stores. Polish markets for Poles. Jewish markets for Jews." After they spoke their slogans, they let the people do as they pleased, but it seemed to me, they would make notes about who bowed to their pressure, and who would defiantly go inside the grocery store.

My father and other leaders of the community sensed the situation would get worse. So, when the Germans tore into western Poland, it was with a double relief that the Soviets arrived. We greeted the Russians by giving them bread and salt—a traditional welcome, along with our cheers.

When the Germans invaded Russia, the Soviets left our *shtetl*, but their leaving was not so benign. In the villages and cities of Soviet Poland, Russian soldiers had rounded up the rich, the bourgeoisie, and political dissidents who had not yet been shot, and put them on transports to journey deep into Russia.

My mother Yentl, a small, frail woman who had never completely recovered from a bout with typhus, feared that her entire family would be separated and taken by train to Siberia. She begged me to go to the lumberyard to hide, but I refused. I instinctively knew the Russians were better for us, and I wanted to go with them. I wanted to become a soldier and fight the Germans.

In a few days, it became clear that the Germans were coming closer to Pohost Zagorodski—would, in fact, march right through the *shtetl*. At first, we heard it from peasants, but then we saw truckload after truckload of Russian soldiers pouring back through the *shtetl* with all kinds of heavy equipment.

When the German proximity became common knowledge, many White Russian and Polish men and women turned on the Jews, even neighbors that had been friends for years. When the Germans crossed the border into eastern Poland, they opened the jails in all the towns they entered, freeing criminals and political offenders alike. Ironically, one of the prisoners they released from Brest-Litovsk was my brother David.

David, he was incredible. Like usual, in everything he ever did, he'd risen to a high position under the Soviets. Someone got jealous and made up some lies about him. The Soviets would call it "denouncing" someone. So David ended up being put in jail by the Russians and freed by the Germans.

Many of these others were hardened criminals with a long history of anti-Semitism. They raided the settlements and took whatever they could from the Jews: clothing, valuables and food. They killed some of their victims.

You realize, boys, I'm jumping around a bit, but I want you to understand some of the background

Nationalistic White Russians turned on the retreating Soviets. They blew up bridges to the Russians' rear, and cut telephone wires and destroyed railroad tracks.

Worse for Pohost Zagorodski were the Poles and White Russians from neighboring villages. They called themselves *militz*. Self-appointed policemen, they aligned themselves with the Germans, swept down on the *shtetl* and started their own pogroms; raping young girls, beating men and boys, looting at will. They were hoodlums, gangsters.

Many refugees came to Pohost Zagorodski in the wake of the invasion. They fled Warsaw and Lodz and Pinsk, hoping the Nazis would ignore the smaller villages.

At this time, I joined a group of young Jewish men who decided to follow the Soviet Army on their retreat.

I felt very strange. It would be the first time I had left my family, and this was very hard for me, but anything was better than sitting around waiting for the Germans to decide my fate. At least with the Russians, I would have a chance to fight. And that's what I planned to do, join the Soviet Army.

On Friday night, July 4th, fifteen of us headed to the railway station at Luninetz, running the whole way through the dense undergrowth of forest. German aircraft were already flying overhead with searchlights looking for Russian stragglers. Other planes were dropping bombs and strafing any targets they could find.

18

At the train station, I found out that a cousin of mine had fallen victim to the German bombs. This was the first of my relatives to be killed in the war.

We boarded a train, but no sooner had we arrived at Bobroisk, the first stop on the line to Russia, than we were turned back. A Soviet general greeted our protests.

He told us that as long as Pinsk was still ostensibly under the control of the Soviet Army, we were not authorized to leave the area.

I asked him—I begged him to let us join up—but he wouldn't budge. He ordered us to return to Pinsk. We ended up hiking back. By the time we got to Pohost Zagorodski, the German army was only four miles from the *shtetl*.

The next day, the trucks, tanks and artillery of the regular German army moved into the area. About one thousand soldiers stayed in and around our *shtetl* for two days. Many soldiers stayed in the *shtetl*, using the houses that were vacated by the villagers when the Soviet Army first arrived in 1939.

Almost immediately, scores of young Polish and White Russian men took it upon themselves to police the Jews. At first they put on armbands of any stripe to designate themselves as police. Later, they were given uniforms by the Germans and made official.

All of these self-appointed policemen were acquaintances of my family, and of most of the Jews in Pohost Zagorodski. Many had been considered to be friends in the recent past.

I had a friend named Zenka Solonievitz. I'll never forget this boy. We knew each other from the time we were about seven years old. We used to play hockey on the Yashelda River when it was frozen over in winter. We played soccer in the summer. We took my canoe out on the Bobric Lake and fished. Sometimes we would sneak into the cemetery at night just to play cards; playing cards was forbidden under Jewish Law at the time. Zenka was Gentile. He didn't care about Jewish Law. He could have played cards anywhere at any time. But he went to the cemetery at night with me because we were friends.

Zenka showed up with a patch.

The first day, they herded the young boys and girls of the *shtetl* into a group and marched them to the Jewish cemetery. I was with them. Zenka saw me, but refused to even acknowledge me.

"It's time you Jews did some honest work," one of the ringleaders said. They told us to pull apart the fence surrounding the cemetery and lay the boards on the ground, crosswise. This was to allow the German heavy equipment—like tanks, trucks and armored cars—to cross over the soft, sandy roads of the *shtetl* and not get bogged down.

When I walked past Zenka to pry another board loose, I spat on the ground. You are the big shots now, I thought, as I labored to pull the wooden boards out of the consecrated ground, but it will not always be so. This I promised myself.

***

Anything you owned could be appropriated by the Germans and it was sheer folly to argue. Your mother's grandfather, Sholom Krugley, a strong, burly man, who had served his five years in the Russian Army as the conductor of the Czar's orchestra and was now a merchant, had the bad luck to pick that day to drive his carriage into the village. It was a beautiful coach and filled with hardware merchandise.

Polish barons from Pinsk had mansions near Pohost Zagorodski, some only four miles away. They used to stay in Krugley's large brick house facing Rynec Square and rent the carriage from Krugley when they came from Pinsk to go hunting. Of course, the carriage was so elegant, and ornately carved, it was only used for rides and celebrations. It even had padded leather seats.

Krugley delivered passengers and mail the seven miles to and from the train station at Parachunsck. He used other, not-so-well-appointed carts for these tasks, and also carriages for the winter with skis instead of wheels.

During the winters, either Sholom or one of his sons would bundle up the grandchildren and take them for a sleigh ride. They put bells and chimes around the horses' necks and took the children through the forest and over the frozen rivers. Grandpa always loved sitting in front with the reins in his hands.

Krugley was stopped in front of the cemetery where we were laboring. When the Germans asked for the carriage, I could see Krugley hold back. He wanted something for it—at the very least, a receipt.

Krugley remembered the Germans from the first war and thought these were probably the same, civilized and courteous. He had not yet understood how truly different these new Germans were. Still, intuitively, he was apprehensive about asking for any compensation.

A corporal pulled the old man aside telling him to get a receipt so he could get the wagon back later. He pointed Krugley to an officer.

As Krugley walked up to the *Standartenfuhrer*, I saw the other German soldiers begin to laugh. I could hear one say, "Imagine a Jew going up to a German officer to get a receipt."

Soon, two men were roughly escorting the terrified Krugley to the marketplace.

After the tanks, trucks and heavy equipment passed, we were allowed to go home. No sooner did I reach my house, than I heard screams coming from all over the village. I was startled. My skin grew cold.

20

The Germans, with the help of their newly appointed policemen, were rousting Jewish people out of their homes and pushing them into the streets. They entered Jewish households, and forced people out with the threat of whips. Over one thousand German soldiers drove the villagers into the marketplace and surrounded them. Now I feared the worst, as my mother and father and I were herded to the marketplace along with hundreds of others. What would happen? Would we be beaten, killed? And what could we do anyway? This was the worst thing; we were helpless.

Everyone in the village had heard rumors about the German treatment of Jews—the deportations, the humiliations, the random shootings.

I saw Julia's grandfather forcibly moved to the center of the marketplace. Following him were soldiers leading his carriage. All of his goods had been tossed off in order to make room for a gigantic log. When they reached the center, the log was rolled off unto the ground. Sixty-year-old Sholom Krugley was handed an ax, made to strip to the waist and chop up the log in the noonday sun.

Other soldiers placed a bench in the middle of the crowd. A slight, fourteen-year-old Jewish boy was hauled out in front of the assembly. The Germans told the crowd to gather in closer. They tore off his shirt, pulled down his pants and forced him down on the bench. Two German soldiers, each carrying a whip, stood on either side of the boy. At the command of the *Standartenfuhrer*, the soldiers brought their whips down on the back and buttocks of the unfortunate boy. Thirty times. Soon, the boy's back was covered with bright red stripes. He fainted from the pain.

When the Germans were finished, they rolled him off the bench and dragged him to the side of the road that ran through the marketplace.

A few people started forward, to help the boy, but soldiers with raised rifles barred their way. No one would be allowed to help him. All of the Jewish villagers were made to stand in the hot sun, but no one was allowed to go to the boy and he lay unconscious in the dirt until the sun went down.

An *Oberst-gruppenfuhrer* walked briskly to the center of the crowd with an aide, and one of the self-appointed White Russian policemen at his side. He spoke in German, while the White Russian translated. The aide pulled a yellow cloth Star of David from his pocket. I'll never forget what he said.

"From this day on, all Jews must wear the Mogan David. If you are found without it, you will be shot. When you are dismissed, I suggest you go to your houses and make one for every family member, including all children. They must look like this." His aide held the yellow star above his head.

All the Jews were made to stand there, in the marketplace. No food or water was allowed. Too much movement by any of the people resulted in the shove from a rifle butt or the sting of a whip. They stood still in the marketplace for over four hours.

When it was finally dark, everyone was ordered to go home.

The next evening, my father called a meeting. To our complete surprise, my brother David walked into the house at dusk that night. Germans were milling around outside, so he had to sneak in. There was as yet, no curfew, but the less the Germans saw of you, the less chance of provocation.

Later that same night, Esther Bobrow and her daughter, Leahle, walked in from the train station. Her husband had made his way deep into Russia by now, but Esther had missed us and wanted to come home for a short visit. Her husband, Asher, had begged her to stay, but she was terribly homesick. It was the first time the whole family had been together since the outbreak of the war in 1939.

Papa wasted no time. I have to tell you, your grandfather is the wisest man I've ever known. He told us that the Germans were moving out tomorrow for the old border with Russia. "But these are not the worst of the Germans," he said. "There are roaming bands of SS, called *Einsatzgruppen*. They are rounding up the Jews from the cities and deporting them. Many Jews have simply been killed. I do not know what they will do in the villages." He said he was not certain if this was true, but it was what he had heard.

Samuel looked at us, catching each of us with his eyes. "I want my sons to leave this place."

"But Samuel…" Mama protested. Tears were running from her eyes.

"We have no idea what will happen in this place," he said firmly. "Not tonight. Not tomorrow. I want my family out of danger."

"Father," David said, "you yourself told us that our people have always come to an agreement with conquerors. With petitions or bribes."

"In the end, they'll need us," Label said. "They'll need the production for the war. And in the cities they'll need Jews in the bureaucracy. To run the cities."

"And Shlomo, do you also disagree with your father?"

"The Russians needed us. The Germans will too. Someone has to work, even in wartime. It will be difficult, but we will survive."

Samuel looked at us with heavy eyes, but I could see that Mama felt better now that she thought her family might still stay together.

"Abram?" Mama asked me. "What of you?"

Not wanting to hurt her, I averted my eyes, but I was angry for what happened the day before and for how helpless I felt. Before I could stop myself, I blurted out, "I don't trust the S.O.B.s! The first chance I get, I'm running off. I'm joining the Russians or the partisans. I mean it."

Papa stood up and walked around the room. "I don't know why, but this time it's different. Our people, throughout their history, have had to accommodate different oppressors just in order to live. From the Egyptians and the Babylonians in ancient times, to the Spaniards and Poles more recently. There was always a way. This time I sense it will not be the same. I've told you what I feel and what I want. You are old enough to decide for yourselves. You should plan tonight and be gone no later than tomorrow morning, early. Go to the Rudna forest. It should be safe there. Yentl and I will stay. We are too old to run. We will try to accommodate our new lords."

That night stands out in my mind for another reason. Shlomo. He wasn't interested in preparing to leave. He wanted to go fishing.

Just like Shlomo, I thought. He joked that he had to have something for his wife and child to eat. He could turn any circumstance, no matter how bad, into something we'd laugh about.

We met in the backyard at midnight and shoved my canoe into the Bobric River. It was against my better judgment, but I couldn't refuse him.

During the spring, the flatlands around the *shtetl* flood so badly that the town becomes an island, and the only way in or out are the bridges over the Yashelda and Bobric Rivers. So my canoe became an important mode of transportation.

I remembered the lapping of the water along the sides of the canoe and how gently the boat swayed to the ripples that night, but I was truly puzzled.

We were not just facing everyday problems, even the worst problems of that sort. I could not understand how Shlomo could keep up his rosy outlook. I asked him, "How can you laugh when our problems are so great? These are your problems as well."

To my surprise, Shlomo replied quite seriously.

"First, you know that there are those who say the Devil is not always as bad as he is painted." He paused. "Of course. I'm not one of those." Shlomo laughed.

I smiled. That was much more like my brother.

But then Shlomo was serious again. He leaned forward and touched my shoulder. I can still feel where he touched me.

"More importantly, we are all given a certain amount of time on this earth. As for me, I'm not about to let the Germans ruin whatever time I have left. Besides, I love to fish."

That night was the last time I talked to Shlomo.

***

There was a subtle change in my father's posture just then, and his voice noticeably lowered and quavered just the tiniest bit. He pulled out a handkerchief and blew his nose. I could see he was starting to cry but that he didn't want us to see. "You're going to have to give your old father a rest. I had a hard day today..."

Bill and I, on either side of him, put our arms around his waist as we walked. We wanted to hear more, but we were beginning to understand.

It was the late summer of 1957. My "old" father was all of thirty-five.

THE SECOND DAY

CHAPTER 3

EINSATZGRUPPEN

"What I'm going to tell you now will not be easy for me," my father said. His voice choked up. I could see he was having trouble getting the words out. Tears were forming in his eyes and he began to cough, trying to clear his throat. He had been very animated during the telling of his story up to this point, but now he grew subdued and his features took on a pallor that I'd never seen before. He spoke in a low voice. One I'd never heard before. He coughed again.
"I didn't think it would be this hard."

***

Now, you remember, when I left off, we were hiding in the barn at this time.

Some of this happened to me, some of it was told to me by others such as your mother.

In the second week of July, on a Saturday, two hundred riders in the dark green and black camouflage uniforms of the SS, spurred their horses along the narrow dirt roads leading to Pohost Zagorodski. As far as I could make out, they must have started out at dawn from Pinsk. The riders we saw were part of this group.

You should know that the Germans had a history of committing their atrocities on the Sabbath, or on the holiest days such as Yom Kippur. They were aware of the close family ties of the *shtetl* and knew they would find most of the families together on these sacred days.

As soon as the farmer's wife warned us, we flew down the ladder from the loft. I doubt if I even touched the rungs. At the time we were no more than four or five hundred yards away from the horsemen.

"We can hide in the tall corn by the river," I told the others as we ran from the barn. We could hear still more rifle shots and screams. Terrified of being discovered, we got down on all fours and scrambled furiously through the fields towards the woods. It seemed that the cries and shots were coming at us from all directions.

"Do you think they will tell?" Ruven whispered.

26

"No. They're good people, honest people," I whispered back breathlessly.

Finally, still crawling on all fours, we reached the edge of the woods. They all looked to me. I was the one who knew the forest the best.

"We should move closer to the Kamener Way, a half-mile from the shtetl. I think it'll be safer to hide there," I told them.

Kamen had been the first Jewish center in the area, before Pohost Zagorodski became a shtetl. The oldest Jewish cemetery was located there, next to the Bobric River.

The village had died after most of the Jews had moved to Pohost. Even the cemetery had been unattended for years.

I used to go swimming in the deep Kamener Holes against my parent's wishes. This was the only place close to Pohost Zagorodski where the Bobric River was deep enough for a careless person to drown.

When we reached the Kamener Way, we lay down and hid in the tall grass, our chests heaving from the exertion.

My back went cold. I remember my hands were clenched so tightly I had scars from my nails for a month.

Now the question of who had left in time once more arose. Ruven was as terrified as I that our fathers might be caught. We felt so helpless.

I saw tears were running down the other boys' cheeks as we huddled together trying to comfort each other. It seemed as though we cringed and started with each new series of gunshots, as if each shot had pierced a loved one's heart.

We stayed there for most of that day.

It was late in the morning and already unseasonably hot by the time the SS horsemen reached Pohost Zagorodski. They had been given two hours to round up every Jewish male over the age of ten. Their orders were to not touch the women and children.

The villagers of Pohost Zagorodski had been hearing shots and screaming from the surrounding areas all morning. Some were resigned to whatever fate the coming of the SS would bring. Others, like my brothers and myself were running to the forest and still others sought hiding places in the *shtetl*—in double walls, or cellars, or underground bunkers that they had prepared for just such a crisis.

My brothers Label and David hurried down Yeziorna Street just before dawn, past the Gentile cemetery and out towards the Rudna Forest, taking a more direct path than I did.

Four Jewish boys were planning to run down to the Bobric Lake, get in canoes, paddle across and then hide in the Swiernishtze Forest. Papa considered going with them, but he could not make up his mind. Even as he

27

heard more shots and could tell the sounds were drawing closer, he still could not make up his mind. The boys lost patience and left.

"Go!" my mother finally cried. "They'll only take the men. I'll be safe. Go and hide!"

My father did not know what to do for the first time in his life. How could he leave her, his wife and partner for over thirty years? What if they took the women as well?

"Please," Mama cried. She started to push him toward the door. "There isn't time to think. Just go. I'll be all right."

"I'll only go if you promise to hide," he told her.

"All right. But I won't go with you. If we're apart, there's a better chance one of us won't be found. Your sister and I will run to…"

"Don't tell me."

"Now go, Samuel Bobrow," Mama implored. "Now!"

Samuel Bobrow ran out the front door, down Dworska Street, across the Bobric River bridge in the direction of the railway station. He had had no idea where he was going to hide, but as he crossed the bridge, he remembered an old abandoned house facing Dworska Street, that was across the Bobric River. Dashing through the weed-infested courtyard, Papa reached the front door, flung it open and went inside. This is how a criminal runs, he told me later.

The old lady who owned the house had converted to Christianity, but decided to leave anyway. She left before the German invasion.

My father slammed the door shut, leaning with his back against it, his chest heaving, and wondering how mankind had arrived at this stage.

He ran up the stairs to the second floor where there was an entrance to an attic, and crawled inside. From the attic, he had a view to the street below. With his heart breaking, Papa would witness much of the gruesome spectacle.

Miriam, Papa's sister and Yentl ran towards the lumberyard and hid in a potato patch about a mile from the bridge across the Yashelda. They could see much of the east side of Pohost Zagorodski from there.

After leaving my house, the four young boys went to gather other fugitives. By the time they reached the Zipperstein residence, their number was eight.

"We're going to the lake," one of the boys said. "You should come with us."

Jeruchim looked at his wife. He was also having trouble deciding what to do.

Leah told him, "Go with them. The children aren't ready."

Jeruchim went to her and kissed her on both cheeks and then on her mouth. He started out the door, but only went a few feet before he turned around and went back inside.

"I'm not going to leave my family," he said, resolutely. He walked to the dining room table and sat down, crossing his arms in front of him.

Who knows what turmoil was going through his and my father's minds? I guess it was a lot like Ruven's father.

Shlomo, and our cousin Kalman, dressed only in their light summer clothes and jackets, headed out Dworska Street towards the lumberyard. As they started to cross the sixty-yard-long wooden bridge over the Yashelda River, they must have heard the sound of horses approaching from the opposite direction. And they must have known it was the SS, because they quickly turned around, ran off the bridge and started half-running and half-sliding down the steep riverbank.

They were spotted by two Polish men. One was a young blond man named Alosha. He was the one who had turned in the boy who was whipped by the Germans in the market place.

Before Kalman and Shlomo got to the water's edge, they must have thought it would be better to climb up the wooden cross-supports of the bridge and hide directly underneath, and that's what they did.

As the SS troops crossed over the Yashelda, Alosha and the other peasant ran up onto the bridge from the Pohost Zagorodski side. They went to the *Obersturmbannfuhrer* leading the soldiers and told him there were two Jews hiding under the bridge. Alosha even leaned over the railing and pointed under the bridge to Shlomo and Kalman's hiding place. He wanted to be sure the Germans found them.

The *Obersturmbannfuhrer* led his horse to the railing and peered over. He ordered ten soldiers to dismount. Splitting up into two groups of five, they started down the slopes on either side of the bridge. Spotting the two men, they ordered them to climb down or be shot.

Shlomo and Kalman started to move down. As soon as their feet hit the ground they were shoved and hit by the soldiers, and prodded back onto the bridge at gunpoint. The Germans then made Shlomo and Kalman run alongside the horses into the village.

From their hiding place, Miriam and Yentl saw the boys climb out from under the bridge and run back to the village, seemingly chased by the SS.

A group of older men, who were Jeruchim Zipperstein's contemporaries, now came to his home.

"You must leave, Jeruchim. This is your last chance," begged Leah. "They won't hurt women and children. Leave us. I beg you. If you stay and are shot, I'll hate you forever for leaving me alone."

Until this time, even after hearing the sporadic shooting and screaming for hours, Jeruchim felt it was wrong to leave. There was no honor in it. This he told his wife and children. But Leah would have none of it.

"Do you hear me?" Leah screamed.

Jeruchim finally saw he could not disobey his wife. She might go mad if he was killed.

Kissing Leah goodbye for the second time that morning, he resignedly followed the group down Mieshchanska Street, through the marketplace, over to Dworska, and past Rublawski's tavern. Their numbers had now swelled to over forty and included young men and children as well.

Nearing the mansion of the Polish priest, Drogomish, they heard the galloping of horses.

The mansion, where the priest lived with a housekeeper, was also the church where he held services for all of the Catholics in Pohost Zagorodski.

Drogomish, in his black robes and white collar, saw them from his window and rushed outside. The priest was old and bent, and known throughout the village to be a good-hearted man. He kept many pigeons as pets and even had three ostriches. People would come from miles away to tour his gardens and catch the smell of jasmine and orange blossoms.

He had been sitting alone in his garden alcove sadly contemplating the growing turmoil in his village and apparently trying to think of some way to help. Now the disturbance had come to his front yard. He rushed out to see how he could aid the fugitives.

Urgently, he motioned the Jewish men and boys into his garden. The garden spread over two acres, but was dwarfed by the potato patch, which was a quarter-of-a-mile wide and a half-a mile long, stretching all the way to Bobric Lake and filled with two-foot-high potato plants.

Quickly, the fugitives left the road, following the priest down the furrows between the plants to the edge farthest from the road. There, in the weeded dirt furrows between the rows of potato plants, they lay down to hide. From this position, they could probably hear the passing of the SS riders moving into the *shtetl*.

Nazis from Borki now entered Pohost Zagorodski from the north, riding past the Polish school on Mieshchanska Street. Both groups converged on the marketplace and dismounted. We did not know there were going to be two groups of SS.

Shlomo and Kalman had reached the marketplace and were ordered to stand and wait there. One soldier stood guard over them, his machine gun pointed at them.

The soldiers started moving house to house, brandishing their machine guns and whips, made of genuine ox hide that looked so shiny and new, as if they were handed out to the men that very morning. Accompanied by the local police force, they forced all the men they found out into the street. The SS men moved so quickly, so efficiently, they allowed little time for protest or defiance.

Stragglers and those who resisted were beaten or whipped. In every house where there were children, the troopers yelled, "How old are you? How old are you?" If the child answered ten or above, he was taken out to the marketplace.

Leah Zipperstein placed her hands on her twelve-year-old son's shoulders. "Listen to me, Avremel. When they come and ask you how old you are, you look them in the eye and say nine years old. Do you understand?"

"Yes, Mama."

"And shrink down," Julia added. "Slouch a bit so you look smaller."

"Yes," Leah agreed.

To their immense relief, when the time came, the soldiers believed Avremel's performance.

In the village hospital, those men who were too sick or infirm to move were shot on the spot.

Almost ninety men and young boys were rounded up and forced to the marketplace. The women and youngest children were ordered to stay inside—to wail and beat their breasts behind closed doors.

In the center of the village, the *Obersturmbannfuhrer* called to his sergeant, "Is that all you found?"

"Yes, *Herr Obersturmbannfuhrer*," the sergeant replied. "That's it."

This was not good enough for him. He must be able to show better numbers. Summoning a ten-year-old Polish boy, who was watching the spectacle, to his side, the *Obersturmbannfuhrer* said, "I will give you ten marks if you can tell me where there are any more Jews."

The boy smiled and said, "Come with me."

Twenty SS troopers mounted their horses and followed the young boy down Dworska Street to the church. When they reached the old mansion that now served as the Catholic Church, the boy pointed to a huge potato patch behind the priest's house.

"There," he said.

As the sergeant and his men started into the garden on their horses, Drogomish ran out once more.

"What are you doing in my garden?" he yelled. "You are stomping on the plants. You'll destroy them."

"There are Jews hiding in the garden," the sergeant said.

"There is nothing here except the potato plants. And you're ruining them," the priest said, moving in front of the horses of the sergeant and his men, trying to block their way.

31

"Get out of the way, Father," the sergeant demanded.

"No," Drogomish said, defiantly. "You have no right. This is a holy place, the grounds of the church."

"Toss him out of the way," the sergeant said to his men. Four soldiers dismounted and threw the frail priest to the ground.

"Jew lover," the sergeant snarled.

The soldiers then searched the field, knocking over the plants, trampling on others and tearing up the dirt and crops. Thus they combed the field while the forty Jews lay trembling in the dirt.

Finding the men, the SS forced them to their feet, whipping and beating them with sticks as they herded them back to the marketplace.

When a hundred and thirty Jewish men and boys were finally assembled in the Rynec marketplace, the SS soldiers mounted their horses and formed a circle around them to prevent any escape attempts. Then they made them run down Dworska Street across the Bobric River bridge out of town.

How ironic that the marketplace, the center of life in the *shtetl*, the location of the merchants, taverns, artisan's workshops, farmer's produce stands—had now been the center of the gathering of death.

My father, in the abandoned house, was so close, he felt he could have reached down and touched them. He saw his son, Shlomo, at the front of the group of men. He's so fast, Papa thought. How could they have caught him? He prayed that he could reach out and lift him away from them.

But he could only watch.

The SS troops took the Jews past the Bobrow lumberyard to an old Jewish cemetery. In the cemetery, the soldiers lined them up in groups of ten.

"Ask your God to protect you, Rabbi," the *Obersturmbannfuhrer* said jokingly. "Ask Him to let you live."

The rabbi would not look at his tormentor, but stood, eyes closed and praying.

Three peasants who had accompanied the forced march from Pohost Zagorodski walked suppliantly up to the *Obersturmbannfuhrer.*

"Please sir," the leader of the peasants said, "we need four of these people. Please don't kill them."

"Which four?" the officer asked.

"The druggist, the blacksmith, the tailor and the shoemaker," the peasant replied.

The *Obersturmbannfuhrer* looked distressed. This would cut back on his numbers. "Are you certain you need them? Surely you can find others to do those jobs."

32

"Sir. Of course we would rather make do with others but unfortunately, there are no others with those skills for a great distance from our village. It would make our lives very difficult."

"All right. You can have them for now." He smiled and called for his aide. "Sergeant."

"Yes sir."

"Let these men pick out the four Jews they need," the *Obersturmbannführer* begrudgingly ordered.

"Yes sir," obeyed the sergeant. Together with the peasants, he walked through the lines of Jews while they picked out the men. Then the peasants started to leave with the four.

"Wait," commanded the *Obersturmbannführer*. "Let your *chosen ones* watch." The *Obersturmbannführer* chuckled at his witticism.

The first people they killed were the wealthy and the religious—the rabbi, the shochet, the cantor, and the gabbai of the temple. The Jews, in their lines of ten, were marched to a row of tombstones, on the other side of which was a small hill. There, they were made to kneel down with their backs towards the soldiers. The SS shot them with their machine guns. A single soldier then walked into the sprawl of bodies and put one bullet into the head of anyone still moving. The next line of ten was now ordered to move up, made to kneel and then shot. This order continued until all one hundred and thirty men and children were dead. Except for the first line, the Jews had to sit, squatting, trembling and listening to the sounds of their friends being murdered, as they inched closer to the same fate. Many prayed.

This group of men included Shlomo and Kalman, Jeruchim Zipperstein, Josef Sosnik and Sholom Krugley.

In a way, they were lucky. For most of them, it was over quickly. In the many massacres that occurred during the *Aktion Reinhard*—the German name for the methodical killing of Jews living in this area of Poland—Jews were toyed with, tortured and humiliated; old men's beards were lit on fire in Jozefow. In Lomazy, elderly Jews were made to run the gauntlet naked, while soldiers beat them with clubs, or made to crawl through mud to their graves which they first were made to dig. Some were buried alive—they were shot, dumped into a pit, and covered with dirt, even though the Ukranian or Polish or German butchers many times missed their mark. In one city, it was said the ground moved for three days with the tormented flailings of the dying who were buried alive. In Bialystok, others were sealed up in synagogues which were then set on fire, burning the people alive. Mothers were told they had to pick which of their children would die and which would live. Then the SS would kill them all regardless.

At least the Jews of Pohost Zagorodski were not physically tortured.

33

The peasants were then allowed to take the craftsmen they had requested away, and the SS remounted their horses and rode off to the east.

***

Throughout the day we listened to the shooting and screaming. It seemed like the shooting was coming ever nearer to our hiding place. The sound of the shooting, round after round, continued for three hours.

We had no idea how many of our friends and families had been caught. Ruven Sosnick kept playing over and over in his mind how his father had gone back. How he could not convince him to stay. And I wished I could go back and yell at my brothers and father to leave with me. Why did they have to take their time? They didn't need so much preparation. They just needed to leave. Of course, you have to understand, that at this time, we had no idea who had been caught or who got away. We could only imagine the worst.

This was to be one of the longest days of my life, though worse days were yet to come.

By the time the shooting stopped, the sun had set and the hot day had somewhat cooled off. I knew I had to take a chance to find out what happened. To find out if I had any family left.

I led the others deeper into the woods to the house of a peasant who was a friend of my brothers, and uneasily knocked on the door. I could feel my heart thumping in my chest and ears.

When I asked him what he knew, he said, "David and Label stopped to get food from me during the day. They are hiding somewhere in the woods. As far as I know they are safe."

"Thank God," I said with great relief. "Do you know anything about Shlomo, or my father, or any of my friends' families?"

"I'm sorry," the peasant replied, looking downcast. "I don't know. But I think I can guide you to David and Label."

An hour-and-a-half later, after trudging through the deepest parts of the forest, with ever dreadful thoughts running through my head with each sorrowful step, I was reunited with my brothers, David and Label.

With them was a whole other group of Jews from Pohost Zagorodski who had run off in the opposite direction and then circled around to the Rudna Forest.

As we sat in the thick grass of the forest and compared experiences, I realized that these people also did not know who had been killed and who had escaped.

There was a great sadness in the gathering. No one knew what to do next. Who could tell when the next group of SS would come?

34

My brother David slowly stood up, his sorrowful blue-green eyes looking at Label and myself. "It is time for us to say Kaddish for all those who perished," he said "Who knows who will say Kaddish for us?"

We all slowly stood up. It was the first time I had ever seen a group of grown men crying.

We gathered in a circle. David, Label and I joined hands. In a beautiful, mellifluous voice that I felt was mournfully crying out to the souls who had perished, David started to chant the Kaddish and the rest joined in:

> *Yitgadal veyitkadash shemei raba bealm divera chireutei,*
> *veyamlich malchutei bechayeichon uveyomeichon*
> *uvechayei dechol beit*
> *Yisraeil, baagala uvizeman kariv, veimeru: amein.*
> *Yehei shemei raba mevarach lealam ulealmei almaya.*
> *Yitbarach veyishtabach, veyitpaar veyitroman*
> *veyitnasei veyithadar veyitaleh veyithalal*
> *shemei dekudesha, berich hu, leeila min kol*
> *birechata veshirata, tushbechata venechemata*
> *daamiran bealma veimeru: amein.*

Tears streamed down the ashen cheeks of the survivors, but I felt a strange calm come from reciting the familiar words of the Kaddish and hearing the soothing voice of my brother. Perhaps there was still some hope left in me.

> *Yehei shelama raba min shemaya vechayim*
> *aleinu veal kol Yisraeil veimeru: amein.*
> *Oseh shalom bimeromav, hu yaaseh shalom*
> *aleinu veal kol Yisraeil, veimeru: amein.*

David sat down on the forest floor, resting his arms on his pulled-up knees. He was completely exhausted.

"We now know the nature of the German," David said in a voice that could barely be heard over the sounds of the woodland.

I looked at my older brothers. I tried to think of the David and Label I had grown up admiring. The brothers who were so wise, so calm and in control, who always had an answer for any problem, and who had so luckily gotten away. But now I could only think of two others: Shlomo and Papa.

Label helped David stand up and said we should not stay so close to the shtetl. We had to go deeper into the Rudna. As we moved into the darkness, David's words kept coming back to me. *Who will say Kaddish for us?*

During the next few days, the victims of the massacre were buried. Peasants from the surrounding area covered the site with dirt. Those men from Pohost Zagorodski who had escaped had not yet returned, and the many new widows and grieving mothers and grandmothers were too much in shock to help.

CHAPTER 4

EMPTY HOUSES

Suddenly, our world was in chaos. Trust, that most innocent and hopeful cement of society and its relationships, was gone. Of the four hundred and twenty families of Pohost Zagorodski, eighty percent had been Jewish. Now those numbers were irretrievably altered.

For the moment, the women and children still in the *shtetl* were safe, but for the men and boys who escaped, any association with the peasants was precarious.

One no longer knew who to trust. There were those rare peasants who would risk their own lives to harbor or protect the Jews, but this was assuredly not the case with most of the people of the surrounding areas.

Certain Polish and White Russian peasants and townsfolk would turn Jews in to the Germans only if the opportunity came their way. Some would go out of their way to help the Germans in their goal to exterminate us. And some from both categories had at one time been friends, or business partners, or at least neighbors with Jews living in the *shtetls* of the Pale, which was the only territory in Czarist Russia where it was legal for Jews to settle.

The Gentiles of Pohost Zagorodski had been good friends to the Jews before the German invasion—at least, that is how it seemed to me. We used to play cards together, play soccer or hockey, go ice-skating or fishing. We would go to each other's homes for dinner, and work together. But this all changed with the advent of war. White Russians whom I had considered my best friends, now looked at Jews as though they were dirt. Friendships of a lifetime were now completely reversed. One day we were close as brothers, the next, we were enemies. The Gentiles acted as if they did not know their former Jewish friends. To me, since the Germans entered the village, it seemed as if the Gentiles thought the Jews were in their way: that, if only the Jews were gone, it would be possible to not feel guilt about their treatment, to not feel remorse about taking their possessions. If not for the Jews, perhaps it would be possible to have peace with the Germans.

They looked upon the Jews as strangers who were only there temporarily. One man who had worked with me at the lumberyard, said

"Abram, your time is running out. They're already building the ovens. And in a short time they'll burn everybody."

But he had his own problems. He was a Communist. The Communists did not have much of a future in the new Germany either. I never figured out whether the man was warning me out of a common fear, or trying to frighten me.

Some acted this way out of a latent anti-Semitism that had never been very far from the surface, some did it out of an irrational, but nevertheless real, hatred for Jews, and some did it for simple greed—the desire to take whatever goods they could beat the Germans to. The Poles and White Russians had heard the rumors from the West as well and figured the Jews would not be around too much longer. In Pohost Zagorodski, all of these conditions became more apparent after the slaughter of the men.

For instance, soon after the massacre, when things had settled down enough that we were able to go back to our houses, one of the teachers from the Polish school walked into my home barely offering a greeting.

The teacher, whose name was Stefco, said "I'd like to borrow your boiling pot," but what he meant was that you won't be needing it much longer because you won't be around. The huge black pot was more than a yard high and a yard across. It sat on slats over a fireplace and was cemented into the wall. When it came time to wash and sterilize the clothes, a fire was built underneath, the water was brought to a boil and the clothes were tossed in. The pot was partially built into the wall and was fastened at the top by bricks. My mother wondered how he was going to borrow something like that? But Papa told the teacher if he wanted it, he could take it. Stefco brought a hammer and started to loosen the pot by smashing the bricks and then the cement, and damaging the stove next to the pot.

Your mother had a beautiful leather briefcase. It was taken in much the same way. Jeruchim had bought it for her while she had been away at school in Pinsk. It was borrowed by a friend. Julia knew better than to protest. The police always sided with whomever was against the Jews, and the Jews could say nothing about it. The Jewish people had little protection after the German invasion. After one hundred and thirty men and young boys were murdered, the remaining people of Pohost Zagorodski had even less protection. Everything became worse.

So it was with some trepidation that my brothers and I went to the house of one of the peasants the day after the massacre.

"Please," David asked the wiry old man, who he had once known as a friend, "would you do us the greatest favor of going into the village and finding out who was killed and who is still alive?"

The peasant did not say a word. He put on a cloak and led us to his barn where we helped him harness his horse and buggy. As he rode by us, we could see tears in his eyes. We knew we could trust him.

It was not long before he returned with grim news. He found out that all the men and boys who had been gathered up in the marketplace had been killed, but he did not know who had been caught. "You boys better stay in the forest," he told us. "I don't know when another SS troop will come to finish the job, but I've learned there are groups of SS roaming the countryside right now, tracking down escaped Jews."

We stayed in the forest for the day, but that night, we decided we had to sneak into the village. We had to find out.

There, at the foot of our mother, Yentl, we heard the whole gruesome tale. Shlomo, my brother was dead.

No one had heard from Papa since the day of the massacre. But Mama emphasized that no one had seen him in the group the SS took out of the *shtetl*, and she hoped and prayed he was still in hiding.

My mother soon became anxious and pleaded with us to leave before morning, and so we did, stealing down back streets and avoiding the marketplace, which was still crawling with Germans. We reached the Polish school before dawn, and felt reasonably safe, but we still moved cautiously until we saw the fields outside of the *shtetl*. Then we ran until we were safely deep inside the Rudna.

For the several days we remained in the Rudna Forest, many of the men became depressed. They were unable to protect the women and small children from the depredations of local bandits from surrounding villages, men who had long had a reputation as vicious anti-Semites. Men who came during the night, grabbing whatever they could and hauling the spoils off in wagons. If an unfortunate girl or woman were found, she was raped and sometimes beaten. This continued until the Germans brought in police to establish order.

All we could do was try to stay too busy to do much thinking. David split the men into three groups. One group would gather whatever was edible in the forest, another would go to friendly peasants to obtain food, and the third group would stand watch. At night, we took turns guarding our little camp. No matter what I did, I always thought of my brother, Shlomo. I also dreamt of him. Sometimes they were good dreams where we were fishing or working at the yard, playing soccer—something that we used to do, but mostly they were sad, or I was trying to warn him about something, but I couldn't make him understand. These dreams would usually haunt me all the next day.

When word came that it was safe to return to the village, some four days later, there was little celebration that we had survived. Papa had returned the day before, hungry and exhausted, but unhurt.

Every man who had survived, now had to face the poor widows whose husbands and children had been brutally murdered.

***

If there had been little chance of escape before, now there was none, though everyday life reached some sort of balance. For almost nine months, life in the *shtetl* followed a set routine. Some people even began to believe they might have a chance of surviving, of reaching an accommodation, much as the Jewish people had done throughout the centuries. Many others simply existed day to day, resigned to their doom. They did not know if they would be alive or dead the next day. They just wanted to be with their loved ones for the present. The Germans occupied every point of the compass, blocking every avenue of escape. Russia was the only possible haven, but by now, it was too late to go east. As I told you, many who had tried earlier, including myself, had been turned back. In the cities, a person could change his clothes, slip out of the ghetto and pass among the Gentiles, perhaps having a better chance to avoid recognition, but still there was no escape. In the small *shtetls*, the Gentiles knew everybody. There was no chance of anonymity. Besides, most of the men that had the strength and will to escape had families: older relatives, wives, and small children that could not survive in the forest or on a hazardous journey that was by no means guaranteed to succeed. And these families were dependent upon them.

You might be wondering why we didn't escape when the Soviets were here, at least during those three weeks before the arrival of the SS. Well, those are some of the reasons. You have to understand, it was not as cut and dried as it looks now, and I'll be the first to admit, I'm a bit touchy about it. After all, we were not that stupid.

Things were so different then. When the Russians and Germans split Poland in half in 1939, and we ended up in the Russian sphere of interest, we were incredibly relieved, even happy. We had heard how the Germans treated Jews.

With the German victories came an opportunity for anti-Semitic Ukrainians, Poles and Lithuanians to organize *pogroms*. These atrocities had ceased with the arrival of the Soviet Army.

In those days, thousands of Poles and Jews from western Poland clogged the roads escaping to the east to be protected by the Soviets, and indeed, the Soviets helped evacuate Jews and members of other national groups that were in danger from the Germans.

But under the Soviets, there were shortages of everything from food to clothing. Shelves in the stores were bare. People were hungry and cold and miserable. Personal property ceased to exist. Everything belonged to the state.

After only a few months of Soviet occupation, refugees, including many Jews, decided it would be better to return to German-occupied areas. After what I've told you, it's pretty hard to believe, isn't it? Well, there were more reasons.

There was the long-established stereotype of the Russians as a backward, anti-Semitic country, with rioting mobs, unruly Cossacks and government-instigated *pogroms*. Germany stood for the civilized West and the rule of law. People who remembered World War I, such as Krugley, your mother's grandfather, were full of praise for the correct and helpful behavior of the Kaiser's soldiers, as opposed to the rioting Russians. Particularly among the older members of the population, the stereotypes persisted and convinced many to stay. The rich even hoped the Germans would restore their wealth and property, end the food shortages, confiscation of property and arbitrary arrests. Many looked forward to the withdrawal of the Soviets.

Those who applied to Soviet authorities in order to return to western Poland, were loaded into trains and exiled to labor camps in Siberia.

Since the signing of the Molotov-Ribbentrop agreement in 1939, the Jewish community was cut off from all sources of information of Nazi attitudes to Jews. Even though there was a constant stream of refugees with stories of atrocities coming from German-occupied Poland, it was forbidden to speak or write about it in public. Some people treated the awful refugee stories as more Soviet propaganda.

Most Jews understood they would suffer under German rule, but they never considered it could mean complete annihilation. People with large families—many children and babies and older relatives—felt it was impossible to carry them into the unknown. Family solidarity was the main reason teenagers and breadwinners did not leave.

Some had reached complete apathy after many months of scarcity and suffering. They were exhausted and no longer found the energy to exert themselves. Others worried about being vagabonds, homeless or jobless in the Russian winter.

Then there were the true believers who maintained God would not forsake his people. Reluctance to become a refugee, and attachment to birthplace, joined with faith and aversion to the Soviet regime.

When the Germans attacked Soviet Poland, many people tried to leave, like myself, but the Soviets did not make it easy.

Local authorities imposed news blackouts. They appealed for calm and warned the people not to try to escape. Little did we know that at the same time they were feverishly planning to evacuate.

While they commandeered all vehicles for their own getaway, they chided people with: "Don't you trust the Red Army," or, "Don't sow panic."

There were official orders against abandoning workplaces or leaving town without authorization, and for a few crucial days, the Soviets refused to issue the required travel permits to any Jews except those who were active in the party and administration.

Finally, when refugees reached border areas, they were threatened or turned away at gunpoint.

Many of the Jews that tried to escape found their deaths on the roads, in the trains or railway stations that were incessantly strafed and bombed. The Germans moved so fast that many escape routes were cut off before people reached them, so they turned back. Some met their death at the hands of nationalist gangs.

***

There were now many empty houses in Pohost Zagorodski. The families of the men who had been murdered moved in with one another. Your mother's family moved in to Sholom Krugley's brick mansion on Rynek Street, on the north side of the marketplace.

The White Russians and Poles were now the employers of Jews, paying them in barter. It was especially hard for the Jews to find food. Jewish girls, such as your mother, were hired to clean houses and paid with small packets of saccharin.

The German occupation force and the regular army required huge amounts of food. Naturally, the first people to be made to sacrifice were the Jews. In the cities, ration cards were issued. In Warsaw, the Jewish people had a daily food ration of 300 calories; Polish people received 634 calories; for Germans it was 2310. In the villages, the Jews were somewhat better off, but in comparison to the days of the Soviet occupation, they were destitute.

We went back to work at the lumberyard on the outskirts of town across from the Yashelda River. It was better than staying home and worrying when the SS would return. The business, which your grandfather and Jeruchim Zipperstein had built up from nothing, had gone from being nationalized by the Soviets to being taken away. Gentiles, who had been friends with us before June 22nd, 1941, had taken over the lumberyard without as much as a sorry, for seizing Papa's life work. The Germans took much of the lumber and flour for the war effort. Now we brothers worked for them.

And we buried ourselves in our work, as someone does when trying to forget a great sorrow. Who owned the yard made little difference to us; staying alive was the important struggle.

This is the first of those aspects I told you about. Not all Jews met their fate at the death camps. Many, especially in Eastern Europe, died at the hands of special police or SS battalions.

As for me, the bitterness was great, all consuming. They had taken Shlomo from us—the sweetest man you could ever have known. Some of the best times in my life I had spent with him.

***

Here my father surprised me, and I'm certain, Bill too. He interrupted the story and spoke directly to us.

"Promise me boys, you will always be close, you will always talk, you will always be friends. You would have loved my brother Shlomo."

Bill and I promised. We put our arms across each other's shoulders and wept with our father.

***

I thought of Shlomo always, but whenever I found myself in the section of the lumberyard where Shlomo used to work, I would begin to shake, my heart becoming a hammer, beating in my throat. And for a few minutes, it was hard for me to breathe.

How could human beings kill for no reason, I wondered? Everyone I knew figured they would not be killed because they were not Communists.

Realizing they would get no help from the local police, the townsfolk set up a committee of Jewish elders, the *Judenrat*. Lazer Lutsky, another lumberman who had his yard by the train station at Parachunsck, but whose family lived in Pohost Zagorodski, was named the head of the committee. Lutsky spoke German fluently. The people thought the stocky, light-haired Lutsky would be able to communicate with the Germans for everybody's benefit.

***

Soon, a different cycle started. As I was resting after work one night, my cousin Beltche, who served on the committee, ran into the house.

"The Germans have grabbed three men for hostages and if we don't collect enough gold, they'll kill them," she cried.

The wives of the kidnapped men approached the committee, appealing to everyone to collect the gold for their husbands' ransom. This was done and the men were freed.

But the Germans kept coming with different demands. Sometimes for war-related materials and sometimes for spoils. It was their idea of sport and it was never-ending. On one occasion, they needed copper; on another, they needed warm overcoats, or furs. On the occasion of the copper, my mother told us to collect every bit of copper cooking utensils in the house. Then, she sent us down to the Bobric River to dump them in. "The Germans won't have my copper," she said scornfully.

The villagers had to supply the needed goods or there would be an accounting. The Germans never came to the *shtetl* without wanting something, the Jews just hoped it would not be for them. This hope became more and more a daydream once the Germans set up their own government, the *Gebietz Kommisariat,* in the buildings of the Polish school in Pohost Zagorodski.

One month after the massacre, the SS came to Lazer Lutsky's committee and asked for seventy men to go to a labor camp in a neighboring village, Honsovich. It was not easy for Lutsky to pick seventy men because there were not that many left from whom to choose. Somehow he found enough men. None of my family were among the men he chose.

As the seventy were marched off to Honsovich, I asked my father, "Are they going off to work, or are they going to be murdered?"

"Beltche told me the Germans said as long as the Jews work, they'll be all right," Papa replied. "But if any try to escape, the Germans will come back to Pohost Zagorodski and kill their whole family. They're holding them as hostages, Abram."

By now, we'd gotten into a routine. We'd work all day at the lumberyard, all the time worrying about what was happening in the village. We would come home late at night, eat, rest, go to bed, then get up early the next morning to go back to work. It was easier that way, to keep busy.

My cousin Akiba positioned himself on an elevation near the lumberyard. Akiba was known for his "eagle eyes." From there he could see anyone, Germans or police coming down the road, or see what was going on in the village, and give warning if need be.

CHAPTER 5

THE LAST PASSOVER

Passover was not the usual joyous occasion in the spring of 1942. I had wondered if we would even celebrate.

In past years, Jeruchim Zipperstein had always arranged to have the matzot baked. He would get the machinery from a friend in Pinsk, and make enough for the whole town. Since Jeruchim was no longer alive, my brother Label found a rural settlement on the outskirts of Pohost Zagorodski that was safe. Yosel Mednick, who was a Cohan, and who used to work with Label, lived in the settlement and had a very good clay oven.

To be a Cohan was very prestigious in the Jewish community. They were direct male descendants of the line of Jewish priests who were drawn exclusively from the tribe of Levi, and in ancient times were separated from the rest of the people by the aloofness of their ecclesiastical role and the laws of purity they had to observe. In those days, they performed the sacrifices to God on Yom Kippur. Now, they said special prayers on the High Holidays.

We brought three eighty-pound bags of flour from the mill, and many in the *shtetl* came to help. The real specialist in baking was Label, and I assisted my mother and aunt in mixing the flour.

It was a very modest Passover that year. There was no wine, no meat and not enough matzot, after it had been divided among the other families. The service was just enough to get by—the four questions were not asked.

The synagogue had already been emptied by the Germans, who planned to turn it into a stable for their horses. No one dared to go near it although the Germans had not yet moved in.

Mama had hidden the special Passover dishes when the Germans had first come. These dishes were only brought out one time a year, to use at the Seder. When I saw the table setting, I went up and hugged her for this touch of normalcy.

After Papa concluded a brief service, we boys wished out loud that they would be able to bake the matzot again next year, and in good health, and Father made the customary toast: "Next year in Jerusalem." By that time, everyone in the house was crying.

Celebrating the freedom from bondage in Egypt and the escape from Pharaoh, was supposed to give hope. This year, throughout the *shtetl*, there was no hope. People were certain that sooner or later, the end would come. Some people were so depressed, they were simply waiting for it to happen. No one looked for Moses. No one looked for a miracle.

This was the last time anyone baked matzot in Pohost Zagorodski.

***

Two weeks after Passover, the German governor for the area came to see Lazer Lutsky. He demanded more men for the labor camp at Honsovich. There were so few men left; it was inevitable that at least one of the Bobrows would be selected. I was the unlucky one.

My sister Esther said, "We'll bribe them, Papa, so they won't take Abram."

"With what?" asked Samuel sharply. He put both hands on his head and seemed ready to rip out his hair at this new misfortune. "We've already used up all our valuables on other bribes. We have nothing left."

"What about the gold watch you gave to David and Shaindel? It's very valuable," Esther said, as she got up and put a shawl around her shoulders. "I'll go get it." She had reached the point of desperation.

Before she could take another step toward the door, I caught her by her slender arm.

"Wait," I said. "And what do you think Shaindel will use for a bribe when they come for David? Well? They will. They'll come for us all. I don't want to use my brother's bribe."

Esther collapsed on a sofa by the front window, pulling the shawl over her head to hide her tears. "I'm sorry. I know," she sobbed. "But I don't want you to go."

"Who can blame you?" my father said, putting his arm around Esther's shoulder to console her. "You meant well."

I sat beside her, trying to comfort her as well.

"It's only a matter of time," Samuel said. "These people are destroying us."

"Papa," Esther said, hanging her head as if she was ashamed. "I envy the ones who are already dead."

"Many of us do," Samuel sadly replied.

***

On the next day over one hundred people gathered in the courtyard of the *shul*, everyone hugging everyone else, wishing each other well, and saying their goodbyes. I knew I would not be seeing most of them again. Your mother hugged me with tears in her eyes. It seemed like it was the first time we had held each other since Shlomo and Esther's wedding, almost two years earlier.

Ukranian and White Russian police, two to a wagon, one to hold the reins of the single horse and drive, and one to guard the human cargo, drove into the marketplace that morning.

The Germans found willing allies in their war against us. Ukrainians, Poles, and White Russians were made policemen in the cities and *shtetls,* and the Ukrainians were often formed as auxiliaries to the German *Einsatzgruppen,* and used in the *Aktions* or massacres and deportations of the Jews.

There were ten carts in all, with a single plow horse pulling each one. Enough for sixty passengers. They loaded six men in each cart.

The White Russian in the first cart snapped his whip at his horse and the doleful column started down Yeziorna Street on the way north to Honsovich. Ruven Sosnik and Beltche's husband, Akiba, also were made to go. At least I go with my friends, I thought.

We waved sadly to our loved ones, as the carts pulled away.

In the group from the village, there were three men who were not completely normal. One of them, named Vigdar, told me his story. He reckoned that his condition was caused by a German soldier hitting him in the head with a rifle butt in World War I. While riding in the wagon, he figured out exactly how many days and hours he had left to live. It took two days and eight hours to travel in the carts to Honsovich. During the trip, Vigdar's hair turned from dark brown to a brilliant white.

It was a gloomy, overcast day when we arrived. The Germans picked out the three men, including Vigdar, and executed them on the spot. It was precisely the time Vigdar had figured he had to live.

Rain started to fall as I looked around the main yard of my new home and I waited for the guards to give the command to get down from the carts. A tall fence topped with barbed wire was the first thing I noticed. And a small square surrounded by meager wooden barracks.

Eight hundred or so men from the surrounding villages were working in the camp, which used to be the Jewish section of Honsovich. When the Germans came, they turned it into a ghetto enclosing some four thousand men, women and children. The Germans built the iron fence, topped it with the barbed wire and surrounded it with Ukrainian guards.

There were no deportations from Honsovich. The SS came in one day and murdered all the inhabitants of the ghetto. Then they turned it into a labor camp. The Ukrainians remained in place as guards.

I saw prisoners being led out of camp to their work, and others being escorted back through another gate also covered with barbed wire. No one was shackled or bound. The greatest guard was the known threat to their families if they should try to escape. I wondered if I would be in this place until they killed me.

My friends and I were put in the barracks-like houses forcibly vacated by the former Jewish inhabitants. The Germans had set up bunk beds in tiers of three. Ruven, Akiba and I shared one tier.

On the fourth night in the camp, we were awakened by loud shouting from the Germans and the policemen.

"*Raus! Raus!*" they bellowed, ordering all of us out of the houses.

Everyone had to jump out of their bunks and run outside. We were put in lines and made to count off, every man counting a number, "One, two, three" up to ten. This was done over and over until all the workers were counted. After two hours, we were ordered back into the houses. The SS was diligent.

I was exhausted, but too curious to go to sleep. I sought out some of the older inmates to find out why.

"This happens every week to ten days to see if anyone is missing. You know, don't you," the older man said emphatically, "if anyone tries to run away, his whole family, everybody in it, will be killed."

I had already heard this too many times. I went back to my bunk and tried to sleep.

One of the hardest things was to stay clean. Typhus-ridden lice were a constant concern. They only gave us time to wash twice a week and we were working hard and getting dirty.

We were given very little food by the Germans; soup twice a day, with a small piece of dark rye bread. If an inmate had nobody on the outside to send him food, the likelihood was that he would starve. Ruven and I had been able to bring food with us, and the first few weeks, my brothers were able to send packages to us by way of friendly peasants. We both shared our food with Akiba and a sickly boy, who was also from Pohost Zagorodski and used to study with me in Cheder.

At first, Akiba would not sit down to eat with us. He sat alone, sipping his bowl of soup, and refused our offer of extra food.

"Why?" I asked one night.

"I have nobody to send me food, and I don't want to take yours. It's not right, Abram. You need all you have."

"Nonsense, Akiba," I replied. "You are my friend. As long as I have food, we'll share it. And we'll share it till the end. That's final."

When I finally convinced him to take a piece of bread, Ruven walked over and gave him a piece of cheese.

"If you don't eat, you won't be strong enough to survive. And you know what that means," Ruven said.

"One of these days," I said in hushed tones, "we'll escape from here. And mark my words, they will not get away with this. There will come a reckoning, and I guarantee you, you will want to be strong for that."

The leader of our group in the camp was a man named Greenbaum, who spoke perfect German. Every day he would get a list from the Germans telling him how many laborers were needed, where they were needed, and for what jobs they were needed. Some were sent to cut trees and clear roads for the German heavy weapons and tanks. Some loaded and unloaded railway cars on the Baranovich-Luninietz line. One group was sent to a tannery to process animal hides and make leather goods. People were sent to take apart buildings, and sort and save the materials. There were also groups that were sent to dig huge trenches that were used for graves to bury prisoners-of-war and others who were shot. The worst job for me was the digging of the trenches. The Germans drank wine, ate, and joked aloud as the execution squads brought up Russian prisoners, murdered them in cold blood and made the other prisoners dump them into the trenches. I vowed I would never do that job.

I was first sent to work with people who used to be in the building industry. I was lucky. These people were experts at demolishing buildings and made sure everything was done carefully so no one was hurt. They saved everything so that the Germans would have no complaints with their work.

Akiba worked in the tannery and tried to convince me that I would be better off working there. Late at night, whispering to me from his middle bunk, Akiba argued, "This is skilled work, Abram. They need the leather, so they need us. I've heard rumors that people working with leather will be spared. I think if we work here we'll survive the war."

The following day I went to the commander of the labor camp and asked to be transferred to the leather department. He agreed, so I went to work with Akiba.

It was a terrible job. Not only was the work painful and exhausting, but the smell from the chemicals was sickening.

The first process was to tan the raw animal skins. The raw skins or hides were put in large containers. Then water was poured over them, chicken fertilizer was added, and the skins were left to soak for awhile. We had to get in the vats, barefoot, and stomp on the mixture for a few hours. The acid from the fertilizer would remove the hair from the hides. Then the hides were transferred to different vats with different chemicals, and we had to stomp on the hides again. The stench was unbearable. If you stomped on the hides too long, the chemicals would not only remove the hair from the hides, but it would also remove the skin from your feet.

We had to work for awhile, jump out of the vat and wash the acid from our feet, then start treading up and down on the hides again.

After a few weeks, I was ready to do anything else, even work on the trenches.

Luckily, I found out the Germans needed more men for duty in the forest and I received the commander's permission to work on the road, clearing trees.

Walking through the woods the first day, I discovered I had to cross an area where people were being hung. The majority of them were women. The Germans claimed they worked with the partisans. I was startled, but realized that the women had at least chosen to resist. Usually the Germans let the same corpses hang for a few days, then removed them when they had new victims. In six months at the work camp, I never once crossed that area without seeing bodies hanging.

You might think this is strange, but in a way, I envied them. I could not help but think, at least they fought back against the Germans.

CHAPTER 6

THE GHETTO

Not long after I was sent to Honsovich, your mother arose early one morning to take the laundry down to the lake, bringing the twins for help. As they walked down Yeziorna Street, they heard the sound of hammers and men cursing and yelling orders. They saw horse-drawn wagons hauling steel poles along with bales of wire and barbed wire down the street. It was early June of 1942.

Most of the houses in this area were already empty since the massacre. The women and small children had moved in with relatives in other parts of the village. Leah Zipperstein had moved her family to her father's house eight months earlier.

Recently, Julia's Uncle Akiva and his family had moved into Sholom Krugley's house to be together with Julia's family. Eleven women and children and one man were crammed into the house.

Workers dumped the bales of wire and poles a little ways down the street from Bobric Lake. The police supervised the sweating workers who dug post-holes for three-quarters of a mile down Yeziorna Street to the edge of the lake, enclosing all the houses on either side of the street. From what your mother could understand, the workers were of two minds: they were pleased to finally be isolating the Jews, getting rid of them so to speak. But on the other hand, they were angry that they had to do the work. Unfortunately for them, by this time there were very few Jewish men left in the *shtetl*. Most of them were in labor camps, or working in protected industries such as the lumberyard, or they were dead.

The workmen drove the heavy metal posts into the ground, unwound the wire and wrapped it around the posts until the entire area was encircled. Barbed wire was then wound around the top of the posts. These fences were seven feet high.

On orders from the Germans, they were readying a ghetto. It took one day to turn an already dead village into a prison.

The very next day, the police rousted all the Jews out of their homes, allowing them only what they could carry on their backs, and brandishing sticks and whips, chased them down Yeziorna Street to the ghetto.

The remaining men, who had escaped the massacre and the labor camp at Honsovich, were locked in the synagogue. Lazer Lutsky, the head of the *Judenrat*, was ordered to prepare another list of men to go to the labor camp, but he refused, saying to the police, "I will not send any more of our men. You can take my sons and myself. That's all."

The Germans agreed. The Lutskys were taken along with whatever other men the Nazis could round up. They were all kept locked up with no food or water for two days until wagons arrived from Honsovich and they were loaded up and carted away.

***

If one thought it was hard to adjust to life without the men, the women and children somehow managed. They accommodated themselves. They became used to the state of affairs, as all people do. They said, "I have lost my husband, or my father, or my son. This is terrible, but I'm alive and I have others to care for—the elderly, the children. I have to provide. I have to make do." Although many of them were certain there would be another violent dislocation. It had to come sooner or later.

Now, here it was; the ghetto. The last station on their descent into the Nazi's world. If they were caught outside, they would be shot. If they became pregnant, they would be shot. If they became ill or were found to have lice, they would be shot. Their new world was guarded twenty-four hours a day by Ukranian and Byelorussian *militz:* police with machine guns. They could not pass through the single gate on Yeziorna Street unless they had a special permit and were being taken to work. They couldn't attend school. They obviously could not travel. They could not own a business or even walk on the sidewalk. All these offenses were punishable by death. If they became sick the Nazis might consider them a burden, not usable as slave labor. Also punishable by death.

There was no food for days, no warm clothes. Most of the clothes had been traded for food in earlier times and children's stomachs quickly became bloated from lack of food. The world of the ghetto dwellers had diminished to only one street, Yeziorna.

After the massacre, many of the Jews had to go to work for the Gentiles of Pohost Zagorodski. They cleaned floors and walls. They cleaned bathrooms. At least they were not made to clean them using only toothbrushes, as did more unfortunate Jews in some of the large cities.

One of your mother's first jobs was to work in the German government offices. She had given clothes to the Polish girl who managed the kitchen in order to get an easy job. The girl brought in three Jewish girls to do the housework—cook the meals, serve the Germans, wash dishes, and clean the offices. The Polish girl kept them in the back, only working in those offices when the Germans were absent. If they were out of sight there was less chance of them getting in trouble.

Julia and her friends were not supposed to receive any food, but Julia bribed the Polish girl with a maroon dress. When the Germans were finished with their meals, the Polish girl brought the food scraps and bones in to the girls, and made them go in a closet to eat. Then she would lock the closet until they were finished.

Looking through a small window in the office one day, Julia saw old men being tormented. The Germans had received a bunch of live red crabs for their lunch. Before having the crabs boiled, they rounded up seven old bearded men, and attached the crabs to their beards, by the claws. The soldiers could hardly stop laughing.

The Germans knew that the Polish girl had helpers, but they had never seen them. One afternoon, when they heard the girls leaving, they rushed outside with their whips.

"How fast can you run?" they asked the girls as they snapped their whips. "*Eins, zwei, drei!*" they bellowed as they chased the girls away. Julia received three bloody welts on her shoulders and back as she ran.

In the winter, the Jews shoveled snow. In the spring, they cleared the mud and dug furrows in the fields for planting. They did all the heavy work that had been done by the White Russians and Poles. They tended the sheep and cows in the fields.

***

On a daily basis, a White Russian man came to the ghetto and said, "I need five workers today," or "I need six workers." Some number.

Then he selected the workers and left. Julia tried to get selected because the girls would be taken away from Pohost Zagorodski to the small peasant villages. On one such day, your mother and twenty other young girls were taken to Bagdanovka and made to plant trees in the snow. A man took them to the site and handed out little plants in boxes. Julia's shoes had already worn out by this time. New shoes and clothes were impossible to come by. Learning from the peasants, she peeled the bark off birch trees and fastened the strips around her feet with twigs and twine.

Every time Julia dug out a hole in the frozen ground and placed a bunch of plants in it, she said, "They should never grow," as if to put a curse on the plants. There was no reason for this work—planting forests in the dead of winter—other than to make the Jews toil. Your mother thought they would freeze them to death just so they could beautify the homes of the White Russians.

Staying with the villagers during the week turned out to be a lucky break. There were no Germans in Bagdanovka or many of the outlying villages, and where there were no Germans, one could at least breathe and have the illusion that one might survive. Also, the White Russians peasants, for the most part, treated them fairly.

If Julia stayed in the village, there was no way to know what the Germans or the police would do. They might strike at people for the most trivial of reasons or for no reason at all.

The hardest part was that there were no set rules that you could live by—rules that if you followed, you knew you would be safe.

Your mother and grandmother and the twins were rounded up one hot, sunny morning, along with thirty-two other women. The police marched them to the hardware store on Rynec Square that once belonged to Julia's grandfather, Sholom Krugley. They were led inside and the metal doors were locked. No reason was given. No charges were leveled. For three days, they remained in the locked store. Very little food or water was brought to them. Three of the ladies fainted on the second day and no one had enough energy to try to help.

After three days in the stifling heat of the shop, the police, led by Stevkos Volodia, a man who had been a friendly neighbor for most of Julia's life, flung open the doors. Ten of the ladies were ushered out and chased back to the ghetto gates with whips.

"You're off!" Volodia shouted, snapping his whip. "You're off! Get out of here!"

This group included Julia and her family. The other ladies were held back. Once the first group was back inside the ghetto, Julia heard rifle shots. The police executed all the rest.

In the eyes of the Germans and the policemen, Julia, with her fair skin and light brown hair, did not look Jewish. She could only guess if that was the reason she was let go. There was no way to know.

***

Before the invasion, if a child was misbehaving, the parents would say, "Behave or a gypsy will come and take you." Now, it was "Behave or a Jew will come and take you."

On the weekends, the girls were allowed to walk the six miles back to Pohost Zagorodski. Julia walked the distance in her *postales,* the birch bark shoes.

Julia brought old clothes that she had hidden away to trade with the villagers for food—mostly potatoes. One lucky day, she traded for forty pounds of potatoes. Covering the potatoes with her thick black Polish shawl, and wearing a peasant's scarf so she would not look Jewish, she carried forty pounds of potatoes on her shoulders, the whole six miles home.

All business was bartering. There was no money for the Jews of the *shtetl*. Everyone worked for food. It was much more important, and it became harder and harder to come by.

***

Before the Soviet invasion, the area on the east side of the barbed wire was rented by different Jewish families in order to plant gardens to supplement their diets. Mostly they grew potatoes. There were still patches of potatoes growing after everyone was moved to the ghetto.

At night, Julia and Avremel snuck down to the fence and Avremel crawled through the small openings on his belly. Julia held his legs to pull him back quickly if anyone came. They could be shot if he was caught on the other side of the fence. This was a twelve year old, around the same age as you boys.

Leah banned them from going, but they went anyway. They were too hungry—almost starving—to ignore the potato patch. Leah shivered in fear for her children every time they left. Finally, she forbid them to tell her anything about it. She did not want to know.

Avremel dug up the plants he could reach and passed them back to his sister. Then he smoothed over the dirt so no one would know better. When Avremel had gathered all the potatoes from a section, Julia pulled him back and they returned to the house. During their time in the ghetto, your mother told me that they cleared whole sections of that potato patch.

My father and his family moved into the same house on Rynec Street. He had managed to take two large bags of flour with him to the ghetto—these were worth their weight in gold—and he promised Leah that as long as the Bobrows had food, the Zippersteins would not go hungry.

Now, instead of your mother living with eleven people in one house, there were eleven in one room.

Yentl and Samuel Bobrow - 1909

Yentl, Esther, Abram, Samuel Bobrow - 1932

Jeruchim Zipperstein (Julia's father at age 18)-1911

Julia's mother Leah (front row right), Julia's aunt Esther (mother's sister, front row center), Julia's aunt Sarah (mother's sister, back row left), dressed in Bylorussian outfits

Celebration of rebuilding of Synagogue and new torah (young Julia far right) – 1930

59

Krugly family (Julia's grandfather, grandmother, aunts and uncles, Sholom Krugly, front row, third from left) – 1929

Shimon Bobrow (center, Abram's grandfather)

Esther Zipperstein (Julia's sister, Shlomo Bobrow's
wife) – 1937

Esther Bobrow (Abram's sister) – 1936

Julia's uncle Avremel and Julia's little brother
(Julia and Esther in background) - 1938

The twins, Sarah and Rachel (Julia's sisters left
to right) - 1938

Julia Zipperstein (second from left) – 1939

Leah and Avremel Zipperstein (Julia's mother and brother) – 1935

David Bobrow (partisan leader, Shlomo's father) – 1932

Shlomo Bobrow (third from right) – 1937

CHAPTER 7

HONSOVICH

Occasionally the police from Pohost Zagorodski came to the Honsovich labor camp, escorting new workers. Often they would bring mail and packages from our families. Once the Jews of Pohost Zagorodski were moved to the ghetto, this became quite rare. A policemen might say, "Nothing but mail for you today, Bobrow. I guess your village is a little short of food," and think it was a great joke.

One day, I spotted a policemen who I knew before the war. At first, Ziml, the policeman, acted as if he did not know me, whether from guilt or embarrassment, I could not tell. But finally, as he was on his way out of the camp, he broke down and spoke to me. Ziml had no detailed information about my family, but he did say that the partisans had occupied Pohost Zagorodski for one night. The policemen had hid in some of the houses, because if the partisans had caught them, they would have killed them. Ziml was not like most of the policemen. He realized the Germans would not be there permanently.

"Will the Germans keep their word?" I asked Ziml.

Ziml looked down at the ground when he answered in a low voice. "I don't know, Abram. I don't think so."

Later, I heard that Ziml had run off to join the partisans.

***

Inspectors from the *Gebiets-Komisariat* visited the work sites from time to time to make sure we Jews were keeping up with the labor.

"Do we need to worry about him?" I asked some of the older workers when I saw a new inspector who I did not recognize.

"No. This one's not so bad," one man said.

"Yes," agreed the other. "He's definitely better than the ten plagues." Then they both started laughing.

I was going to have to be there a long time before I found any humor, I thought.

But this German was a little better. Trying hard to look at it objectively, I reasoned that most of the Germans were so amoral and villainous that any act of kindness seemed like a godsend.

The German spoke a little Hebrew, and that in itself made me a bit more comfortable. Still, as soon as we knew he was coming, all of us picked up the pace, working faster and more energetically.

The first day, he said to us, "Friends, don't work so hard. Tomorrow is another day and the work won't run away from you."

In a quiet moment when my group was allowed a brief rest, he really surprised me. He actually warned us. "The SS is coming closer to camp. These people wear the black uniforms, with crossbones and skeleton skulls on their hats as their insignia. They mean business. They're extremely evil people and you have to be careful."

After he left, all the workers huddled together excitedly. Everyone already knew about the proximity of the SS, but we were all surprised to receive fair warning from a German.

Coming back from work the next day, I noticed a new face among the workers, and was curious. There had not been any truckloads of new workers in some time. The first chance I got, I went up to him to see if he had any news of life outside the camp.

Cautiously, but with an obvious bravado, the man whispered, "I was with the partisans for awhile. Look at this." He raised a pistol part way out of his pants. Just enough so I could see what it was.

"Why are you here?" I asked. "They'll hang you if they find out."

"Don't worry. I know what I'm doing." He eased the pistol back under his belt and patted it. He gave a little smile. "I got tired of the forest. I needed a change of pace so I came here. Believe me. Living off the land in the forest isn't so easy. You're cold all the time, or wet. And there's never enough to eat. I'm always cold, and hungry. That's why I came to the camp. But I promise you, soon as I'm rested, I'll go back to the partisans."

A few days later, as the man prepared to go back to the forest, I brought Ruven and Akiba to meet him.

"Could you take the three of us with you when you go back? We want to join the partisans," I said.

"I'd like to. You have been good to me, but frankly, they won't take you unless you have weapons. Weapons are harder to get than bodies. They only want people with weapons. To get weapons isn't that easy. I'm sorry. But look, before I go, I want to give you some news. It's not good, but you better listen. The SS are slowly making their way to Pohost Zagorodski and to Honsovich. They're slaughtering whatever remnants of the Jewish communities they find along the way. This I know for a fact."

After the stranger disappeared as quietly as he had arrived, we were more depressed than ever.

"Why did you even bring it up?" Ruven shouted. "I sign the death warrant of my mother and sisters if I run. I've already lost my father. And you, you have people to protect as well. You know we can't leave here."

"As much as we talk about running away to join the partisans, our hands are tied," Akiba said despondently. "How can we leave? Every Jew here faces that same dilemma."

I knew it as well. "Should a son leave elderly parents to their fate, or younger brothers and sisters, so he can run off to join the partisans? Should a husband leave his wife and children to save himself? How did we know that the partisan was even telling the truth? I was sick of the questions. The better question," I told them, "is can we trust the Germans to keep their word?"

***

The men in my barracks kept the windows opened when they slept. It was much more comfortable that way. The summers in Honsovich were hot and very humid. In the next building was my cousin, Berel Denenberg.

The night after the partisan left, I was awakened by a sound from Denenberg's building. Quietly, I got down from my bunk and went to the window to listen.

Denenberg often talked in his sleep. Sometimes he would go on for half an hour without stopping. When people woke him, he would not have any idea where he was—whether he was still dreaming or awake. This night as he spoke, I heard him saying goodbye to everyone he knew.

***

The next day, I helped roll logs into the mud to make a *Nakot*, a road through the swamps for the passage of heavy German equipment. After working most of the day, my crew stopped to rest and eat. Two young boys we knew from the camp approached us. The boys were trembling with fear.

"The SS have killed all the Jews in the town of Lenin. Every last one. Women and children and babies," said the first boy.

"The people from Lenin are planning to run," the second boy said. "They only stayed here because their families were held hostage. Now the hostages are dead."

It didn't take us long to realize the ramifications. "If they killed those people," I said, "they obviously don't care if we work or not. They'll kill the people in our towns and they're probably planning to kill us all as well."

"Besides," the first boy said, "if the workers from Lenin run away, they'll kill us anyway. That's the way they work. If some escape, we're all in danger."

"But if we try to escape," argued Vanya, one of the older men, "we'll be shot. Certainly. There are guards everywhere. We're safer staying and working."

"Safer. Are you crazy?" asked the boy. "Do you know where you are? Do you know who your keepers are?"

"We know our situation here," Vanya replied, barely keeping his temper. "We don't know the circumstances in the forest. They need us."

"They don't have to shoot us. They're starving us, or working us to death," the first boy argued.

The older man turned away angrily.

"Didn't you listen?" the boy continued. "The SS is coming. The partisan told Abram, and now a Jew from Lenin told me. The Lenin Jews are bent on leaving."

"This is going nowhere," I said. "We've argued this way since the first days of the Germans and this is where it's got us. For me, this does it. They're going to kill us all. We have to break out and try to warn our families. You do what you want. As for me, I'm working until our shift is done. Then I'm going back to camp. I'd advise you to not make a move until it's dark. If I see one Lenin man heading towards the fence, I'm off. As for you, Vanya, stay. And God be with you."

The boy motioned for me to come closer. "We have an escape committee. We've planned a raid on the police station and post office."

I stared incredulously at the boy. I'd been there four months and never heard of such a committee.

"One of the men has promised he can get a truck for the escape."

"Well," I said, "it looks like he better have it by tonight."

At dusk, I returned to Honsovich and sought out a man I knew from Lenin. He told me the same story as the boys. I went to my hut. Finding Akiba and Ruven, I brought them near a window facing the camp's eastern fence so I could keep watch on the prison yard. Then I told them what had happened.

"We have to start planning a way to escape," I said.

"The SS could be in Pohost Zagorodski right now," Akiba realized.

"Then we have to go to warn them…to try to save them," Ruven said.

Although hazy, there was still enough light for me to make out people in the courtyard, moving tentatively toward the fence. One was my friend from Lenin.

"That's it. They're going. We have to move. Now. Get your things," I said urgently.

70

Ruven and Akiba nodded in agreement and gathered their belongings and some food. I put a hatchet that I had stolen from the leather factory in my bundle.

Exiting the building, we met Greenbaum, the camp leader, and explained the commotion.

"I'll go with you," Greenbaum said, not even bothering to get his few possessions.

Three other men joined us on the way to the barbed wire fence. Ruven quickly cut the wire in two places and Akiva held the strands open while we slipped through. Then we threw away all sense of caution and began to sprint to the woods, a hundred yards away. As I ran, I tore off the hated yellow patch and threw it to the ground. An immense weight seemed to lift from my shoulders.

By the time we reached the outskirts of Honsovich, we could hear shooting behind us. Many other groups of men were also running to the forest.

In the camp, SS and police rode out of the camp gate on horseback, heading to the forest to cut off the escaping prisoners. Soldiers in the watchtowers were shooting anyone that was outside in the yard. Workers who decided to take their chances in the camp, obviously stayed inside and ducked down.

We were surrounded. Reaching the tree line, I ran thirty yards and dove into some bushes. I prayed as SS troops rode by so close, I could almost reach out and touch them. I could smell their unwashed bodies. As soon as the soldiers passed, I jumped up and ran again, diving into another patch of bushes if I heard a shot or men shouting or the sound of horses. The night was very dark. As I ran, I clutched my hatchet and resolved that I would go down fighting. I wasn't afraid. In fact, I felt exhilarated that I was no longer under the Nazis' control. I was free, and if I died fighting, that was okay. But I promised myself that I would take a few of the sons of bitches with me.

One of the men, a blacksmith who had been my neighbor in Pohost Zagorodski, stopped running. He grabbed his chest and fell to the ground. I ran over to him, but he was dead. Heart attack.

As I got further into the thick forest, two other men from Pohost Zagorodski joined me. Luckily, one of these men, Kalman Brevda, had worked in the woods with me, and knew the area. I was only familiar with the forests closer to Pohost Zagorodski and that was fifty miles away. I knew the woods better than Ruven or Akiba, but I was certain I could not lead anybody out of this forest.

To get home, we would all have to rely on Brevda.

Brevda said the main roads were out of the question. He was certain the police were concentrating on them, and by now would have checkpoints on all roads leading from Honsovich.

He led us three hundred yards off the main road. It took an hour just going this distance into the forest. This was an area of swamps, trees, lakes and mud. The going was very slow, until Brevda found the trail he was looking for. When we were finally on the path, we moved quickly, half running, half walking.

Now I stopped worrying so much about being caught. Instead, I wondered if we would get to Pohost Zagorodski in time. I had become so cynical. How could one not be? I expected the worst. I was certain the SS were headed toward Pohost Zagorodski to finish the job.

I told you that there were two times in my life when I was terrified out of my mind. This was the second time. As I look back on it, I realize that the first time I was so scared was because I had no idea what was going to happen. This time I was frightened because I knew what the Nazis were capable of.

We had gone six miles when we came to a small village. Avoiding the houses, we moved closer to the road so we would not lose track of each other. Just then we heard three shots. Everyone dove to the ground. There was another shot.

"Where's it coming from?" Greenbaum whispered.

"Don't ask dumb questions," Brevda yelled as he stood up. "Let's get out of here!"

In the excitement, Brevda ran one way and I ran the other. Now I was the only one of my group with any knowledge of the area. Akiba and Ruven had disappeared as well.

We had no choice except to walk all night. I could only hope I was leading us in the right direction.

By the time we came to the outskirts of the village of Rotinsh, we were exhausted. Stopping to rest in a field of shrubs and weeds, we couldn't help ourselves—we all fell sound asleep.

As day broke, I was awakened by the sound of peasants talking, as they grazed their cattle. I cautiously got up on my knees and peered through the tall grass. I saw peasants and their animals on one side of us, and two Germans soldiers talking to a policeman about fifty yards away on the other side.

"Abram," Greenbaum whispered, "I can't run anymore. My legs are killing me."

Bolt, the third man in our small group agreed. "I need more rest," he said.

I took another look at the Germans. "I think it's best if we stay put anyway. Here in the weeds. We can't move while the soldiers are this close."

For three hours we stayed, lying in the tall grass and shrubs, not able to make any noise. Even a sneeze could give us away. Bolt and Greenbaum fell back to sleep, but I could not. What if one of the cattle wandered over, bringing a shepherd into our midst? Then that shepherd would alert the Germans. What if the Germans or the policeman decided they wanted to talk to the farmers? We were directly in their path.

That was not my worst fear. For three hours, I lay there helpless, unable to move, dreading what I would find at home—that I would be too late.

Before the night was out, rewards for us were posted around the countryside. I saw one of them early the next morning. Some of the escapees were caught this way. Peasants would offer them food, take them in, and turn them in to the Germans. As I told you before, we had no idea who we could trust.

I heard later that all the Jews who stayed behind in Honsovich were gathered into the main courtyard of the camp and shot.

THE THIRD DAY

CHAPTER 8

POHOST ZAGORODSKI

Today was rather strange. Papa was very secretive, and insistent on Mama being out of the house; even, it seemed, out of the neighborhood. After a huge lunch, he sent her out, not even letting her clear away the dishes and clean up the kitchen. He promised that we men would see to it. Since she was very involved in temple fundraising and other activities, Papa knew she would have plenty to do. He as much as handed her the car keys and ushered her out of the house. Obviously, I was curious. What could be worse than what we had already heard?

I learned later that Mama had not talked about this for many years, and Papa was worried about what effect it might have on her. Before speaking to us, Papa waited till the sounds of the car receded into silence. Then we did the dishes, and only after we were finished did he resume the story.

***

The three hours that I was hiding in the tall grass seemed like an eternity. When the policeman and the Germans finally moved off in a different direction, I quietly led Bolt and Greenbaum deeper into the woods, further from the grazing area. It was still too dangerous to resume our journey.

"There're too many shepherds out here. They might help us, but it's more likely they'd report us to the Germans. We have to wait," I told them. It was disheartening. All this for the sake of a few dirty little cows.

Five more hours were wasted, hiding. It was that long before the peasants herded their animals off to their enclosures, and we could safely start out for the *shtetl*. There were just too many people on the road. We still had to keep to the deep woods to stay out of the way of both the peasants and the Germans. To our misfortune, this part of the forest was as thick as a tropical rain forest and the going was excruciatingly slow.

***

This time the Nazis sent trucks to Pohost Zagorodski. I can still imagine the great clouds of dust stirred up by the gray trucks and the roar of the diesel engines breaking the serenity of a summer afternoon.

It was August, 1942. The ghetto of Pohost Zagorodski had been in existence for four months.

Shlomo's wife Esther—this was your mother's sister—was probably among the first to hear the trucks. She had been given a job with a Polish family that lived on the outskirts of town.

The lady of the house wanted to hide her; she begged Esther to stay, telling her she would only be killed. But Esther insisted on going back to get her baby—blond, curly-haired four-year-old Aviva. Esther had a feeling that this time, the SS had come for the women and children.

The Polish woman told her husband to go with Esther to help her get back into the ghetto.

The two of them ran down Yeziorna Street until they were almost in sight of the guard at the ghetto entrance. Then they ducked out of sight behind a brick house and continued running along the east fence of the ghetto. They found a small hole in the fence, only big enough for a child.

Esther thought she would never get through, but the Polish man stepped on the bottom part of the barbed-wire fence, holding it down. He said he would wait for her.

Esther managed to squeeze through, only ripping a small piece of fabric from her dress.

She ran into her house and yelled, "Mother! They're coming to kill us all! Give me Aviva. Hurry!"

Leah quickly ran to get the little girl, and lifted her to her mother's arms.

Tears running down her cheeks, Esther Zipperstein gently caressed her mother's face with one hand, then hugged and kissed her. Julia ran up and hugged Esther tightly.

"Give the twins a kiss for me," Esther said with profound sadness in her heart. Julia could tell Esther wanted to stay a few more minutes with their mother.

"Go!" Julia shouted. She had no idea where the courage came to shove her sister out the door for what she was certain was the last time. "Please hurry!" *Please survive.*

Esther and Aviva made it back through the fence with the Polish man's help. Together, they ran to the Polish home before the SS reached that part of Pohost Zagorodski.

The Polish couple hid them in their basement.

As the *Einsatzgruppen* came to a halt in front of the walls of the Jewish ghetto, a *haupsturmfuhrer,* or captain, rode up in the sidecar of a motorcycle. Getting out, he ordered his men down from the trucks.

It was not really necessary to signal the drivers to leave the engines running, they knew the program—they had already done it so many times.

Soon, fifty SS troupers, resplendent in their dark green uniforms with yellow trim, and each carrying either a whip, a machine gun, or a rifle, were gathered in a circle around their *haupsturmfuhrer*. First, he assigned non-commissioned officers to take their men and surround the ghetto to ensure there would be no escapes. Next, he informed the rest, another fifty soldiers, that anyone trying to escape should be shot, as well as those too sick or frail to walk to the marketplace, or infants, or those trying to hide or resist.

Divided into teams of two and three soldiers, they entered the ghetto. Polish and White Russian collaborators, who had been made policemen, entered along with the SS.

Avremel Zipperstein was playing field hockey with a six other children when he heard the engines. He smacked the ball as hard as he could, then dropped his stick and ran home to warn his mother.

A small contingent of soldiers stayed near the gated entrance to the ghetto, while the rest, going from house to house in groups of two and three, combed the fenced-off ghetto area, rounded up all the women and children and brought them to the marketplace.

Little sporadic pops, like the sound of firecrackers going off, were heard in the air as the Nazis shot anyone who was sick, too feeble to move, or just plain slow. They were shot in the bed where they lay or the chair where they sat. It did not matter if they were old or young, a child or an adult, they were shot on the spot. Babies that cried were also shot. They were "offering resistance." One baby, crying in its mother's arms, was pried away, held at arm's length, shot and dropped to the ground like litter. The screaming young mother, made to watch her precious infant's death, was shot immediately afterward.

***

Esther Bobrow screamed at her father, "Papa! Get to the cellar. The SS is here!" Esther gathered her young daughter into her arms to soothe her fears.

"But what about you?" my father asked hesitatingly. "You and mother come as well."

"No. They'll only want the men, like last time," Yentl said. "If they don't find anyone here, they'll start to search. You know that."

Against his protests, Esther started pushing Papa towards the cellar. Samuel took my mother's hand and pulled her close. He embraced her. "You are the strong one." He slowly turned and walked down the stairs. Esther followed him into the cellar to cover the false floor.

She then returned to our mother's side. They held each other and waited.

In another part of the ghetto, Label was also persuaded by his wife to head for the double cellar that had been secretly constructed for this very purpose.

In his house, David Bobrow had built a second wall about one and a half feet wide, out from the windowless bedroom wall. As Shaindel, cradling their baby, told him to hide, David grasped her trembling arm.

"What if they're the ones who kill everyone?" he asked. "Come in with me. There's enough room."

"Who'll close it if we're both inside?"

David smiled grimly. "We'll manage. If they make any kind of detailed search, they'll find us anyway."

"What about the baby? If he cries…" she asked.

"Shlameleh," David said softly, taking his son from Shaindel and caressing his baby's arm, "you'll be quiet for us, won't you?"

The baby smiled and gurgled at his father's soothing voice. David knew his baby would not give them away. The three of them hurriedly slipped into the opening of the wall, and David wedged it shut, flush with the adjoining wall.

Down the street, Avremel Zipperstein burst into his house, yelling, "Mama! Mama!" He ran up into his mother's arms and hugged her.

"I know," Leah said. "Be brave, my little man. Go get your sisters. Down by the lake."

Avremel left her embrace and raced out the door.

By the time he returned with the twins, Leah had brought her mother to the front of the house. The whole family gathered together, and Leah, with tears streaming down her cheeks, ushered them outside, before the soldiers could have a chance to shove or beat them.

***

Julia knew that death had finally come. It was almost a relief to her. The waiting over the last year had been unbearable. Life in the ghetto had been so terrifying, the conditions so wretched, that she had actually wished for death many times during the last year. Still, goosebumps of fear rose on her back and arms. Her only comforting thought was that she knew Esther was safe with the Polish family.

Outside, Julia was struck by the incongruity of her people being driven like an unwanted herd of animals on such a beautiful summer afternoon. The blistering heat of midday had abated. The sun still shone brightly, though there was now ample shade from the trees. She could smell the air off the lake. There was a faint, pleasant smell of wood-burning fires and Julia wondered who would put out the fires.

Throughout the ghetto, people cried and prayed. Some screamed and begged for God's intervention, for a miracle. The sound of their laments was shrill and helpless. *"Shamah Yisrael"* rang out from every quarter as the Germans shouted back "Where is your god? He's not with you. God is with us!" Some of the SS soldiers even wore belts on which those words were written: "God is with us."

Walking next to Julia was a white-haired, old lady. A soldier screamed at her to move faster. He kicked her with his heavy boot, driving her to the ground. Then, as if without a second thought, Julia saw him draw out his luger and shoot the old lady in the head. He acted with no more remorse than if he was swatting a pesky fly.

Father, Julia thought, you were the lucky one. You didn't have to live through this. Seeing your family murdered. Your whole village destroyed. Annihilated. You were the lucky one.

A shudder ran through her body as she thought of Avremel and the twins. She kept them all close together and moving quickly.

She could not help but notice the sharp contrast between the tall, well-fed soldiers in their crisp, dark uniforms and the starved, hollow-eyed women and children of the ghetto.

Others were being shoved along by the blow of a rifle butt or the sting of a whip. The fortunate ones were those who moved fast enough to be ignored by the Nazis. SS troopers laughed and made crude jokes as they pushed and whipped the helpless women and children through the ghetto down Dworska Street towards the waiting trucks.

The old, the sick, and the young children and mothers with babies, were pushed onto the trucks, while the others were grouped and made to march in columns of four. This, so the SS could keep better track of the numbers. Your mother walked in a column with her brother and two sisters. Her mother and grandmother were in the row behind.

In the same columns were my mother, my aunt, my sister Esther and her daughter. Many other relatives were also in line. David Lutsky, a student, and his mother, Chaska walked in the row in front of Julia. The fact that they were blond, even their eyebrows, and the family of Lazer Lutsky, meant nothing to the SS. The Germans marched them all down Dworska Street, prodding and kicking them.

As they crossed the bridge, one young girl started to run, then another. For a second, Julia was struck with the urge to run. She quietly slipped out of her shoes so it would be easier for her, but Avremel stopped her, grabbing your mother by the wrist.

"Don't Julia," he cried. "Please. Don't you see what they're doing? They'll shoot you right now."

Guards were just then leveling their machine guns. The two women, and then a third would-be fugitive, were machine-gunned in the back as they ran.

They were marched past the Jewish cemetery where the men and boys had been killed a year earlier, and past the lumber mill to an area of low-lying hills.

Julia heard a soldier yell out, "Who do I shoot first?" as they approached a deep ravine. The trucks, their engines still running, had already arrived. One five-year-old boy was sitting in the truck, whining for his mother. An SS man grabbed him by the neck, lifting him up out of the truck. He laid his pistol against the boy's neck, and without a second thought, fired.

The soldiers unloaded the trucks and started shooting everyone that had ridden up in them, babies included, and throwing them into the abyss. One soldier took a baby, threw her four feet up in the air, and, positioning his rifle under the falling toddler, caught her on his bayonet.

The women and children who marched up were made to strip. All of the clothes were neatly put in piles by the SS men. Once naked, the women were then moved up to the edge of the ravine in the same columns of four by which they arrived.

Julia could not bear the thought of taking her clothes off one piece at a time in front of these men, so she angrily ripped her clothes off, shredding them.

We look so pathetic, Julia thought as she viewed the pale, clammy bodies walking up to the edge of the hill. Months of starvation had done its job. It had all been so gradual. She had never realized how far they had fallen. Look at these people. There's nothing to them. How weak and pitiful they had all become.

As a row of four Jews reached the edge of the pit, they were forced to kneel down. A soldier went down the line shooting one bullet into the neck of each person, and one by one, their bodies tumbled into the deep ditch. Then the next four were ordered to walk to the edge, also forced to kneel, and shot.

Julia and Avremel, and their twin sisters, Sarah and Rachel, walked up to the rim hand in hand. Avremel said, "Don't cry. We will soon be with Papa."

Throughout the ordeal, Julia had kept telling herself Esther was safe. In this she took comfort. But here was Avremel, trying to comfort her, always trying to protect her. And even though she had not wanted to give the Germans the pleasure of seeing any tears or weakness, she began to cry.

The four of them were made to kneel. Julia's skin crawled as she thought of falling naked on top of the naked bodies of her loved ones. As she knelt, she thought about Leah having to witness her children's deaths, and she felt worse for her mother than she did for herself. Then Julia felt a kick in the back. An SS man had kicked her instead of shooting. She heard a Polish policeman sneering at the German, "What? You are hesitating to kill a Jewess?" The SS man looked at the Pole and smiled in contempt. Then he raised his gun and shot at Julia.

There was so much screaming and crying and gunfire, that Julia did not even hear the shot. She felt what seemed like another kick. This time, to the back of her neck. There was no pain as she felt herself somersault over and over down the hill, only a numbness encompassing her whole body. As she tumbled over the rough ground, Julia thought if this is death, it is not so bad—certainly far better than the existence they had been forced to live since the coming of the Nazis.

She blacked out and fell into the jumble of naked bodies—most of whom were already dead when they hit the bottom of the ravine. But the marksmanship of the SS was not always true. Some of the women and children were wailing and writhing in pain—the ones who could, still crying out, "*Shamah Yisrael.*"

Julia was bewildered to realize she was still alive when she came to in the ravine. But the clawing and biting on her arms and legs, as other victims tried desperately not to be buried alive under the new victims falling on top of them, convinced her that death would not be so easy after all. More bodies fell on her. In horror, she realized the bodies now pressing her down might even be someone from her family. Perhaps her own mother. My God, she thought, horrified beyond comprehension. She bit her lip severely, then jammed her fists against her mouth to suppress the urge to scream. She did not want to give the soldiers the satisfaction.

A few of the soldiers walked down into the ditch and fired their pistols at anyone who was still groaning or moving.

Julia prayed for a second bullet to end her misery. She had been shot in the neck, but the bullet continued out through her left cheek and missed her vital spots. In her right hand was a bullet. She wondered if it was the bullet that hit her or if it had come from someone else.

The SS men down in the ditch that were finishing off the victims soon tired of it, and climbed back up the hill. There was too much blood and too many bone fragments splattered on their nice uniforms after such close range work.

***

81

Back in the field, I was in a state of unbelievable worry and anguish. I could still hear the stirrings of the peasants, but at least now it was getting dark, and that allowed us to move closer to the highway where the ground was cleared of trees and debris and we could move faster.

After three hours of fast walking and jogging, we came to a fork in the road. I had no idea which fork led to Pohost Zagorodski. I picked the left fork and it turned out to be the wrong one. In another three hours of walking, we stopped quickly and ducked down behind some large trees. We heard voices that we thought were speaking German. Carefully edging closer, I recognized the language. It was German. But this was another group from my hometown, using German for safety's sake.

Moving closer yet, I could see my cousin, Yosel Danenberg, and motioned for my friends to come forward.

"Yosel," I whispered loudly. "It's me, Abram."

At first puzzled, Yosel soon recognized me and we hugged each other. His joy at seeing me was mixed with tears.

"Abram. You took the wrong fork as well," he whispered, hugging me all the more tightly. "We did the same. We're about two miles from Malkovich.

"How do you know?" I asked.

Now Yosel started crying. He could barely speak. "My brother Berel went up and knocked on the window of a peasant's house. They opened the window and shot him. Right there. No questions asked. He was dead immediately. I ran up to help him, but he was dead. They pulled me away," he said, indicating the other men.

I tried to comfort him, but what could I say? I knew what it was like to lose a brother to these butchers. Yosel was beginning to suffer the same sort of depression I did after Shlomo's death, and I had not been able to stop thinking about Shlomo for nine months.

Berel's dead. Another cousin dead, I thought. How many of my family before this is over? All, I wondered? If I thought too much about it, I was certain I would go mad. We were so helpless. I knew we had to find guns, weapons, something.

"Let's start back to the fork. Quickly. We have to hurry. It's the only way back home and we've already wasted too much time," I told them with a new determination.

***

The slaughter of innocents continued. There was now so much pressure and weight from above that Julia felt the same fear as those who had gone before her. She might be buried alive. It was becoming hard to breathe. She was choking. She could feel the painful movement of bodies both above and below her. Again, the thought of who these suffering beings could be, caused a deep revulsion, even sickness, inside her. Please God, she prayed, let me die.

The shooting in columns had continued into dusk until everyone, all eight hundred women and children from the ghetto, except the few who had managed to hide, had been led to the edge of the ditch and then murdered.

Before the Germans could once more go down the hill of the ravine to finish the job, or even gather up the discarded clothing, they heard shots coming from the other side of the *shtetl.*

They figured it must be partisans, and quickly boarded the trucks and headed in the direction of the shooting. They would finish this job later.

In the massive grave at the bottom of the pit, there were still people that were alive, screaming and kicking.

It took all of Julia's willpower, but she waited until the sound of the trucks receded. The weight of the people on top of her was crushing her. She could not breathe. The heat was suffocating her. Draining her. The fear of being buried alive now outweighed her desire to die. Julia had to fight the feeling of panic. When it seemed as though the only noise was the groaning of the other still live victims, she used all of her strength to claw and crawl out from under the dead weight of bodies. It seemed interminable. As if she could only measure her progress in inches and hours, and every movement was over and through the quagmire of loved one's bloodied bodies.

When she reached the top, she saw there were others, five in all, who had been strong enough to inch their way to the surface and emerge. One was Julia's cousin, Rivka, whose grandfather had overseen the building of the new temple in Pohost Zagorodski after the fire had destroyed the first one. Rivka's three-year-old daughter was one of the children who had ridden in the trucks. Now the child was dead.

Faigel was another girl Julia knew. Raven-haired and twenty years old, Faigel's father had been a blacksmith in town. Rivka had been wounded in the head. Faigel had been shot in the arm.

The six women climbed to the top of the ravine and scattered, running to different White Russian farmhouses near the Kamener Way. At each house, the girls begged to be taken in. All six were completely naked, blood streaming from their wounds.

Julia was exhausted. Her neck was bleeding slightly and aching. She had no idea how she was able to keep running from house to house, furiously pounding on the wooden doors till her hands were bloody, only to have the peasants slam the doors in her face or lock them as she approached. No one would take her in. In desperation, she grabbed some scrub rags that were hanging on a fence to dry, and covered herself as best she could.

She saw one more house, one more hope. She ran up to the front and pounded on the door. Will no one help me, she screamed. No one did. Julia gave up and ran back toward the brush leading to the woods.

Three of the women who survived found Byelorussian families willing to take them in. But in the morning, all three were turned over to the Germans, who immediately executed them.

Julia entered the thick covering of forest and found a dense thicket in which to hide. The two other women who had not found refuge with the peasants also wandered aimlessly in the woods, not knowing what to do or where to go. Along with your mother, they had realized that they could not go to the Poles or White Russians for help, or at least had given up.

After many hours of soul-searching mixed with an almost paralyzing fear, Julia finally knew what she had to do. Since she left the Kamener area, she had been hiding in her wet rags in a field near the woods, trying to rest. Now she got up and set about finding her way back to the ravine, but she was disoriented.

After wandering around the forest in what seemed like circles in the dark, she found her way back to the hill, using the anguished voices of the dying to help guide her. But this raised feelings of hope. If there are voices, she thought, they might be of my family. *Some might still be alive.*

At this time of year, it was cold after sundown and she was shivering. Finding the clothes pile, she grabbed the first jacket and dress she could find. Not bothering to rip off the yellow patch that identified the wearer as a Jew, she put on the jacket only to be horrified when she looked at the passport in one of the pockets. It belonged to a woman she knew.

Steeling herself for what she would find, she edged down the hill into the ravine. The dirt and grass were sticky from blood.

She quietly whispered out the names of her family: "Avremel, Sarah, Rachel, Leah," as she groped her way around the mass grave. None of those she called answered. There were only weak, inhuman voices, suffering from pain and thirst.

As she waded out into the piles of bodies to call their names once more, she heard a voice.

"Help me," the woman cried. "It's not for myself, but my baby. He's buried under here and I know he's alive. I don't want him to be crushed. Please," she sobbed. "I know I'm dying, but I want my son to live. Please help me move some of the bodies off him."

Julia knew the woman. She was Michle Rudnick, very attractive and from a well-to-do family. Her husband, who was killed in the first massacre, had been an accountant from Vilna. Her son was only seven years old.

"He might still be alive," Michle pleaded.

Julia struggled to move aside some of the naked bodies. The woman was too weak to be of much help. Michle tugged at some of the various entwined limbs around her, then finally fell back exhausted. She knew she was dying.

Julia was so undernourished from living in the ghetto, that with the addition of her wound, she also soon became exhausted. Tracks of tears must have shown on her gaunt face in the moonlight.

Looking up at Julia for the first time, Michle exclaimed, "Oh my God! You are so bloodied yourself. I'm sorry. You must get out and save yourself. You must have no strength to help us. Go. Save yourself."

Julia struggled with the bodies, but she was too weak. The woman's child was never found.

As Julia left, Michle cried out one last time, "God help us."

Three times that night, Julia went back to the pit. Not able to find her way in the blackness of the woods, she headed toward the sounds of the dying. Three times she crawled down the hill and called out for her family. Three times she ascended the hill with nothing but a profound, heart-wrenching sorrow and emptiness, the last time because it was starting to get light, and she knew it would be too dangerous to remain any longer.

Your mother no longer wanted to die. She wanted revenge.

***

After having chased away the partisans, the Germans returned to Pohost Zagorodski and searched the ghetto area for hidden cellars and double walls. They were successful in finding some Jews, who were immediately executed. They sent out teams to sweep the nearby forests for others that had escaped their net.

***

I can't even begin to imagine how terribly alone your mother felt. She wandered around the thick forest looking for other survivors, but did not dare to call out. She wanted to sit down and cry, but she knew there were German patrols in the area—she had heard the distant sound of their trucks. She thought it would be safer on the other side of the Bobric River.

As she approached the banks of the river, she heard faint voices speaking Yiddish. It was the two other survivors, Rivka and Faigel, huddling by the river.

"We should cross the river," Julia said as she came up to them. But the two girls did not want to.

"It's too deep," said Rivka. "We could drown."

"It's better to try it than to be shot by the Germans," Julia argued.

Faigel started to cry. "I think the current is too swift for me. I'm not a strong swimmer."

Finding strength from somewhere deep within herself, Julia urged them to at least try. She felt it was better to drown than to fall into the hands of the Germans.

Your mother headed into the water. Once she waded in, the water was soon up to her knees, then waist. It got deeper and deeper until it was up to her chin, but she kept going. She could feel the coolness of the water against her wound—seeming to ease the pain.

Behind her, the other two girls stood still, terrified that she would drown. It looked like she was disappearing with each step away from shore. Somehow, they managed to plunge into the water and follow Julia, swimming across the river without incident.

But as soon as they were ashore on the other side, a shot rang out. Panicking, all three ran to a nearby potato patch and dove into the furrows dividing the plants. In the confusion, they became separated. From the potato patch, Julia could hear dogs barking from all directions. In horror, she realized the dogs were barking at the sounds of the people dying in the ravine. Julia finally fell asleep in the potato patch, from exhaustion.

That same morning, two truckloads of SS men drove back to the site of the slaughter. They got down from the trucks, one group going over to the mounds of clothing, sorting it and loading the clothes onto the trucks. Another group took handfuls of grenades, walked over to the edge of the pit, and tossed them in, tearing up the bodies with the explosions. The cries and moans of the dying finally stopped.

Julia was awakened by the explosions. She knew what it was and cried silently, trying to blot out the sound by covering her ears. She was afraid to look for the other two girls.

When the Germans left, Julia made it back to the woods by herself. In a clearing she saw a haystack. She crawled on her hands and knees towards the hay. Worried that someone would notice the stack was disheveled if she crawled inside, she wriggled her way under the wooden platform holding the haystack above the muddy field, and placed her hands under her chin to keep her face dry and out of the mud.

Even from under the platform, the smell of the newly mown hay was invigorating to her. She breathed in deeply, and in her weariness, as she fought to keep her eyes open and her wits about her, she prayed that it had all been a dream.

As sleep inevitably overtook Julia, her mother Leah appeared to her in a vision.

"Don't worry, my darling," her mother said. "You are safe here. And in the morning, a peasant will bring you milk and bread."

Julia reached out to touch her. "Mother," she cried, but as she reached, the vision disappeared.

Julia slept fitfully there, under the haystack, until early the next morning. Just as the skies began to lighten, she crawled out from under the wooden framework.

Even though it was the dry season, enough water had seeped under the platform during the night, to chill her thoroughly. Standing up and trying to wring some of the cold water out of her coat, she saw a man on horseback in the distant field. He waved to her. Puzzled at first, she realized he was motioning for her to move back to some bushes behind the haystack. This she quickly did. The man rode toward her.

Crouching behind the bushes, shivering from the damp cold, and in fear of the man approaching her, Julia said a prayer.

The man drew nearer and your mother recognized him. It was Sholomitski, a friend of her grandfather's. He rode up to the bushes, once or twice looking behind him to see if any of his workers were watching. Satisfied they were not, he pointed to Julia's coat and the yellow star on the front.

"I know you, don't I?" Sholomitski asked.

Julia started to rise but he motioned for her to stay down.

"It's too dangerous for you to be seen. What is your name, child?" He had come to the field to see his workers who were cutting and stacking hay.

"I'm Julia Zipperstein. Krugley's granddaughter," Julia whispered.

"Yes, yes. I thought it was you. I haven't seen you since you were little," he said, as he held his hand down low to indicate a small child. "I knew your father and grandfather. You are in danger here. Promise me you'll stay in the bushes until dark. My workers might see you."

Julia nodded.

"Tonight, when it's safe I'll bring you food. Here," he said, handing her a damp leather flask filled with water. "This will have to hold you till then." Then he turned and rode off.

By this time, your mother was not sure she could trust anyone, but she had to trust Sholomitski. There was no other choice, no other place to go. She could not just wander around until she was discovered by the Germans or turned in by peasants. Julia prayed that he was a true friend.

**

The Germans moved into Pohost Zagorodski, destined to become a garrison town. Eighty SS occupied the vacant Jewish homes and buildings.

Some moved into the Bobrow house and some into the Zipperstein house. Horses were stabled in the synagogue, purposely desecrating the holy edifice with manure. The SS put out a proclamation to the peasants that anyone who brought in a live Jew would get five hundred marks; many Jews were turned in to the Germans in this manner. Two days after the massacre, and after all the trouble and risk the Polish employers of Esther Zipperstein Bobrow had undertaken, they turned her and little Aviva in to the Germans. Forty other Pohost Jews that had hidden during the massacre were also turned in. All were murdered. Some were tortured before being killed.

Three days after the massacre, signs reading "This City Is *Judenfrei*" appeared on posters all over the *shtetl*. *Judenfrei* means free of Jews.

CHAPTER 9

JULIA

For the second night in a row, we jogged as far as we could before hunger and exhaustion forced us to slow down and walk. When we were the least bit rested, we pushed ourselves to run again.

It was almost dawn when we came to a single small farm on the edge of the forest. Even though I had known Alexi since I was a little boy, and his farm was only four miles from Pohost Zagorodski, I was still nervous about approaching his place.

I told my exhausted comrades to wait while I found out what had happened in the town. I walked up to the house cautiously, the story of Berel Danenberg still fresh in my mind, but the apprehension of what I might find overshadowed any fear.

Knocking on the window, I called softly, "Hello, hello. Alexi."

"Is that you, Bobrow?" the peasant answered, as he opened the shutter to the window.

"Yes," I answered.

"You can't stay here long. You shouldn't even come in. The SS is everywhere. Wait just a second. I'll bring some food. You must be hungry," Alexi said, and he turned away from the window.

As the man left, I felt my heart pounding. How on earth could I even ask the question? I wasn't sure I wanted to know the answer.

Alexi returned quickly with a loaf of bread, some cheese, and some biscuits, stuffing them into a bag that he handed me through the window.

"I have to tell you something. You must prepare yourself," Alexi said very slowly, deliberately. He could not look me directly in the face. "I am about to cause you great pain."

I remember feeling a wave of heat trail down my back to my thighs. During two nights of walking, I had tried to prepare myself for this, but now I knew how miserably I had failed.

"They took the whole town out yesterday," Alexi said solemnly. "Everyone in the ghetto. All the women and children. They took them out past the lumberyard and shot them. I'm not certain, but I think your father and brothers are still alive. A friend of mine told me he saw them in the

89

woods, not too far from his farm. Now, you better go deeper into the woods. Good luck to you. May God take care of you and your father and brothers."

"Thank you," I said as tears started streaming down my cheeks. "You are a friend."

Then Alexi closed his window.

I walked back to the others, who were hidden in a gully near the road. *Now I had to tell them.* I edged down into the ditch. It took me quite awhile to find the words, any words.

"He says my father and two brothers might still be alive, so maybe there is some hope that others escaped as well," I said first, trying to keep their spirits up. Then I repeated the story.

Even with all they had been through—all they had seen, heard about and suffered themselves, they were stunned.

"If only we didn't get lost," Yosel cried, "we might have saved at least some of them."

Most of them broke down sobbing.

***

Every step on the way to oblivion, from the first day the Germans entered Poland, we had told ourselves, "Well, this is bad, but I can live with it. Life will be hard, but I can survive it."

From the first order to put on the yellow patches, we said, "I can handle this."

Then the next step downward would come in an order from the SS to the police. We would comply and say the same thing: "I can live with it. I can survive it. Just tell me the rules, and I'll live with them. Murder? Out of the question. Life may be severe, but murder?"

With each step, more of our humanity was taken from us. With each step, the Nazis degraded us a bit more. We said to ourselves and our loved ones, "This cannot last forever. A point will arrive when there is stability."

Even in the labor camp, we thought, the Germans need us for labor. They've given their word. We can endure. Even the Nazis could not be so irrational as to kill working Jews who were making an essential contribution to the war effort.

The spiral went down and down until now, when we were certain we had reached hell.

Every one of the men harbored in his heart the hope that someone in his family remained alive. But that hope seemed to diminish with each passing minute.

Now we cried. We beat our breasts with our closed fists. We wailed. We railed against an uncaring God. We blamed ourselves for not moving faster,

90

for not knowing, for not guessing. But how could we? How could anyone suspect the scope of this barbaric revolt against all the traditions of a rationalist, humanist, Western civilization?

Lastly, we swore vengeance.

This is what my nightmares relive. Every night. This is why you heard me yell, "If only I'd gotten there sooner." Every night for twelve years.

***

Bill and I were sitting on the brown sofa in the living room and Papa was sitting in a chair next to the window. Papa had opened all the windows and set a fan to blow on me and Bill. The heat did not seem to bother him, but then nothing ever did.

Mama was still out so we had been alone listening to Papa's story for much of the afternoon.

"Boys," he said abruptly, "I have to take a small break."

He got up and went into the kitchen for a glass of water. It was only then that I noticed how ashen his face had become. He had been sitting with his back to the window while talking to us, and his face had been in the shadows. I don't think either Bill or I realized at the time how hard it was for him to tell us about the war.

Perhaps Bill did, but then, he was older.

When Papa returned with his water, he started in immediately as though he had never stopped.

***

"We can't stay here," I said finally. "There are parties of SS looking for any escapees. Alexi called them search and destroy missions. We can walk to another place I know…we'll talk to another peasant and see if he tells the same story."

Other houses, some two to four miles away from the outskirts of a village, were also called *chutos,* for single peasant's house, and the peasants living in them were called *chutoransas.* We kept to the side of the road bordering on the woods, as we walked to one of these *chutos.* I led them to another farmer that I knew from working at the lumber mill.

To our horror, the peasant verified everything that we had heard before. He added that some of Pohost Zagorodski's Jews saved themselves by hiding in the woods. "This forest goes on forever," he said to me, "so it is very safe, and it's likely that your family is here somewhere close by. A lot of Jews who escaped were from the work camp at Honsovich."

91

After thanking the peasant, we moved deeper into the Rudna Forest. After trudging another four miles, we ran into a group of Jews from Honsovich who were hiding with some people from Pohost Zagorodski.

"Abram!" I heard in a familiar tone. My heart leaped. I wasn't alone! This was now the happiest moment of my life.

I looked around to see Papa running towards me! With him were Label and our Aunt Yentl, who had escaped with her two daughters and her son. We grabbed each other and hugged until we were almost suffocating one another.

With his voice cracking from the pain, Papa said, "Abram. Your mother and sister are gone." He grabbed me and held me tightly as if he needed my strength to stay upright.

Samuel spoke slowly, sadly. "We dug a cellar under the floor of the old cellar in our house in the ghetto. You didn't see it because this was after you were in the work camp. We had a rope attached to the cover, so when we closed it, a rug would come down over the wooden cover to hide the entrance. I guess the Germans were in a hurry. They didn't even search. When it got dark, we surfaced and found an empty village. Nobody was there. The townspeople must have been so frightened, they all stayed in doors."

"Or maybe they were off celebrating," Label added cynically. "We didn't want to stick around to see what would happen, so we ran to the forest. David also built a false wall in his house, but I don't know what happened to him. I don't know if he escaped."

"There might be other families that managed to escape as well," Samuel said sadly. "But I can't tell you who or where they got to. Some hid in their basements in false walls or dugouts. Some hid in their attics. They were waiting for nightfall to escape. Like us. When the partisans started to shoot near Pohost, the SS ran away, otherwise they would probably have come back to search for us." Now his voice choked up. He started to sob. "Abram, your mother and sister, and Aunt Miriam—they wouldn't hide with me. I'm so sorry. I should've made them. There was plenty of room. But you know your mother. Never thinking of herself. Esther pushed me down to the cellar." Samuel collapsed on the ground, sitting cross-legged. Label and I knelt down beside him. My father looked at me as if for forgiveness. "They said they would only take the women and children again. Yentl was certain…she said if they didn't find someone home, they would search more thoroughly. I'm so sorry."

***

Sitting near the edge of Sholomitski's field, Julia was not in any pain, at least not from her wound. Everything that had happened in the last day and night had completely numbed her to her physical pain. The pain she felt was in her heart. She was in shock, unable to comprehend the events of the last thirty-six hours.

Though your mother was weak from her ordeal, the farmer Sholomitski said it was better for her to leave the vicinity.

Coming back to the edge of his field where he had left Julia earlier that day, he handed her some bread and milk. Then he pointed in the direction of the forest.

"There is a woman who lives in the forest. She is very poor, but very good and kind. I want you to go there," he told her. "Listen very carefully and I'll tell you how. Yes?"

Julia understood.

"There is an irrigation canal you have to cross," he said very precisely. "It's only four yards wide, but very deep. If you go straight as I point, you'll find a canoe that you can paddle across. The canal borders my land. You'll see a big oak tree. The canoe is floating on the water by the oak.

"By the time you cross the canal, it'll be dark, but you should be able to make out some very tall trees. You'll see a light. It comes from a peasant's hut. Go towards it and knock on the door. In this house there is a good woman who will help you."

Julia followed his directions. She came to the canal, but there was no canoe. She worried that she had veered off course. But she couldn't go back. She took a deep breath, edged down to the water and swam across. Struggling up the other side, she spotted the oak tree and was very relieved. Twenty minutes later she saw the light beckoning through the dark night. Julia headed directly toward the light and came to the hut. She knocked on the door, involuntarily shuddering with the remembrance of the last time she had knocked at someone's house.

The peasant woman motioned for Julia to come in, but raised her hands over her mouth in horror as your mother came into the light.

"Take off that coat!" the lady said in a shrill whisper.

Julia had forgotten she was still wearing the clothes discarded at the massacre. She looked down at her breast. The yellow, cloth Star of David was still sewed on to the jacket. It looked so large to her, so visible, that again she shuddered. Julia tore off the jacket and threw it to the ground.

Without a word, the woman pointed to the yellow patch, shook her head sadly, took the coat and cast it in the oven to burn.

She gently washed the blood from Julia's neck and bandaged the wound, and then gave her an old skirt, home woven and full of lice. Julia could feel the bites as soon as she put the clothes on. Then the woman braided Julia's long hair and put pink ribbons in it.

"This will make you look more like a Gentile," the old woman said. She put a gray scarf on Julia's head and led her out to a neglected, broken-down barn.

That night Julia stayed in a hayloft with the horses. The next morning, the woman gave her a beggar's bag filled with bread.

"Go to Bagdanovka," she instructed Julia. "It's farther away and safer there, but it will take you at least a day of walking, maybe more." The woman handed her a cane. She stood with her hands on her hips and looked over Julia. "I think you should stoop over when you walk, like a little old peasant lady.

"On the road, when you are walking, don't say good morning or goodbye, don't talk to the peasants. It's too dangerous," she told your mother. "It's their habit to always say good morning and goodbye, but if you return their greetings, you might give yourself away."

The old woman walked Julia to a well-worn cow path.

"Follow this trail until you come to a second road. The first road you'll come to leads back to your home or southeast to Dubnovich. Don't take this road."

Julia nodded.

"The second road starts north, but curls slowly around in the direction of Bagdanovka."

"But what of the Germans?" Julia asked.

"The trail goes on for some distance. By the time you reach the second road, you should be well out of their way." The old lady hugged Julia. "Now go. And Godspeed."

As she walked, Julia only nodded when peasants greeted her. She tried to look straight ahead, focusing on the path. In truth, she noticed little. She found herself thinking about her family. She thought about them when the children were young, and that was some comfort. Thoughts about the present were crushing. How could a Polish boy give up my father and forty others for ten marks, she wondered? Poor Mama. She never forgave herself for not letting Papa move the family to Cuba. And Avremel, her brave little brother, trying to shield her and comfort her all the way to the grave. He was always like that, even though eight years younger than her. She remembered how he had saved her life when she was fourteen. It was the first time she had taken him skating. There he was, all bundled up—only six-years-old— and complaining that he could hardly move, or breathe.

Mother had warned them to stay away from the *tiche*, the only soft spot on the lake. It always stayed soft, even when the rest of the lake was frozen over.

It was early in the winter, only November, and Jeruchim had gone out and stomped on different parts of Bobric Lake to make sure the ice was solid. Julia and Avremel, holding hands, trudged through the snow drifts down to the lake. Their house was only a few yards away.

They had not been skating long—Avremel was just beginning to find his balance—when Julia felt one skate go through the ice. She had never forgotten that feeling. The ice around her other foot began cracking as well. And tiny six-year-old Avremel, with his bundled up golden curls and his blue eyes peeking through his red scarf, would not let go of her hand. Even as she pleaded with him to move away, even as she sunk to her neck in the icy water, he would not let go.

I remember this well, boys. I was playing hockey with my friends, not too far away. I had seen them skating ten minutes earlier and waved. Then, I don't have any idea how or why—I just had this feeling—I knew something was wrong. In that instant, I suddenly stopped playing the game, and began to scan the surface of the lake. I saw little Avremel but I couldn't see your mother. Immediately, I knew what happened and skated as fast as I could across the lake. I got down on the ice and extended my stick to her and managed to pull her out. But if it had not been for Avremel, she would have gone under way before I got there. I lifted him up over my shoulders and called him "the little hero."

That was the first time your mother ever kissed me.

Julia told me that she also thought of me during that walk to Bagdanovka. She had no idea where I was or if I was alive or dead. We had not seen each other since the day I was loaded on the cart for Honsovich. She worried I would come to the *shtetl* and think that she was gone, with all the rest.

***

Julia knew there were kind people in the hamlet of Bagdanovka. She had been sent there as a worker during her months in the ghetto to collect pine cones in the forest.

She reached Bagdanovka early the next morning and went straight to one of those people, a peasant who was a Seventh Day Adventist. Ushering her inside, he scolded her. "How could you wear these clothes? They're filthy. You'll get sick. Come. My wife will find you something suitable."

After Julia undressed, the man took her clothes to the backyard and burned them. His wife heated some water for the wash basin, gave her a bath and scrubbed her to get rid of the lice, dried her off, and gave her clean clothes. Then, they took her to a small building in their backyard, and told her she would be safe inside. This building was their church.

Julia was frightened to be alone and the days she spent in the church seemed to go on endlessly. The small room felt like a prison, and though she trusted these people, she could not help thinking that she was helplessly at their mercy. There were many times she went to the door and edged it open a tiny bit to make sure she was not locked in.

The peasants gave her more food than she remembered eating the whole time in the ghetto. She slowly recovered her strength.

After four days, these people heard that a group of partisans was going to pass through the village, and they convinced Julia it was best for all concerned if she go with them to the deep woods and safety. Who knew how soon the Germans would get this far into Byelorussia?

***

My family stayed one night in the Rudna. The next morning, Label woke me up.

"There is a partisan group rumored to be near Bagdanovka. We have to make contact with them. There's a chance David and his wife are there as well."

Our small band of refugees now started on the trek to Bagdanovka. The going was slow. There were many older people, and they were so weak and exhausted. Some had been walking and running for three days and nights by this time. They had had no food since their escape, and had been already starving in the ghetto.

Not too far from Bagdanovka, we ran into the first group of partisans I had seen. They numbered about forty young men. Most of them had been Soviet soldiers and had escaped from prisoner-of-war camps.

This particular group was the one that had forced the Germans out of Pohost Zagorodski for one night, and compelled Ziml and the other policemen into hiding.

The moment I saw the partisans, I felt the adrenaline begin to course through my body. These were real fighting men. An organized force. This is what I had been waiting for since the first day of the German invasion.

"Now Label. Now we will show the Nazis a different side of the coin," I told my brother.

"Come on then," Label replied, walking toward the leader, who was standing off the side of the road under tall dense evergreens, looking at a weather-beaten map.

"I am a master sergeant in the Polish Army," Label said. "This is my brother. We want to join you and fight. The very next engagement. We're ready."

The head of the partisans looked us over.

96

"We appreciate your desire to fight," he said, hesitantly. "But you have to understand, we are looking for people with weapons. The cold facts are there are many dispossessed people in this forest and many of them just want to fight. Can you blame them? They want revenge. But whoever we take on in our group, we're going to have to support them, feed them." He looked quickly into Label's eyes, then looked away. "I'm sorry." He went back to studying his map.

Label and I walked dejectedly back to our father.

"Yes, I know," Samuel said. "And I can't blame them. Too many mouths to feed. They would have to spend all their time foraging if they took on everyone. They wouldn't be able to fight."

"But we *are* soldiers," Label said angrily, kicking the ground with his heel in frustration. Label had been in Warsaw when the fighting broke out. A master sergeant in artillery, he stripped out of his uniform when the provisional government surrendered, put on civilian clothes he got from a friend, and snuck out of the city, carefully making his way home through the German lines.

We had to move on. We had to get closer to Bagdanovka, which was deeper in the forest and less likely to be approached by the Germans. Another long march was started.

About four miles from Bagdanovka, there was another tearful reunion. My oldest brother David was with a group that had escaped from Honsovich, and had later met up with a few people from the ghetto. With him were his wife, Shaindel and his infant son, Shlameleh. They had hidden in the cellar until dark and then stole out of the ghetto before the *Einsatzgruppen* soldiers came back to search for stragglers.

Hardly had the tears ended and the stories begun, when David, standing erect and looking every bit the natural leader, put up his hands to ask for attention. Even under the Soviets, though he had started out as a lowly receiving clerk, he had soon risen to be in charge of all the operations for his region.

"We can't stay here," David said. "The Germans are looking for partisans in this area. We should clear out and go further into the woods."

Everyone was in agreement.

"Luckily, they can't barb wire all the forests," my brother said with a cynical little laugh.

CHAPTER 10

THE FOREST

Hiding under the trees during the day and resting, we would start moving as soon as the sun went down. It was cooler then too, so walking was easier for the old people and children. The fall in Byelorussia can still have days of intense heat. And it was the only time we dared to move on the dirt roads.

I was out in front by about a hundred yards when I heard voices nearby. Quickly I passed the word down the line to get off the road.

We waited in the darkness. We had no weapons. All we could do was hide.

As they drew near, I heard Russian words and I figured they were other refugees or even partisans. And your mother was with them. They had taken her from the family in Bagdanovka, but now wanted to leave her with her fellow Jews.

I had not seen her for almost five months and I couldn't believe how small and frail she looked.

I could see she was cold, so I draped my jacket over her shoulders. She cried as she told me the whole story of the massacre. I cried with her.

"Julia, I think that right here are most of the people that escaped," I said.

***

The partisan group your mother was with called themselves *Mishkins*, and numbered about one hundred, again mostly young men. Some of them were Russian soldiers who had escaped the German encirclements and refused to surrender, and others had been captured, but had managed to escape.

They were too small in number to engage the Germans in anything other than ambushes, so they had to be content with tearing up rails, and burning bridges, mills, dairies—doing anything that would disrupt the German war machine.

Once more, we approached a partisan leader with the hope of being able to fight with his group. Once more, we were turned away for the same reason—no weapons.

"This group will only allow us to stay with them a few days, perhaps a week," David said to us. "We need to form our own group, or organize a Jewish division."

"We still wouldn't have weapons," Label said.

Greenbaum said, "They should let us stay. We'll fight. We can carry our own weight. They have no right to make us go."

"I think they have the power to make us do whatever they please," my father answered. "They say they want people with weapons, but I think it's just an excuse. I don't think they want Jews."

"Then the hell with them. We should split up into small groups," Avremel Feldman, a short, stocky young man, said. "It's easier to survive that way."

"And who'll make up the groups?" Label asked sarcastically. "You?"

"Boys," Papa said. "We should not argue about this now, and we should not split up. We're much stronger together."

Unfortunately, rifts were forming amongst us refugees. Different, smaller groups formed with each new disappointment, and my father's advice was ignored. The others viewed him as just old, not wise.

"I am a burden to my sons," he said one day. "Abram and David and Label—try to go with the partisans. If they take even one of you, don't you others feel bad. You go with my blessing."

Each day, David went to the leader of the partisans, trying to persuade them to take us with them or at least give us some weapons so we could defend ourselves. I don't have any idea what he said to them, but I guarantee you, my brother could be very persuasive. David always felt that he could come up with the perfect argument that would convince anybody of the rightness and reasonableness of his views. And he was usually successful. This time, his success was only partial.

On the tenth day, David came back to us, carrying a burlap bag. He no longer looked hopeful. Reaching into the bag, he took out a sawed-off rifle and handed it to Label. He gave me a revolver, stuck a second pistol in his belt, and handed out two more weapons to other Jewish men.

"Father," he said. "They gave me these few weapons and very little ammunition. They said they might take me and my wife and Shlamelah. They will not take any more people with them. That's final. They're moving out and we'll have no defense if we stay here.

"To form our own unit doesn't make sense. There simply aren't enough weapons. We have to keep moving farther into the forest.

"Father. I ask you to make this decision for me. I will stay with you if you want."

Although he felt a profound emptiness, as though his very heart was being violently wrenched from his body, Papa somehow outwardly managed to appear calm. It was so much more difficult to keep his earlier resolve now that one of his sons might actually leave, but with little hesitation, he said, "If they will take you, you must go. You have to save your own family first. And it's a blessing that they will take you with a two-year-old baby. We'll move deeper into the woods. We'll be all right."

"Yes, we'll be all right," I said, knowing full well that one word from any of us and David would remain. "It's better for you to go. It'll be safer for you with such a big group, and safer for us without the baby. One scream from him and it's the end for all of us." I could feel a solitary tear drifting down my cheek. My heart was breaking.

Everything was so peaceful out there in the forest. Birds sang and crickets chirped, bees and flies buzzed in and out of the trees. If I took a deep breath, the smell of the tall evergreens blocked out every other scent. In essence, everything seemed normal. How could this be, I wondered? Should not time stop? Should not the animals and insects mourn along with us? Should not a horrendous cataclysm rend the rest of the earth and make others wail and gnash their teeth as I was doing? And now David was going. In these circumstances, I might never see him again.

***

The next day, as David and his family were leaving with the partisans, a tall blond officer mounted on a dark brown stallion, pulled in his reins. He turned the horse around and motioned for two of his men to approach him.

"We should not let our situation overly harden our hearts. Take the wounded woman with us," he ordered. They rode back to get Julia, who was sitting with me near one of the slender birch trees that interspersed the pines.

As I watched, the soldiers lifted her up on a horse, to sit behind one of them.

"Abram," Julia called out to me. "Your coat…"

I stood up and walked over, reaching up to her to put my hand on her waist.

"You keep it. It's cold at night. Don't worry. I'll see you again. I promise. You'll give it back to me then."

Julia leaned over and kissed me, once on each cheek, and rode away with the soldiers.

***

Six others decided to go to the city of Pinsk. They had heard that no one had been killed in Pinsk.

100

Frustration was growing among those who were left. We numbered almost fifty people. Many could not decide between the forest or the city. Once again, rifts began to form.

Samuel, Label and I were so broken-hearted by David's departure that we paid little heed when Avremel Feldman strode up to the group like a glad-handed politician gathering in his flock.

Someone said, "Our leadership is strong. Before the war we knew this part of Bagdanovka better than any of you. Avremel Feldman bought and sold calves here, and peddled goods all over the area."

"So?" Greenbaum said. He was used to being a leader himself, and he would be damned if he was going to listen to this martinet. Wolf, who had been his assistant in Honsovich, nodded in agreement.

Feldman was adamant. "I spent many months in these forests. I know where we can hide safely."

He looked around at the refugees, particularly at Label and me. I guessed he had already sized us up as strong and valuable men, and he wanted Label to join his group.

"My one concern is that we are too many. We must split up into smaller groups."

"How small?" asked Label. "Do you want to take the responsibility for splitting us up?"

"Look," Feldman said. "If the Germans find this one group, we're all dead. But if we split up into groups of two and three, and they find one of us, the others would have warning. The others will hear shots and have time to scatter."

"How will we split up, Papa?" I asked my father.

"We shouldn't," he answered pointedly.

"Label should come with me," Feldman broke in. "He is a soldier and we will do more fighting. You," he pointed at me, "should stay with your father."

"I guarantee that I will be fighting," I said angrily.

"And who will Yentl and the children go with?" asked Papa, now becoming angry as well.

"They will go with their own group," Feldman replied. "We aren't trying to send people off to summer camp or the village social. We're trying to survive. I think this is the best way. We'll split up, but we'll still be close enough to communicate. Do you think it'll be easy to survive in the forest? To feed everybody? In winter?"

"I know the forest and the difficulties as well as you," Samuel answered. "And I think there's safety in numbers."

For Label, the decision was especially hard. Should he choose the stronger group with Feldman, or stay with his father and brother? He already felt tremendous guilt that he had failed to convince his wife to hide with him. How could he bear the responsibility of taking on his aunt and her children? Or leaving Papa and me?

Finally, Label said, "I will stay with my father. As for the other questions, I can't answer."

At the time, I must admit I was certain that Feldman was right, at least about splitting up.

"Make the damn Germans work harder to find us," I said. "Keep the groups small, but we want our aunt and the children to go with us."

Feldman's face was turning red. He was not used to being questioned.

Yentl sat on some grass nearby and huddled with her arms around her children.

"I don't think you understand. This is the way it's going to be," Feldman said emphatically. "These forests are like a jungle. I know where to hide. I know where to get food. If you don't do it the way I say, fine. I won't take you."

"That's enough," Greenbaum said. "I'm going to follow the partisans."

"Right," Wolf said. "We'll make them take us."

"I'm not going without Yentl," Samuel said. "The hell with your forests. We'll find our own way."

Yentl walked up to Papa and me.

"No, Samuel," Yentl said. "Just as you told David. You must save your family first. He said we'll be close enough to communicate. We'll go with the group Feldman assigns us. You do the same. We'll be fine. It's best this way."

The arguments continued for some time, but Yentl had the final say. Papa could not make her budge.

I hugged each of the children in turn, then, at dawn on a clear September day, we moved off in our respective groups, following Avremel Feldman northeast into the great forests of Bagdanovka.

***

This is the other story that has not got much notice; the Jews who escaped to the forest and fought back. At first, for Label, your grandfather and myself, it was mostly just trying to survive the Russian winter. The fighting came later.

***

Your mother told me this story: Greenbaum, Wolf Bolt and one other man left, moving fast, in the direction of the partisans. All originally from central Poland, they had been forced into the labor camp at Honsovich, like me.

The partisans went northeast in the direction of Malkovich to try to reach the receding Soviet lines. Greenbaum and the others caught up with the rear guard just south of the village, near the River Cna.

Greenbaum hailed the partisans in Russian. Three of the rear guard soldiers stayed with Greenbaum and the others, while two soldiers went up to the main group to ask instructions.

After an hour passed, the two soldiers returned.

"We are to tell you to go back. Leave us and don't follow us again. Those are orders."

As the partisans departed, the three refugees briefly talked it over, then started running, once again catching up to the partisans.

"We can't go back," Wolf Bolt pleaded.

"We can't fall into the hands of the Germans again," Greenbaum said.

The partisans gave them one more chance to leave. When they refused, all three were shot.

Quite a few other Jews were killed in this manner. There were many instances of Polish Fascist partisan groups, such as the *Armja Krajova*, who lured Jews out of the ghetto with promises of weapons, only to shoot them when they appeared. And other groups of partisans, or bandits, who shot Jews on sight. At least Greenbaum and the others were given the opportunity to leave.

***

Even though the *Mishkins* accepted Julia Zipperstein and my brother David and his family, I was certain that the reason the Russian partisans did not take more Jews was due to anti-Semitism and not the lack of weapons.

Most Jews in partisan groups that I talked to, found that life was much easier if they kept their Jewishness to themselves.

***

Once the partisans had left, Feldman led the remainder of us towards the Mizelyshchatz Forest, part of the deep woods surrounding the village of Bagdanovka. When we reached the forest, he split us into small groups.

My group consisted of just three men—my father, Label and myself. Now we were really on our own.

There were no roads where we went, not even cart paths or cattle tracks. We kept to narrow footpaths that the peasants used to get wood or to do some illegal hunting or trapping. But we had to be careful to avoid those

103

same peasants. Being in an unfamiliar area, we had no way of knowing which peasants to trust. Some took pleasure in working with the Germans, who paid a bounty for turning in Jews. Many of the Jews living in the forest were caught this way. And some of the people who helped Jewish refugees were executed as well.

Other peasants were friendly due to past associations and favors, such as when Label and I helped them hedge on their quotas of wood when the Soviets were in power, or due to longtime friendships. These people would give us bread, potatoes, and sometimes meat. They bravely ignored the threat to their own lives by helping not only us, but other desperate Jews. They saved many lives by the simple humanitarian act of giving food.

We moved so deep into the forest, we had to walk eight miles back and forth, at night, just to get closer to Bagdanovka where there were friendly peasants.

We were not any worse off in terms of food, shelter or weapons—we still had very little of these—only in numbers and possibly safety. Still, the greatest obstacles to our survival were: how to get food and how to avoid or defend ourselves against the special units that were hunting both Jews and partisans.

Since the escape from Honsovich, we had existed on potatoes stolen from local farmers or a chicken if we were lucky. Water was not a problem—it was all around us. It was just dirty and crawling with worms. When we had the luxury of a few hours of safety, we were able to boil the marsh water. We learned to carry a cloth, or use our clothing as a sieve, through which to pour water to drink. At those times, dysentery became a problem.

We did not dare shoot game. Ammunition was scarce and the noise would tip off the peasants or the Germans. Also, we could not set traps because they left a trail. If you came back to check a trap, it was very likely that you would be the one that was caught.

It was not even winter yet, but just like the partisan had told me in Honsovich, we always seemed to be wet and cold and hungry. We would somehow have to find shelter for the winter.

The reason the Germans had sent the 1st Cavalry as part of their right flank was that horses were necessary for traversing the marshy areas. These forests were part of the Pripet Marshes and in many places were no more than a giant swamp. Armored forces could not get through. This was the same reasoning used by the partisans. If it was hard for us, it would be hard for our enemies.

***

104

In October, Label's brother-in-law, Hershel Jezuk, showed up in our part of the forest. Label's wife and Hershel's wife were sisters—both victims of the Nazis. Accompanying Hershel was his brother, Aron and their Uncle Sholom. They agreed to stay with us, increasing our group to six.

"You know that some people from your *shtetl* went to Pinsk?" Sholom said one day out of the blue.

"Yes," my father said, and gave Sholom a puzzled look.

"Those people were killed on the road. They never reached Pinsk."

"They were all killed?" Samuel asked, as though it was a surprise. He knew it was not a surprise, but he always hoped.

"Only one survived, but I don't know his name. I'm sorry," Sholom said.

"You don't know," Samuel mumbled. Then he turned his back and walked off into the forest to sit under a huge oak tree. My father had not thought anything else could make him cry. He found out that the human capacity for suffering was well beyond his previous beliefs.

***

When the *Mishkins* finally made camp, your mother collapsed. Three days later, she awakened in a *sanchast,* a few dingy cots and makeshift beds set underneath canvas anchored by ropes to pine trees. This served as the camp hospital.

Even though the area was shaded by the tarpaulin, the light inside seemed bright to Julia. It took her a few moments to get used to it. Why, she wondered?

"You've slept for three whole days," said a gentle voice. It belonged to Ivan Vasilievich, a Russian veterinarian who had been drafted into the army as a doctor.

As Julia opened her eyes, it also took her a few minutes to realize where she was and that she was safe. One of the things she remembered that calmed her was the faint smell of smoke wafting through the tent.

The doctor removed the bandages around Julia's neck. "Ah-hah. Progress. We're doing fine. Does it hurt?"

"No," Julia said. She could not help bringing her hand up to touch the wound. "A little bit."

Vasilievich had cleaned and dressed Julia's wounds, and applied clean bandages every day since the *Mishkin* partisans had accepted her into their group.

Many of the *Mishkins* had been prisoners of war. They had had the foresight to realize they would have to surrender, and managed to bury their weapons and ammunition in the forest before giving up to the German forces. Once they escaped from the prisoner-of-war camps, they headed straight for these caches of weapons. They formed their partisan group as they met up with other soldiers who had also escaped.

Many of the early partisan groups were formed in this way. The groups were usually small, weapons were scarce and they had no way to replenish their ammunition.

There were also bandits who formed groups of guerrillas. These were usually Ukrainian, Lithuanian, Latvian, and Polish. These people would sometimes fight the Germans and sometimes the partisans. But they had one thing in common: their hatred of Jews.

Vasilievich was very kind to your mother. He nursed her back to health and taught her skills she could use with the partisans. He would always push her to get better. "You have to eat and get the strength back in your legs. You have to start earning your keep," he would say.

***

Boys, you have to understand that at this time a lot of us looked little better than skeletons with flesh hanging on. We had been surviving on so little food, we were lucky we didn't die of starvation, disease or exposure, let alone the Nazis.

***

When your mother finally got up and went out that morning, she was surprised to see a small village of people going about their business around her; cooking food, bringing in firewood, laundering clothes and cleaning weapons—a few women were peeling potatoes. Some of the soldiers had been able to hide and recover their tents, others parachutes, which could be stretched between trees for use as cover like the *sanchast*—all of these were camouflaged with branches and grass so they could not be seen from the air. The camp almost looked like a regular army bivouac.

At least people here can breathe free, Julia thought. You don't have to worry about the Nazis. For days, she had been afraid to look at anyone, afraid they would recognize her as a Jew and turn her in. Now she was surrounded by strangers, but they were kind, and beset by the same fate. As she followed Vasilievich around the camp, people greeted her, smiled at her and inquired about her wound and health. For the first time in what seemed like years, she felt calm and safe.

Soon, your mother was put to work peeling potatoes. Then, Vasilievich began to train her, and all the other women in camp, to apply first aid. As many people as possible had to learn this, no matter that the education was brief and medical supplies were pitifully scarce.

There was no alcohol, and they usually didn't have time to sterilize wounds anyway. If they were on a mission, and a partisan was injured, all they could do was wash the wound out and bandage it, and pray they could get the soldier to the *sanchast* in time. The only advantage at the *sanchast* was they were able to boil water to clean the wounds and sterilize the bandages.

Julia found the first day back on her feet to be very exhausting. She received permission from the doctor to retire early. But once there, lying on blankets on the ground, she could not sleep. The few cots had been given to the more seriously injured. Your mother could be compulsive about the most trivial things, whether changing the hem on one of the twins' skirts over and over until she got it just right, or rewriting a letter to her parents six or seven times until it was perfect, no smudges, nothing crossed out. And she had written many letters to them when she was away at school in Pinsk and very homesick. She lay there on the ground, going over and over the events of the last few days. The skin on her back would prickle, her eyes would grow hot and her hands tighten into fists. She prayed that there was some mistake, that it was a horrible nightmare. She was alone in the world, in the forest. Her whole family had been destroyed, some of them before her very eyes. There was a tightness in her chest making it hard to breathe. She still could not believe it happened. Disbelief and sorrow were soon replaced by anger and then fierce hatred.

Your mother wanted to live to take revenge. She told herself she would fight to survive so that she could avenge her family.

That night she vowed to herself: *I will never be caught alive by the Germans. It would be better to die than be captured and tortured again.*

Many people committed suicide rather than be taken alive by the Germans. One doctor she knew threw himself into a canal and drowned himself rather than be caught.

She had heard that a friend of mine was tied to the tail of a horse and dragged for miles before the Germans beat him with sticks and then hung him. Even early in the war, everyone knew the Germans would torture partisans, especially Jewish partisans.

The Germans constructed wooden scaffolds to use as gallows. They hauled a prisoner up in a truck, put a noose over his head, then drove the truck away, leaving a sign: "Cooperated With Partisans," on the victim. They left the corpse, whether a man or a woman, hanging for a few days, then they would hang someone else. Once, they forced five brothers to hang each other.

Julia finally fell deep in slumber, but for the next three nights, she cried during her sleep. Vasilievich slept under a tree nearby. On the third night, he crawled inside the *sanchast* over to Julia.

Vasilievich shook her gently on the shoulder. "Wake up, little one," he whispered. "Wake up. I know you have been through much, but you are crying in your sleep. If you don't stop, I'm afraid the partisans will kick you out. It's too dangerous for them…the noise."

Julia dried her tears and nodded. She told him, "Doctor, you are the finest man I have ever known. I swear it."

From that time on, your mother slept quietly.

***

In my group, the first necessity was always food. I'm certain it was the same for most of the survivors in the forest. With more men now in our party, it was easier to take turns going out to get provisions. I would usually go with Aron and Label would go with Hershel. The older men usually stayed in camp gathering firewood and edible plants.

It was getting colder, always colder. One dreary overcast day, in pouring rain, four of us headed in the direction of a small village called Rudne. As we emerged from the woods, after hiking for three hours, I spotted a bridge with two German soldiers standing guard. I quickly halted the rest of the party, knelt down and motioned for them to slip back among the trees. Then, I quietly crawled after them. We moved deeper into the woods, away from the bridge, but got so turned around in the heavy rain and gloom, we were unaware that we went in a circle. An hour later, we ended up back at the same bridge where the Germans were stationed. This time they saw us and started firing. Luckily, no one was hit and we escaped back into the woods. We wandered around in circles for four or five hours. It was freezing. We were starved. And now it was dark.

The sound of rain on the roof of my house had always been comforting to me. But then I was inside. Now I prayed for it to stop.

Label looked around, trying to get his bearings. Then, exasperated, he abruptly sat down. He said, "The forest can get your head all mixed up, even for people as familiar with it as we are."

"We should not move anymore," he said. "Let's sit and wait for the dawn, so we can get an idea of where we are. Otherwise, the best that can happen is we'll remain hopelessly lost. Worse, we might run into the Germans again."

I'll never forget it. We sat in that cold rain for another five miserable hours.

108

From the time we first went into the forest, there were agonizing days without food, and months without a change of clothes. We stank. We had no soap. And we were always at the mercy of the weather. Now we would have to stay in our wet, smelly clothes until they dried with the help of the wind. There was no sun.

Every part of me was chilled—my fingers and toes were numb, my teeth were chattering. I had no idea how I'd fall asleep, but eventually I did. We all did. The human body can get used to almost anything, it's the mind that has trouble.

On a night like this, we didn't worry about posting a sentry. And this was still only the fall. How were we going to survive the winter? I had no idea.

There was a chilly dawn the next day. Label woke up first. His clothes were still damp and cold, his movements stiff and slow. Waking us up, he allowed us a few moments to stir, to get our blood circulating.

At the first light, Label began to get a better feel for directions. He led us deeper into the forest. The lighter it became, the deeper into the forest we moved. Finally, we made it to the area around Rudne and located a friendly peasant who gave us something to eat. It was just the usual bread and potatoes, but it was a godsend.

The farmer invited us inside, taking our clothes to dry over a wood fire and giving us blankets to cover ourselves.

"It is amazing that none of you got sick," his wife said.

I wolfed down a half a loaf of bread, then started on a raw potato.

The lady laughed. "I'll boil that for you if you want."

The others were eating just as voraciously, when a few local men wandered into the hut.

"They can't stay here," the leader of these men said to the peasant. Quickly, with an anxious look, he turned to us. "You can't stay here. The Germans are preparing a search-and-destroy operation. They're looking for partisans and Jews."

"Where can we go?" Label asked.

"They're coming from the south. From Pinsk," the man answered. "Go any direction out of this area except south and you should be safe."

During the first months we were in the forest, this happened numerous times. As long as we stayed deep in the forests of Bagdanovka, we were fairly safe. We were always at risk venturing outside. Peasants were usually in the fields picking berries and mushrooms for the winter, and gathering hay to feed their animals. If we did not personally know the peasant, we had no way of knowing if he or she was sympathetic.

But we had to have sustenance, and for that, we had to leave the woods. Usually setting out at night when we went for food, we were forced to keep moving, always changing areas, always at the mercy of the peasants. And always so hungry. I was a wiry boy, but I knew I had lost a lot of weight in the first two months in the forest. Looking at Papa, I thought he was wasting away to nothing.

As we left Rudne, I asked Label, "Are they telling us the truth?"

"Do you want to take the chance to find out?" Label asked in return. "At least they gave us food for Papa and Sholom."

During the day, in the relative safety of the Bagdanovka woods, we would gather dead, dry branches for our fires. Green branches would cause too much smoke that someone could notice from a distance. Many Jews were caught because of this simple mistake.

When we were out of the deep forests, we watched the peasants to see what direction they took. I usually made a fire at twilight when we could see the peasants had already started for home. Then, we could sit down, cook our meager portions and eat. When in camp, at least two of us would always be on guard duty, perhaps a mile out from the camp, two hours on, then four hours off.

For our group, the first year in the forest had nothing to do with revenge or fighting back. We were only concerned with adapting and surviving.

After eating one night, I went out on watch. Standing silently behind a tall oak tree, I heard a stranger approaching. Quietly, I drew the revolver from my belt and waited. As the solitary figure drew closer, I recognized his face.

"Sander," I whispered.

The boy jumped. He had already been scared out of his wits by a recent escape.

"Sander Hoffman," I whispered again, as I edged forward from my hiding place. "Come here. Over by the tree."

Sander Hoffman was a fourteen-year-old boy from Pohost Zagorodski. He was so skinny, he looked worse than us.

"Oh my God," he cried as he recognized me. He fell to the leaf-covered ground and crumpled up, sobbing for a good ten minutes.

"We were in a small village, not far from here," Sander said, when he stopped crying. "There were eight of us. The Germans found out about our bunker. They surrounded us at dawn. Yelled at us to get out. I was just waking up. I heard gunfire. Next thing I knew, I was running. They threw grenades into the bunker. When people came out, the Germans made them lie face down, then they shot them in the neck. I started running again and I've been running all day. I don't know how many escaped, but Mule Lutsky was running with me some of the way. I don't even know how we got separated. He might be somewhere around here."

"How many were killed? Anyone I'd know?" I asked.

"Mule's father, Lazer, was killed," Sander said, still trying to regain his composure. "I think most of them were. I just don't know."

We were to hear countless stories like this the whole time we were in the forest. I now realized that we had to always be on guard. Always.

I walked Sander back to the camp and gave him something to eat. Then I went back to my watch point. In another hour, Mule, tall, broad-shouldered and fierce, and a friend of mine from home, came through the forest, painstakingly making his way.

Mule Lutsky and Sander Hoffman joined our group, making us eight.

With this warning, and such proximity to the village where the ambush took place, we knew we'd have to pull out in another direction. It was not easy to keep changing places, and already, after only some two months on the run, we had changed camps four times. We had just learned our way around, and more importantly, knew where to get food. Now we had to leave.

We couldn't go too far away from the peasants who were friendly to us. New, safe contacts were hard to come by. So carefully, we erased all evidence of our stay, burying anything not a necessity and smoothing over the ground with dirt and weeds, and then spreading newly fallen leaves over that. We loaded the remaining food onto our shoulders and started the hike . deeper into the forest.

THE FOURTH DAY

CHAPTER 11

THE BUNKER

We started late on the fourth day of the story. On our chicken farm, it was the end of the molting period—many of the hens had laid a second round of eggs and they couldn't wait.

Papa had the chickens elevated in row upon row of cages, one chicken to a cage so they wouldn't peck at each other. In between the cages were troughs which delivered water for the chickens, one for each row of cages and running 70-80 yards in length. On the other side of the cages were funnels through which the eggs would gently drop into a different metal trough. Papa drove an electric cart down the aisle between the troughs. Steering with his legs, he gathered in the eggs with his hands. Bill helped him.

They came in about four in the afternoon. The warm aroma of baked chicken and potatoes wafted in from the kitchen as Papa and Bill cleaned up.

***

In late October, the days began to grow shorter and colder. Wearing the same light clothes I had worn during the summer in Honsovich, I realized that if something was not done, we would all die of exposure before we had a chance to fight. I never slept well, drifting in and out of sleep, but mostly lying awake, shivering. Watching my father and some of the others tossing and turning, shaking with the cold, I knew we had to dig a bunker, similar to the trench that Mule and Sander had hidden in. But Papa did not like the idea. It was too dangerous. It would leave a footprint of our existence that could be traced.

There were local informers and trackers, and special platoons formed to hunt partisans. The Nazis waged a relentless campaign in which the hunters systematically hunted down and killed their prey.

I'm not sure you boys can fully appreciate this in all its magnitude. *We were being hunted!* Continuously. Like some rabid dog. We always had to be on our guard.

I was sure that in a bunker we would be like sitting ducks, lined up nicely for the Nazis. But it had to be done, or we would perish from the cold without firing a shot.

So one morning before dawn, Label and I scoured the ground looking for strong branches or pieces of wood—anything we could use to dig.

That day was spent digging a deep trench. It took five hours to dig a hole large enough for all of us. For the most part, my father sat the whole time with his arms folded in disapproval. He was not used to seeing his sons disobey him. And I didn't want to. Neither did Label, but we also didn't want to freeze to death.

The most difficult part was digging through the topsoil, but the dirt became softer underneath. While some of us dug, Aron and Label fashioned a cover out of branches and leaves that we could pull over the hole at night. Once the hatch was in place, our new home was well disguised. A peasant would have to walk right over it and fall through the "roof" before he knew there was a bunker.

Papa was surprised. He grudgingly admitted it wasn't such a bad idea after all.

Only a few days later, we heard rumors of the approaching Germans, so we left our bunker and went further into the forest and dug another shelter. Now that we had some experience with trenches, we dug even deeper so neither the fire nor the smoke would be visible.

Winter came, and snow began to fall. Footprints in the snow could lead the Germans directly to us. We had to get more food at one time so as not to go through the snow too often.

It was becoming so cold I would have sold my soul for one warm night in a real house instead of sitting all night in the trench. Papa, usually so rational, spoke about actually stealing into Pohost Zagorodski for one night's sleep in his old bed.

In spite of the danger of discovery, the next day Label and I collected as many dry twigs as we could find, and piled them in the trench to make a fire for the night.

When we got up in the following morning, our eyes were red and swollen from the smoke; too sore to open in the bright light of day. Label, who was coughing badly, threw off the cover of the bunker to let the smoke escape not caring who might spot us. We were all coughing until Label finished brewing a weak tea. This soothed our raw throats. It was the first time the cool, brisk air felt good on our faces and flowing into our lungs.

What was worse? Heat that brought with it blistered eyes, noses and throats, or freezing in the cruel winter air?

Not able to stand this torture for more than a few nights, I asked no one in particular, "Doesn't someone know where we could get a small stove?"

Sholom Jezuk held his chin in his hands. "I know of a heater. I just can't remember..." He sat in this position for ten minutes, focusing on what would be in normal circumstances, the most trivial of memories. He tortured us. Finally he said, "That's it. I knew it. I remember—there's a school in Bagdanovka that's been closed for some time. I'm certain they had a metal heater."

That was enough for me. I stood up. "Who's coming with me?" I asked.

"I'll come," Aron said. "But can we wait until dark? It might be safer then."

"Right." I chuckled for the first time in months. I realized I was just a bit too eager.

Almost all our movements, except for foraging near our camp, came under cover of night in the forest. We hated the moonlight. We wanted darkness.

We learned to move silently. Any time we heard a sound, we froze until the sound was identified. If it was an animal, we moved on. If the noise was made by a human, we waited until they left. We were not aggressive. We had so few weapons and ammunition that we avoided fights if possible. We decided early on that until we had more weapons, the only time we would fight was if we stumbled upon some Germans and there was no possible escape, or if we learned that some peasants had betrayed us.

The snow presented a new problem. Now we had to learn to cover our tracks. Most of the time we would walk backwards to confuse our enemies.

Using the stars to guide us, we trudged for four hours through the forest. Finally, we spotted the lights of the village through the dense mass of pine trees. We climbed to a vantage point on a wooded hill just outside Bagdanovka, and sat for an hour. Snowflakes were swirling through the brisk air.

We had kept warm during the walk, but now, crouching down in the cold night air, we were freezing. The wind was picking up, blowing snow into our faces like little darts. It seemed to go right through our light clothing.

"I'm so cold, I'm going to get sick," Aron complained. He slowly stood up and began stamping his feet on the ground to stay warm.

I blew into my gloves to try to warm my fingers. Then I laughed. "Just be grateful it's warmer under the trees," I told Aron. "We could be in an open field. Then you'd really cry." I rubbed my arms. "I used to love weather like this," I said. "I'd be out on the pond, skating or playing hockey with my friends."

"I know," Aron replied. "God. I hope the stove's there."

There had been no movement in the town for the whole time we watched.

115

"I think it's safe now," I said as I stood up stiffly. My bones ached from the cold. "It's as good a time as any. Let's go."

"No townspeople, no Germans," Aron said. "I guess we're the only ones crazy enough to be out in this weather."

Going into the village, we found the school was locked up tight, with boards nailed across the windows. Breaking a window would make too much noise, so we pried off the boards and then the moldings, taking off a whole window and setting it down against the wall of the building.

Aron and I climbed in, one behind the other.

It was so nice and warm inside, out of the wind, I don't think either of us wanted to leave.

The school was small, only one room, and the stove was right in the middle.

"That looks pretty heavy," I said. I wondered how the hell we were going to get it back to the camp.

The stove was small, but made of cast iron—I estimated it weighed about a hundred and fifty pounds. But I wasn't going to leave without it, so we got to work quietly disconnecting the pipes. Aron followed my lead. He was a city boy and had no idea how these things worked. I took off a big sturdy burlap bag that was tied around my waist, opened it, and with Aron's help, wedged the stove into the bag. Taking a long pipe as well, we dragged our precious cargo outside, this time opening the back door from within, and headed back to the forest.

It was eight miles back to camp and we had to alternate carrying the stove or pipe, switching every three hundred yards or so.

Back at the camp, Label lowered the stove into the ditch, using ropes, and with the help of his brother-in-law, Hershel, extended the pipe away from the hole. Aron and I rounded up some dry twigs and branches from dead trees.

"You do the honors, Papa," Label said, handing our father one of the few remaining matches.

Samuel got down into the ditch and lit the wood. Closing the heater door, he smiled and put his hands in front of it. In a few minutes, the fire caught. I don't think I'd ever seen him so happy.

"This is heaven," Samuel exclaimed. "Come. Join me."

The rest of us climbed down into the trench.

"Aron thought he was going to be sick," I jokingly told the others. That was a mistake, opening my big mouth.

"I don't think you should make fun of Aron," Papa said, and then started to laugh. "You, my little fighter, you had the worst case of measles I ever saw. Right, Label?"

"Right," Label agreed.

"When Abram was ten, the measles were going around, and Abram got a light case," Samuel told the others. "So, after four days, my bright one here, thinks he's all right and goes swimming with his friends."

"Yes," Label added. "Mama found you down at the river, hauled you out and sent you home to bed."

"The next day, the poor boy couldn't straighten his head," Samuel said. "But he's so stubborn, he didn't tell anyone. Mother saw his head leaning to the side, and when she asked him what was wrong, he said, 'Nothing. I feel like doing that.'"

By now, everyone was laughing.

"Finally, he admitted that he couldn't hold his head up and it hurt," Label said. "By the time the local doctor saw him, his left arm was also so swollen, the doctor suggested we take him to Pinsk. By the time we got him to Pinsk, the swelling had spread to his chest. The Pinsk doctors wanted to operate, but they were afraid, so they wanted to send him to Warsaw."

"I was really busy at the lumberyard," Samuel said, "so Yentl and Esther took him to Warsaw. The doctors there also couldn't decide whether to operate or not. Abram had an enormous amount of pus in his chest. Finally they sent him to the most famous doctor in Warsaw...I can't remember his name...and he said we should wait and had better send him to a country villa, a *dacha*.

"While he was being treated at the *dacha*, one of the doctors stuck a needle in him to see what was developing."

"By this time, he was unconscious," Label chimed in.

"A couple of days later, he woke up," Papa went on. "All the pus came out when the doctor stuck in the needle. That's the moment I arrived."

"Papa spent a lot of money to keep you well," Label said, chuckling.

"And I lost a lot of money as well, taking time off from the business," my father said. "By the way, when are you going to pay me back?" Samuel then gave me a good-natured push.

"And don't go swimming tonight," Label said, laughing once more.

Everyone joined in the laughter, even me. It was the first time we felt halfway comfortable in many months and now it was my turn.

"Kalman came over to our house one day," I said. "He yelled my name. He was quite excited, but you know Kalman."

Label said, "The strongest person I ever knew."

"Yes he was," I agreed. "So he says, 'You know how I've always wanted an owl?'"

Oh boy, I thought. Trouble is not far off the horizon. "Yes," I answered.

"Well, yesterday," Kalman says, "I met a peasant in the Swiernishtze Forest. He told me about a large owl nesting close to a clearing by his farm."

"So?" I said.

117

Kalman says, "This peasant...he tells me that owls, even though they see so great at night...maybe because of it...they can't see a lick in the daytime."

"So?" I said, fearing the worst.

"I already talked to Lazar Moshe," Kalman goes on. "Why don't the three of us go find that owl and bring him home? Isn't that a great idea?"

Samuel and Label were already laughing out loud. They knew our cousin Kalman all too well.

"Lazar agreed to this?" I asked Kalman. I always considered Lazar Moshe to be very smart. He was not about to do anything stupid. "Well, I guess with guys as big and strong as you two, we ought to be able to handle the owl. Especially if it can't see." Of course I was thinking I'll believe it when I see it.

"Of course you were," Samuel said. And Label doubled up in laughter.

"And you can keep him," Kalman tells me. "We'll build a cage and put it in your barn. She can keep your pigeons company."

Two days later, Kalman and I paddled my canoe across the Bobric Lake. Lazar sat low in the middle, barking out orders like a Roman galley master.

After about a mile walk, we reached the clearing. I'm sure we looked fearless, but I don't think we were too well prepared. Hell, I only had a small hatchet and Kalman had a knife.

"I thought you were bringing a net," I said to Kalman. "How are we going to catch an owl without a net?"

"So I forgot," Kalman answers me. "Don't worry. I'll take care of it."

"That's why we're worried," Lazar says.

Both Label and Samuel had to hold their sides they were laughing so hard. The others were also laughing helplessly.

I stood up and pointed to a nearby tree. "There it is," Kalman shouts. "Look at the size! It's an eagle owl." Across the clearing on the tallest pine, maybe sixty feet high, Kalman pointed out a large brown owl, streaked and specked with bits of darker and lighter brown. It had tufts of lighter feathers on either side of its head, which stood up like ears.

"I'll go first," Kalman said. He walked up to the tree and put his hands on either side, feeling the bark as if to take its measure. Then he stepped up on the lowest limb and started to climb. No sooner had he climbed six feet, than I started up after him. Lazar followed me.

Climbing from limb to limb, Kalman drew near the nest on top in fifteen minutes. Lazar and I were right below him.

"Can you see her?" Lazar whispers to me.

"I'm too low," I whisper back. "Can you see her?" I whisper to Kalman.

I put my finger to my lips as if to mimic Kalman. "Shsh," Kalman whispers back. "I'm right below her."

Kalman was trying to figure out just what he was going to do. He could see the long, sharp talons of the bird right above him, and I could see just a little bit of indecision. I bet now he wished he'd remembered the net.

"This isn't going to be so easy," he whispers to me.

"What?" Lazar asks.

I grabbed a lower branch and leaned down. "He says it's not going to be so easy," I whisper to Lazar.

Near the top of the pine, I could see Kalman slowly moving his hand toward the owl's leg. He was just about to grab it when the owl lunged down at him, shrieking wildly and spreading her wings to their greatest span—almost five feet.

I guess Kalman had a sudden change of mind. He didn't want any piece of the owl. He started to shinny down the tree, but in his haste, he began to slip. Soon he was falling pell-mell. He held onto the tree trunk as he fell, both arms spread around the pine's trunk as though he was hugging it. Kalman's so big, as he slid down, limbs and branches broke off under his weight. Soon, he fell into me and I started to fall. I fell down on Lazar, who had started shinnying down the trunk as fast as he could. But he wasn't fast enough. Now we were both falling into Lazar—all three of us, screaming and shouting all the way to the ground.

All of the men were laughing hysterically. My father cried out, "Stop! Stop! You're killing me."

By the time we hit the ground, the pine was completely shorn of all its boughs and branches.

Slowly, we got up. Kalman and I dusted ourselves off and I saw Lazar open his shirt to shake out small twigs and branches, some still with the pine needles attached.

I checked myself up and down to see if all my body parts were still in the right places.

"Are you all right?" Kalman asks us.

Lazar pulled a branch from the back of his trousers and glared at Kalman. "No thanks to you two."

"Why don't you lose some weight?" I asked Kalman. Then I started to laugh, and collapsed on the ground.

Kalman, with a sheepish expression on his face, felt his stomach. He was surprised anyone would think he was too heavy. Then he pushed his stomach out as far as he could. Kalman and Lazar began to laugh. Pretty soon they were rolling on the ground with me.

We laughed until there were tears in our eyes and our stomachs hurt. Then, as quickly as the laughter had filled the air, there was silence.

Label looked at me and Papa. "I miss Kalman," he said.

***

A heavy snow fell that night, the sign of a long, cold winter. The more snow on the ground, the more dangerous it was for us. Food would have to be rationed out. We decided that we should not leave camp to secure more food. It was too risky to leave tracks.

There was a little creek within a mile from the new camp. Label and I searched the nearby forest for a particular kind of branch. We wanted something solid with a knob on the end. When we were kids, we would find such a branch, and use a knife or other tool from the lumberyard, and fashion it into a hockey stick. Both of us were pretty good hockey players. I was playing hockey the night I pulled your mother from the ice. This time, I shaped the branch using the hatchet I had taken from Honsovich.

My grandfather had taught us another use for the stick. Reaching the stream, we tested the ice and walked out into the middle.

Label brushed the snow off a small area where the ice was not too thick. Then we waited, watching the ice intently. For an hour we waited. Abruptly, Label pointed to the ice. I saw it as well. Through the ice, I could just make out the silhouette of a fish. Raising the stick, I brought it down violently on the surface. The fish, a type of sanddip, was stunned. Hurriedly, Label cut a hole in the ice and grabbed the fish with his bare hands. Another reason to celebrate.

For the next few months we lived on *zitefke,* a soup made with flour and water, potatoes which we either baked or removed the skin from and boiled, and if we were lucky, fish.

None of us kept up our strength with so little nourishment.

***

During the next heavy blizzard, food was so scarce we decided it was necessary to go under cover of the storm and get food. We also craved news. We had heard nothing of the war for months. We did not know how the bleak summer for the Soviet armies had turned into a hopeful winter: that in November, the Soviets had counter-attacked in Stalingrad and captured three hundred thousand German soldiers, and in mid-December, they routed the Italians on the Don. That war was far away for us. We had enough trouble with mere survival.

This time it was Aron's and my turn to go for supplies.

Coming to a *chutor* late at night, one of the peasants invited us in. "They killed a couple of Jews in the village of Borki," the slack-jawed man said. "Several of them were women."

120

A sharp pain went straight to my heart. To this day, I have no idea how I knew. But I knew. It was my aunt and her children. There was no explaining it. I *knew* it. There was no doubt.

The *chutoransa* gave us food that we took back to camp.

"Label, Papa," I said sadly, when I returned. "Some Jews were killed in Borki. I'm certain it was Aunt Yentl and her children."

After questioning me, my father said, "Boys, you have to find out what actually happened there. We must know for sure."

Both of us agreed, but we were too tired to leave that night.

Early the next morning, Label and I started the twelve mile walk to Borki. It took us a whole day. We had to be very careful not to be seen and it was not easy—a lot of peasants were out hauling their hay in wagons.

At Borki, I knocked on the door of a peasant I had heard of named Nicolaichik.

"We are the Bobrow brothers," I said.

The bull-necked man let us in and gave us food.

Nicolaichik, who was a great bear of a man, looked at us with downcast, teary eyes. His sadness increased with each word of his story.

"Six people were executed, including Yentl and her children. Several people ran away…" Nicolaichik now broke down, sobbing. "Little Michle. She was badly wounded, but still breathing. I carried her here, and tried to save her. I couldn't."

Wiping his face with the sleeve of his coat, he rose. "Come. I will show you her grave."

Together we trudged through the snow at the rear of his hut. As we walked, Label said he didn't understand how this could have happened to our aunt and cousins. "They were hidden in an underground bunker," he reasoned. "Far out of the way of Nazi patrols."

Twenty yards from the house, we saw a tiny mound. Nicolaichik brushed some snow off so that we could see the surface of the dirt. Stuck in the middle of the grave was a stake, and in defiance of the Nazis, there was a crudely fashioned, wooden Star of David.

Both of us began to cry. "How could this have happened?" Label repeated as he glared at the big man.

Nicolaichik walked closer to us and spoke in a low, angry voice. "There is a fellow named Boychik. He told the Germans where they were hiding. He collected blood money for their hiding place."

After more detailed questioning, I said, "I know this Boychik, Label. He worked with me on the riverbank. When the Soviets were here. We ate together, drank together. I hired him, for God's sake."

With this, Label's hatred of the Nazis, that had been building in him since the death of his wife and child, suddenly made him violently ill. He doubled up, clutching his stomach in fierce pain and collapsed on the ground. He vomited over and over.

I put my hand on his shoulder to try to comfort him. "Get us some water—please," I asked Nicolaichik.

The *chutoransa* hurried inside.

"Are you all right?" I asked Label. "We should go to the bunker…take a look."

"You're right," Label said. He was not sure he would be able to stand it, but he could not let his brother go alone. "I'll be okay. But it's going to be hard to go in there."

After Label drank the water, he felt a little better. Nicolaichik then led us to the underground bunker.

Inside, it was dark and hard to see, but we could smell something had been burned. Perhaps a fire to keep warm, I thought. I was trying to not think the worst—of the grenades that Sander had told me about.

"Where are the bodies, Nicolaichik?" Label asked. "Where did they hide them? Did they at least bury them?"

"Not far from here, I believe, but I don't know exactly where," Nicolaichik answered, again hanging his head. "I'm sorry."

Leaving the bunker, we thanked the peasant profusely, and began our trek back to the forest. We had walked a good distance, when Label said "Abram, I don't think Nicolaichik told us the whole truth. The part of the story about Boychick revealing Yentl's hiding place—that I believe. But there's something not right about that man, Nicolaichik."

"I don't care about him. He certainly went out of his way to tell us what a grand fellow he is, but I don't care. I care about finding Boychick."

"Now we're going to drive another stake into our father's heart," Label said sorrowfully.

We never should have separated. We never should have listened to Feldman. I blamed myself. I should have listened to Papa. Then they might still be alive. I don't know why, but I really believed it was my fault. I felt terrible. Nothing Label could tell me could convince me that I wasn't to blame.

Label put his arm around my shoulder as we walked, but neither of us said a word the rest of the way.

Outside the camp, our father was nervously waiting. As soon as he spotted us, he ran up.

"What happened?" he whispered, afraid of the answer.

"It was Aunt Yentl," Label said, gazing softly into Papa's eyes. "And the children."

"Little Michle was wounded," I told him. "One of the peasants took her in, but it was too late. She died in his home."

Papa grabbed me by my coat and screamed, "See! I told you not to listen to Feldman! We never should have split up." Then Samuel Bobrow started sobbing.

"If you'd got there sooner, you might have helped little Michle!" The old man crumpled into a disheveled heap. All the strength, the adrenaline that had served him in his own escape, that had helped him aid others in their escapes, that had seen him through the endless hikes to safety until his torment was relieved by the reunion with his sons, now drained out of him before our eyes. He looked as though he had aged thirty years in the last few months. The father was now the child. The sons were now stronger than the father.

Label crouched down beside him and put his arm around Samuel's shoulders.

"Father," he said gently, "it wouldn't have helped. We wouldn't have come in time anyway."

I also knelt down. It was hard for me to see my father—who had always seemed to be the strongest, bravest, wisest man I knew, who always had just the right answer, the right solution to any problem, and the vigor to carry it through—now, reduced to a sobbing shell of a man. And, I felt so guilty about their deaths, I just wanted to crawl into the nearest hole and die. But I knew Papa needed me, and I didn't have the luxury of wallowing in my own problems. I took hold of Samuel under his arm, helping him to rise. "Let's go back to the bunker," I said. "It's safer. We don't even know what will happen to us. We have to be strong."

"Yes," Samuel agreed in a soft voice. "We have to stay alive, if for nothing else, to bear witness when this is all over."

***

In the same region of the forest, not far from our camp, there was another group of eight Jewish refugees. These people had not dug a bunker. They thought it better to build a *kurang,* a dwelling on the surface, also disguised with twigs and covered with sand. In the middle of the primitive hut, they could make a fire and the smoke would go straight up through a hole in the top.

One night the twigs they gathered for their fire were so dry, the fire spread too quickly and burned down the whole *kurang.* Worse, it created a lot of smoke which spread widely. They were certain that the local peasants would smell the smoke and realize there were Jews or partisans nearby.

A few days later they made the decision to pull out. They didn't want to bet their lives on the benevolence of the peasants.

We too had to make a decision because of that fire. Naturally none of us wanted to leave the bunker, with its warm oven that funneled the smoke out of our eyes and lungs. But there was really no choice. If we wanted to survive, we had to find a different place. Worse, there was no time to haul the heavy oven around.

It was now nearing the end of 1942. We had been homeless, stateless, for barely four months, but it seemed like an eternity.

So far it had been an extremely cold winter with plenty of snow. Before we had the stove, we could never get dry enough or warm enough, and colder weather was on the way.

Gathering what little bits of food we had, and the few weapons, we left everything else and prepared to move off to a safer part of the forest.

As we headed out, my father said, "Five months ago we could not imagine having to live like this, like animals. We'd have given alms to any beggar who had to live in such a ditch. Today, we weep over leaving our warm, cozy ditch, and pray we can find a place as warm and safe. Sometimes I think the people who have already died are better off than we are. We don't know that we'll escape the same fate anyway."

***

One thing I learned in the forest was that given time, people can get used to anything.

Two gigantic black kettles, mounted on wheels, were in the center of the *Mishkin* camp. Every week, your mother and some other women would pile kindling under the pots and fill them with snow to do a wash. They had to boil their clothes frequently to kill the lice. Typhus was a constant danger.

One day a woman said, "We should throw our clothes into the snow so the lice will freeze."

"Yes," Julia said, laughing, "but when we put them back on, the lice will defrost."

Another lady said, "Then the lice will be resurrected."

As the women laughed, Julia noticed a young farmer walking past the wagons and the makeshift horse corral into the camp. As he came closer, she saw the boy had a deep scar running down his left cheek to the corner of his mouth. He strode past without looking at them and walked up to the commander who was sitting near the kitchen tent.

"Four or five Germans are coming to inspect machinery in Malkovich tomorrow at eight a.m." the boy said.

"I see," the commander said.

"They will have to take the road from Zadub'e to Malkovich," the boy added.

The commander got up and walked to a nearby tent. The boy stared after him. His parents had been killed in a German reprisal for the ambush of a two-man patrol. Thirty men and women from a small village were taken out and shot. The young boy had his face smashed by a rifle butt for protesting. He was now a part of the *Mishkin* intelligence system.

Soon, thirty men had grabbed their rifles and were rushing out of camp.

The partisans frequently got information from friendly peasants or from White Russian spies that infiltrated the villages and lived with the peasants. They needed to know about the German movements; when they were coming, where they were going, how many were there, how heavily armed, the location and size of their garrison towns. They tracked the police units as well. Most of these were not regular police, but groups of Ukrainians and some Poles, appointed and trained by the Germans. They needed this information not just for operations, but for security. There was no way they could stand up to a German force and fight it out. It was much more intelligent to run into the Germans only when you wanted to.

Life with the *Mishkins* was not that much safer than life with my small group. They were larger and so left more signs of where they had been. It was hard to remove all evidence of a camp of two hundred people, and they made mistakes.

When the Germans approached the vicinity, they had no choice, they had to move. For the first few months, it seemed to Julia that they were moving camp almost every week. If there was enough warning, they packed the whole camp up on horse-drawn wagons and trudged through the rutted tracks of the forest like some forsaken Gypsy troop.

German special units dogged their every step. These units were under the command of German officers, and consisted of Ukrainians, Latvians, Lithuanians, and White Russian peasants who were trained to track down the partisans. Native to the region, they hated the Soviets and knew the various areas as well as or better than the partisans. Most of the time, the troops were distant enough so that their presence was felt, but not seen. There were times, however, when they managed to get close enough to fire into the *Mishkin* ranks.

With the right information, the partisans could stay a step ahead of the larger German units, and lay ambushes for the smaller units.

By nightfall, some thirty *Mishkins* had set up positions on both sides of the road, some six miles west of Malkovich. When the Germans were in the middle of the position, most of the partisans started firing, while three of the fastest and strongest men rushed the lone officer and knocked him off his horse. The other Germans were dead before they hit the ground, so surprised they had not gotten off a shot. The officer was blindfolded and taken back to camp to be interrogated.

Later that day, when the partisans returned with their prisoner, your mother was summoned to the commander's tent. She was the only one in camp who could speak and understand German, so she was asked to translate.

Upon seeing the handsome, well-fed officer seated on a cot, his hands bound behind him, Julia began to shake with hatred and fear. She was surprised to hear the German ask in a kind voice, "Why are you bandaged, young girl?"

"One like you did this to me," Julia said as anger crept into her voice. "One of you."

"Why?" he asked.

Julia looked at him incredulously. "Because I'm a *Jude*," Julia said, now trying to fight back tears.

The soldier was skeptical. "Couldn't you hide?" he asked. "You don't look Jewish. Your hair is very light."

"They did it to me," she yelled in German. "Your kind. I promise you."

The soldier shook his head in disbelief.

After the interrogation was over, the officer was asked to join the partisans.

Julia translated. "He said he will join, but with the provision that he will not have to fire on German soldiers, or go on ambushes where he might be forced to fire on his countrymen. He will shoot only the Ukrainians or Poles that are on the German side."

Later, while they were left alone in the tent as the *Mishkins* talked over what to do with him, he asked Julia to let his wife know he was still alive so she would not remarry. He took out several worn photographs of his wife and children to show Julia.

At the time, Julia was not aware that the *Mishkins* made a similar offer to most of their captives. They said they would let them live if they either joined or cooperated by giving away the German plans and positions. They had no facilities for keeping prisoners, most of whom were executed by bayonet. They could not afford to waste bullets. Since this officer would not answer any of their questions, he was executed.

The *Mishkins* knew they would not find any shred of mercy at the hands of the Germans or their allies. Why extend that courtesy to them?

Among the partisan groups, it was common knowledge that, in 1942, Hitler had issued a directive telling all soldiers they had the right to use any means, even against women and children, as long as they were successful.

> *No German participating in action against*
> *bandits and their associates is to be held*
> *responsible for acts of violence either from*
> *a disciplinary or judicial point of view.*

Sometimes the *Mishkins* would offer life to a prisoner simply as a cruel joke—then kill them. A payment in kind.

CHAPTER 12

FIRST BLOOD

Brisk winds blew out of the northeast for the next two weeks, depositing mountains of snow, and piling it in high drifts throughout the forest. I was too cold and miserable to worry about my old friend Boychik—there was too little food and we were all chilled to the bone. In the mornings, our clothes were so stiff—sometimes encrusted with bits of ice—it took an effort just to move our arms and legs. Without our beloved stove, I once more thought we would all die of exposure, without having fired a shot.

I remember Label saying he would kill just to have a *ushanki*, one of those round Russian fur caps with the earflaps. It took every ounce of energy just to stay alive and healthy.

New people kept appearing in the forest, haggard, with hollow eyes and empty bellies. Some of them were from the groups that Feldman had organized during the first days after the massacre at Pohost Zagorodski. There was nothing for us to do but take them in.

Soon there were some twenty-five people in our camp, all shivering, all weak and hungry. Papa insisted that all the food should be shared. And it was not long before it was all used up. Every conversation seemed to be about the lack of food. Warm clothing was a distant second. With so many hungry mouths to feed, the only choice was to leave the safety of the Mizelyshchatz Forest to try to get food.

On a crystal-clear night, with a beautiful starry sky, I found Label shaping a stick for fishing.

"Give me the revolver," I said to him. It was my turn to go for food.

We shared the one weapon. Whoever went out of camp on a mission took the gun.

I left with three other men. One of them was Sholom Lan, who had been in the bunker with Yentl and her children, but had managed to escape. The others were Itzik Denenberg, my cousin who, in another life once had two brothers and had been a musician, and Mulia Kozushnik, once a mountain of a man, now only a tall, thin reed.

After brushing out our tracks for the first half-mile out of the camp, we started to walk backward in the snow.

Night fell early this time of year, and the starlight reflecting off the deep white snow made it easy to see. I hated to leave the woods on such a bright evening, but the camp was completely out of food.

I led them to a pasture covered with snow, where there was a farmhouse, once red, but now almost buried in giant snowdrifts. The owner of the now white house was a farmer I had known for a long time before the war.

I knocked on the door. A gaunt, tired man in a heavy wool overcoat and high black boots, answered. We shook hands. "We need food, desperately," I said quickly. "I hate to beg, but we are over twenty people now."

The farmer lowered his eyes and said in a pained voice, "Abram, I have very little food for even my wife and children. I know it's not your fault, but I can't do this any more. There are so many refugees and partisans. Do you know that last night they stole two sheep from my flock and one cow? How can I manage? I can't feed everybody."

I was embarrassed. "I'm sorry. I didn't know." I had only thought of my own problems. This is often the case with people, they only think of their own problems and our problems were great. But this was a severe winter. This man had helped us ever since the first time of trouble.

I knew that difficulties with friendly farmers had arisen as more and more Jews escaped from the labor camps and ghettos and made their way to the forests. These newcomers did not know the peasants at all. Their only hope for survival was to steal or die a slow death of starvation. But one of the great advantages we had was the many years of friendship and dealings with the peasants. I thank God every day for how honest and fair my father had been with everyone. We never would have survived without the good will he had built, but we could not afford to spend that capital foolishly.

These thefts started to turn our peasant friends against us. Worse, some of these good people had been executed by the Germans for helping Jews.

What could I do, I wondered? I couldn't stop the newcomers from stealing. They were starving. They had to get food somehow.

As time went on, it seemed that the newcomers were robbing the farmers blind. There were killings of them as well, when a farmer would stumble upon the desperate thieves.

I vowed right there that when the war ended, I would make sure I repaid every one of the peasants who helped me—double what they did for me.

In later months, when I was forced to leave this familiar area and go to places where I did not know anybody, I found out just how hard it had been for the newcomers. Meeting some peasants for the first time, I asked them for food. They refused and said they would give me nothing. I had no choice except to use force or starve.

The peasant brought out one loaf of bread to me.

"We've been friends for a long time, and I want to give you something, but you must understand…it has been a hard winter."

I almost felt guilty taking the bread, but I had no choice. I thanked him. He had been more than generous to us. "I have an idea," the man said, brightening a bit. "You know. I have a friend in Borki. Yes," he said. "Go to Dmitri in Borki. He has a large estate. Use my name. He will give you enough food for everyone."

He motioned for us to follow him to the stable.

"You can take my sleigh."

Though no one would admit it, I bet we were all thinking more of the man's coat, jealous of its warmth. No one had more than a light cloth jacket. I was sorely tempted to ask for a coat. I resisted the temptation. One could not afford to be greedy.

The farmer tethered one of his horses to a sleigh and gave me the reins.

"You will be careful, Abram?" he asked. He was having second thoughts.

"Certainly," I replied, patting the great sorrel on the chest.

"And you will return it? It's my only sleigh and one of my best horses."

"Of course," I said. "You know my family. We are greatly indebted to you."

"Right. I'm sorry. I can only guess how bad it is for you. You will have better luck in Borki. It is close to Pohost Zagorodski. I'm sure you know some of the people there. They'll know you are coming to ask for food and not to steal."

As we drove off, I had a sick feeling in my gut that quickly turned to fury as I realized who lived in Borki. I turned to Sholom, slapping him on the arm to get his attention. "Borki is the village where Boychik lives. He's the S.O.B. who turned in my aunt."

"I know. Remember? I was there. He turned me in as well," Sholom said coolly. "I say we worry about food later."

"I agree," I said. "Mulia?"

"Right."

"Itzik?"

"They were my cousins too."

"Then let's go," I said as I whipped the reins and shouted at the horse.

We reached the outskirts of Borki around nine at night, and went to the first hut we saw. A man was looking out the window.

"Do you know this fellow Boychik?" I shouted. "Do you know where I can find him?"

"Of course," the man replied. "Are you going to the wedding?"

Wedding, I thought. The S.O.B.'s getting married while we sit out here freezing to death. "Yes," I said, trying hard to remain calm. "We've come a long way for his wedding. I'd hate to be this close and get lost and miss it. It should be one grand affair."

"You're right about that, son. Tomorrow's the day and he's marrying real well. He got to be a real big shot with the Germans...made a lot of money from them."

"So I've heard." *Blood money.*

"The family he's marrying into has a big estate. A *mayuntik* about five miles from here," the man added. "Come inside and I'll draw you a map."

Of course, I knew the area like the back of my hand, but it was as good an excuse as any to go inside and warm up a bit.

"Aren't you boys cold?" the peasant asked, looking somewhat puzzled.

I laughed. "We're from north of Minsk. It's so cold up there, we come here to get warm."

The rest of them tried to laugh as well, if for no other reason than to cover up the noise from their chattering teeth.

After studying the map for twenty minutes with the peasant, we left, happy to have been out of the cold for such a long time.

We reached the estate in less than an hour. It was easy to find. As we came closer, we simply had to follow the noise and the mass of people. It was a grand celebration with lots of guests coming and going. We could see there was a full house of merrymakers. Everyone was eating and drinking sumptuously.

I pulled in the reins, stopping the sleigh. I'm sure my expression was grim. There would be dirty work this night.

"Kozushnik should go in," I said. "If I go in, Boychik will recognize me immediately. And he might know Itzik. Would he know you, Sholom?" I asked.

"I don't think so."

"So, you go with him. Say you're partisans who've lost your way and need to be guided back to the main road. We'll wait out here."

As Kozushnik and Sholom got down from the sleigh, I whispered, "Insist that Boychik guide you. Don't accept anyone else. Get him out here."

Itzik and I walked with them until they were halfway to the house, and waited in the darkness as they knocked on the door and went inside. I stayed ready, keeping my hand on the revolver in my pocket, impatiently stroking it. Would I actually use the gun on the S.O.B.? I had never killed a man, never even shot at one.

Kozushnik and Sholom were in the house for a long time. Outside, it started snowing, lightly at first, but soon it turned into a blizzard. The fierce, bitterly cold wind stung our faces like tiny knives.

"God, I hope they hurry," Itzik said.

My ears and nose were already burning from the freezing wind.

131

Inside, Kozushnik and Sholom were not making much progress, but after letting it be known they were partisans, they were quite popular.

"You'll have to go to Bobric. That's another village around here," Boychik said, raising a glass of wine to the partisans. The other peasants toasted them as well, and once more touched glasses with the groom.

Peasants brought wine, liquor and ham to Kozushnik and Sholom, and even some wedding cake.

We had been spotted by a woman who asked Kozushnik, "Why don't your two friends out there in the snow come in and join the celebration?"

"Someone has to stand guard, Miss. Who knows when a German patrol might show up," Kozushnik replied.

"Well, we can't have them starve on a night like this," Boychik's soon-to-be father-in-law said. "Then I'll take you myself to Bobric. I know the way better than anyone." He snapped his fingers like a medieval lord, and motioned for his servants to bring food and drink to the partisans standing out in the snowstorm. Four servants rushed outside, their hands full, and filled the sled with liquor, ham and breads. Depositing their loads, they quickly ran back to the warmth of the manor.

"Sir," Sholom said, "With all due respect and many thanks, our elders should be honored. It is late and I guarantee you, being out in this weather is miserable. You could catch your death. We would feel bad if we made you go out on a night like this. Before your daughter's happiest day. Let your new son-in-law take us. He is young and a man is full of energy on the night before his wedding."

Boychik obviously did not want to leave his party. He looked out the window.

I recognized him immediately. I ducked back out of sight and stayed hidden, thinking this might be my first and only chance. I was by now shaking all over, but not from the cold. From rage.

Everyone inside the house was quite intoxicated. Boychik was too drunk to resist, and Kozushnik and Sholom were able to slowly edge him closer to the door.

"Come now, Boychik," Sholom said. "You wouldn't make an old man go out on a night like this? And he's your father-in-law."

"My wedding's tomorrow," Boychik protested. "I need to rest."

"Just lead us to the road and point us in the right direction," Kozushnik said. "You'll be back in twenty minutes."

"And you'll have acted like a patriot, Boychik," Sholom added slyly.

"Yessss. A patriot," Boychick slurred. By now they were at the door and protests no longer mattered. Kozushnik opened the door. Both he and Sholom shouted goodbye to the revelers as they strong-armed Boychik out the door.

As they reached the sleigh, I ordered, "Hold him tight."

Boychik must have recognized my voice first, then he saw my face and sobered up quickly. He blurted out, "Bobrow, I am not guilty. I know what you think, but I had nothing to do with what happened to your aunt and her children. You and I were friends. You must believe me."

"We'll discuss it later at our camp and decide what to do with you," I said coolly, but now, face to face with the villain, my anger was almost uncontrollable.

I wrapped a cloth around Boychik's mouth. After gagging him, Kozushnik and I hoisted him up into the sleigh. Kozushnik and Denenberg sat, one on each side of Boychik, holding him firmly by his hands and arms. I got into the driver's seat and snapped the whip at the sorrel until it reached a gallop. I remember turning and glaring at Boychik.

"Didn't we take you in? Didn't we give you work? Didn't we feed you? How could you do this?"

I turned back to watch the road, my face flushed with hatred. "They were my family!"

Boychik's face showed terror. He knew he was a dead man. We had not gone far when he pulled his hands away from his guards and jumped from the sleigh. Kozushnik was just as fast. He vaulted out right after Boychick, ran him down and tackled him by the legs. They rolled over and over. Boychik struggled to regain his feet, but Kozushnik held him down with a vice-like grip.

I reined in the speeding horse, trying to stop the sleigh. Sholom could no longer control his desire for revenge. He reached over to me, grabbed my hatchet, and jumped from the sleigh while it still was sliding to a halt. He grabbed Boychick by the hair and brought down the blade, square into Boychik's forehead. Then, he stood back, breathing heavily.

"Thus to all informers," Sholom said as Boychik lay bleeding on the ground, but still alive. They watched as he turned on his belly and tried to crawl away.

"And to all Germans," said Kozushnik.

"Shoot him!" Sholom screamed at me as I reached them.

I took out the revolver and pointed it at Boychik's head.

"This is for the people in the bunker," I said. "But especially for Michle." Then I pulled the trigger.

"They'll think they're dealing with partisans," Denenberg said. "They don't think Jews have weapons. He'll go down as a traitor."

Sholom pulled the blade from the informer's head. "Good," he said, bending to wipe the blade off in the snow near the body. He handed the hatchet back to me.

"We want them to know who did this," I said adamantly. "It might make them think twice before crossing our path again."

"Yes. Just take his clothes and leave him. Someone could've heard the shot," Kozushnik said. "Let's go."

As I watched, the others pulled off Boychik's boots and took his fur coat. Sholom tried on the coat and was quite pleased. Then they stripped him completely, dumped him in the snow, and returned to the sleigh.

I lingered for a time, staring down at the dead naked body. I had avenged my aunt and her children. I had killed my first enemy. But there was no exhilaration, no lessening of my anger, only sorrow, only emptiness. Revenge doesn't revive the dead, I thought. I would still never again feel my mother's arm on my shoulder, or see little Michle's sweet smile. I quickly traced a Star of David in the snow and ran back to the sleigh.

Later, we drove rapidly along the road, I let out a cynical laugh. "Now I only have four bullets left in my pistol," I told the others.

They knew what I meant.

I figured on only being able to use four. I was leaving the last for myself, if I was in danger of being caught.

None of us would ever let ourselves be captured by the Germans.

We had ridden six miles, when Itzik reached up to the driver's seat and shook my shoulder.

"Abram, let's stop," he said. I'm starving. It's safe now. Let's see what they gave us."

"We're all starving," I said as I pulled in the reins and steered the horse into the woods.

Kozushnik and Denenberg quickly broke off a few branches and walked back to the road. Finding the place where we entered the woods, they started brushing the branches back and forth over the snow until the sleigh tracks disappeared. They continued this, walking backwards, brushing the snow, until they reached the spot where I had turned off, and then followed the path back to the sleigh.

"At least we can eat in peace," Sholom said.

And eat we did. We took out the ham and bread and gorged ourselves— we were too starved to worry about the ham not being kosher. We washed the food down with liquor. It had been a long time since we had been able to eat until full and we relished every morsel.

"We should bring some of this back to the others," I said. I began to feel better now that I had my first real taste of revenge. It also did not hurt that I had a full stomach for the first time in months.

"I think we should continue on the main road instead of through the woods," Kozushnik said. "It's a lot faster."

I shook my head. "I'm not sure that's a good idea."

"Come on, Bobrow. Don't be so serious. No self-respecting German is going to be out on a night like this."

"And certainly no Poles or White Russians," Sholom exclaimed.

"All right," I said, "but I don't like it."

We got back into the sleigh and started toward the road. Kozushnik and Sholom continued to nip at the liquor and after about a mile, they were both singing Russian songs. Itzik joined them. Even I got carried away, singing at the top of my lungs.

Suddenly, we heard shots.

"Germans!" I yelled. I pulled tightly on the reins, causing the horse to lurch violently into the woods. I drove the horse hard as bullets whizzed by our heads. After flying through the woods for a mile, I pulled the horse to a stop. The four of us leapt out and started running, leaving all the supplies, the horse and the sleigh behind.

After a half-hour of running we stopped to catch our breath.

Sholom was suddenly self-righteous. He said, "If we didn't stick to the main road, and we didn't sing those Russian songs, none of this would've happened."

"You know," Kozushnik replied, "that you sang louder than any of us."

"And," Itzik said as he held up his hand to speak, "if we didn't sing the songs and just continued on the road, we would've run straight into the Germans."

All four of us laughed so hard we collapsed on the ground. A full belly can do wonders for you. Then we laboriously began brushing out our footprints before heading the two miles back to camp.

"What was that shooting?" my brother asked as he ran out to meet us.

We told him the whole story and precisely where we had left the sleigh. We looked so tired and intoxicated that Label said he would let us rest while he went to retrieve the horse and sleigh.

"That's a very nice man you borrowed them from," Label said. "I think it's important we return it if we can. We can't afford to alienate people like him."

My brother and another man, left right away, not wanting to waste the cover of night. When they found the horse and sleigh, the sorrel had gotten his reins tangled around an oak tree. All the bread, ham, and liquor were still there. They untangled the horse and rode through the forest to get back to the camp, and then divided up the food and spirits among everybody.

When I returned the horse and sleigh to the peasant, we took along some ham and liquor for gifts. The peasant was very pleased.

***

For our small group, life in the forest consisted of endless periods of boredom, grief and struggle, laced with fear, and sometimes, brief moments of terror. Most of our activity was concerned with food and simple survival, but as we grew hardened and got more used to life in the forest, we began thinking about other things; how to get weapons and how to take part in the war, to claim our right to vengeance.

One night in February, four of us went out to the railway line between Malkovich and Honsovich. After midnight, we found a section on a curve that was hidden from sight of any patrol coming up or down the line. While Kozushnik and Itzik stood watch, about fifty yards apart, Label and I used a long, sturdy wooden bar to pry up the wooden ties. Once the ties broke from the leverage, it was easy to loosen a section of eight-foot rail and bend it in half. If a German patrol happened on the scene, Kozushnik or Itzik would give a signal—whistle or hoot like an owl—and everyone would run back to the safety of the forest.

I laughed as I said to Label, "Pretty ironic, ripping up these ties, huh?"

We used to shape them out of raw lumber at the lumberyard.

Label was not as amused. "This was our work. Our father's life work. Let's do it and get out of here."

"Right," I said. I had not meant any disrespect, but I understood how bitter my older brother was.

The Germans had bunkers and checkpoints all along the rail lines. Soldiers in small, two-man trolleys constantly cruised up and down the lines looking for sabotage. Trees were cut down on both sides of the tracks so that there was little cover. Every five hundred yards there were guardhouses with flares, reflectors and lamps to illuminate the entire length of track, and rockets and flares to summon more troops. There were also guard dogs and mines. Often, the guards would find the breaks in the line before any damage was done. This time, after all the risks we took, we found out the train did not even run that day.

A number of times, we cut the telephone lines between Parachunsck and Malkovich. This was more difficult, because the telephone poles were always located along the main roads and German patrols were everywhere. All our missions had to take place on the darkest of nights, sometimes so dark you had to hold onto the person directly in front of you or risk losing him and getting lost.

Every excursion from the camp was fraught with danger, whether we were trying to do damage to the German war effort or just trying to fill our bellies. For the most part, we would leave only for the necessities—food and information. During this period, the total extent of our arsenal was two rifles and a pistol.

CHAPTER 13

SAMUEL'S MISSION

Everyone in the *Mishkin* camp was in poor health. Gradually, the lack of a sufficient diet and sanitary conditions, the stress from constant vigilance and fear, compounded by the lack of sleep, could lead to illness.

Viruses, fungus, infections were also a constant battle in the forest, and there was little the partisans could do to protect themselves.

After peeling potatoes for weeks on end, your mother's hands broke out in boils from a virus. She could not work in the kitchen, so they gave her a rifle and let her stand watch. She stood watch for two hours every night until her hands heeled.

On top of that, in the six weeks before the spring thaw, the *Mishkins* were forced to move camp four times, as German auxiliaries closed in, dogging their every movement. The whole camp would pack up, pulling most of their necessities on ten horse-drawn carts.

My brother, David, was one of the men in charge of withdrawals. He so zealously guarded the welfare of the horses that Shaindel had to beg him to let their own son Shlameleh ride. Julia, slogging barefoot over the rough ground of the cart paths on these long, nighttime treks, was not so lucky. David would not let her rest on a cart for even a few minutes. He was worried the extra weight would wear down the horses. The horses were more important to the *Mishkins* than the "extra mouths" of women or a small child. Julia knew that David had too much integrity to play favorites, and in addition, the fact that they were Jewish, and dependent on the good will of the *Mishkins,* he felt his honesty and fairness had to be above suspicion.

Your mother would get so exhausted on these night marches that she was in danger of being left behind. She was aware that the partisans sometimes shot stragglers, much as they would shoot someone who fell asleep on guard duty, but she was too weak to help it.

The partisans had acquired six oxen from local farmers. They drove the oxen with them and slaughtered them for meat when they had the luxury of time. Sometimes your mother held onto the tail of an ox and fell asleep as she walked, letting the ox guide her along. Once she got too close and the ox stepped on her leg. Even in her fatigued state, she knew she better not scream. Shaindel saw her distress and bandaged her leg as they walked, but Julia no longer dared sleep walk on the midnight journeys.

One night, toward the end of her sentry duty, Julia began to feel weak and had a headache. She remained at her post until relieved, stumbled back to camp and collapsed on the twigs and leaves that made up her bed.

The next morning, after a feverish sleep, she could barely walk to the stream for some water. Her throat was completely dry and a red rash broke out on her back and upper arms. Shaindel rushed to her. As she asked, "What's wrong?" she touched Julia's head and a clump of light brown hair came off in her hand. "Oh my Lord," Shaindel exclaimed, automatically holding it out to Julia. "This is yours!"

Shaindel took Julia back to her bed and brought her boiled water. She found Dr. Vasilievich and brought him to Julia's tent. She had a fever of 105 degrees. Typhus. This could be a death sentence.

After making her as comfortable as possible, Vasilievich sent her by wagon to Sbychovo, where the partisans had set up a house as a sanitarium. Later Vasilievich followed her to make sure she got good care. After two terrible weeks, the fever finally broke and she was able to return to camp. Considering her overall weakness, your mother was very lucky.

***

One of the partisans who seemed to have a boundless supply of energy was David, my eldest brother.

He was one of those gifted people, who, no matter what they did or where they started, they would soon rise to the top. Tall, with thick, dark hair, he was a natural leader. Clear-sighted in assessing problems, strong and resolute in devising solutions, and unruffled in any situation—so much like our father had always been.

It was not long before he became the quartermaster for the *Mishkin* partisans, in charge of getting supplies from the local farmers; oats and hay for the twenty horses, and potatoes, grain, flour and cabbage for the two hundred people in camp. The very survival of the camp was dependent on his acquisitions.

The one partisan who was upset with David, was your mother. She had told the leader of the *Mishkins* that she would do all the women's work they asked for, and do it without complaint, as long as they promised her she could eventually go on missions. But David would not let her go. He was protective of her.

While she was in the sanitarium, the *Mishkins* had been busy. In Stoschan, they captured some Germans. The partisans had surrounded a house, and told the Germans to lay down their weapons. The Germans were so afraid they became confused. Most of the time, the Germans realized that if they surrendered, they were dead anyway, so they fought to the end. But this time, even though surrounded, they could not decide if they should fight to the death or not. If they surrendered, there was still a chance to maneuver—still a chance to survive. If they fought, they would certainly all die. They threw their guns and ammunition out the windows, then came out with their hands up. They were brought back to the partisan camp and later executed.

On another mission, the partisans dressed up in German uniforms and marched into a village police station at Telehan. They had taken the uniforms from soldiers whom they had killed or taken prisoner in ambushes. Many Russian soldiers had these uniforms with them when they first joined the partisans. They preferred German uniforms because they were better made and much warmer.

***

Early every morning, David would go from cart to cart, checking fittings, halters, reins and wheels, making certain one more time that everything was in order in case there was a sudden need to evacuate the camp.

It happened so often that I'm just going to give you one example your mother told me about.

A gunshot would be heard. Then two, three. In seconds, the calming voice of David Bobrow was heard throughout the camp, encouraging people to move, ordering, coaxing. The horses had to be hitched up to the carts and kettles. As many supplies as possible had to be loaded onto the carts; ammunition and food first. They were the priorities. People had to be awakened. Even the noise of gunfire was not always enough for these worn-out souls.

Sentries had been posted every thirty yards around the perimeter, about a half-mile out from the main camp. From the sound of the shots this time, David figured they had eight to ten minutes to move out.

"Get up!" he yelled. "We've got five minutes to get out of here!"

Julia and her tent-mate hurriedly pulled the ropes holding up their tent. They had fastened them with slipknots. Quickly folding the tent, they threw it on one of the carts, then looked around to see if there was anything they could carry, something important like a rifle or bullets.

Scouts hurried off to the east to make sure they were not heading into any German ambushes or farming areas, where they could not be certain of the loyalties of the peasants.

Fourteen sentries, coming from all directions, ran into the camp and found their tents and belongings already packed.

In six minutes the whole camp was on the move.

Ten Soviet soldiers, without receiving orders, grabbed their rifles and moved ahead of the others. They followed the scouts until they found a good position for an ambush, preferably within a mile of the camp. They did not want to let the Germans get too close. Finding a spot, they dug in and waited, watching as their comrades filed past. They only had twenty rounds apiece. Their orders were to surprise the Germans, kill as many as possible then pull back. If they got out quickly enough they would set another ambush.

***

One morning that first winter, Label came up to me in a cheerful mood. Now that we'd been in the forest for a while, I guess all of us had more confidence.

"You know," he said me, "I gave a lot of clothes, some pretty nice suits to Jas Seluzistky, a *chutos* who lives half a mile from Pohost. I asked him to keep them for me. You remember him? He was a machinist at the lumber mill."

"Of course," I replied. "I worked with him sometimes."

"It's so damn cold," Label said, rubbing his arms to emphasize the point. "Abram, why don't we see if we can get some of them back?"

Pohost Zagorodski was now heavily guarded by the Germans. There was a large garrison of eighty soldiers in the town. Basing themselves in the *shtetl*, they constantly were on patrol in the surrounding areas, including the nearby forests and roads.

"Well," I said, "it's not going to be easy. And we better not tell Papa where we're going. He won't like it."

The next night we started walking the twelve miles to Pohost. We told Papa we were just looking for food.

We arrived without incident about four in the morning. When Label knocked on the door, Seluzistky ignored the noise. When we knocked on the window, he looked out, and recognizing us, let us in.

"I need some of the suits you hid for me," Label told him. "I don't mean to be rude, but we cannot stay for long."

Seluzistky understood. He left the room to get the clothing.

In a few minutes, he returned carrying a few suits and other clothing, and gave Label a bag to put everything in.

When we left, we moved through side streets to be less visible. Label was not sure he could trust the man, now that he thought about it. We gave the impression of a false direction by going to Kamen, an area to the east, before heading back to camp.

We returned to find our father quite upset. Somehow he knew where we had gone.

"It's not smart to risk your lives going after insignificant things," he said. He lectured us for twenty minutes for taking such a "foolish risk."

***

The next morning, I went to chop some wood for our fire. Somehow, I slipped, and one of the benches I used to bracket the log fell on my left arm. I could not move and shouted for help. Someone finally heard, and came over and lifted the bench off my arm. It swelled up immediately, and although my brother bandaged it, I could not use my arm for some time.

When our food supply was once more depleted, Label said he would go to a peasant he knew who would give us some bread. We knew many peasants, and tried to not go to the same people too often. This particular man, lived twelve miles away in the village of Botow.

Label did not want me to go. He said it was too dangerous to take someone with only one good arm, and Hershel and Aron were already going with him. But I was stubborn and insisted on accompanying them.

When we got to Botow, we went to two different peasants' houses until we had gotten almost enough bread and flour to meet our needs. Then we went to a third man's house. Just as we entered, the man's wife ran in from the field and shouted, "The Germans are patrolling in the village!"

The dawn was quickly approaching. Soon we would lose our cover of darkness.

"My friends," the woman said breathlessly, "you'd better run as fast as you can through the back door."

The four of us hurried in the direction she was pointing, only to discover that the couple's land was surrounded by a wooden fence. The only way to safety was over the fence and back into the woods.

Label and the others had no trouble getting over the fence, but when I tried, my left arm was useless and I couldn't make it.

"I can't pull myself up!" I yelled through the fence.

"Abram," Label called from the other side, "hang on! I'm coming back over."

Label climbed the fence again and pushed me up while I used my good arm as much as possible. Label was so strong, he literally threw me over the fence. Hershel and Aron caught me on the other side.

Then we scrambled away, half running, half crawling to the cover of the woods.

It was a near miss. Someone told the Germans that there were partisans in the region. We could have fallen into their hands simply because of my bad arm.

It was a revelation to me. When you are young, you never worry about hurting yourself. You take all sorts of risks. But here in the forest, in our circumstances, the most insignificant injury could lead to capture and death.

***

"Every time you leave the camp for provisions, you endanger your lives," Samuel said two weeks later as we were about to leave. I remember the three of us sitting around a small crackling fire in the bunker. "Do you have any idea what I go through when you're gone? I can't take this. I need to go with you once…to experience the ordeal."

"Papa. It's too dangerous," Label said.

"And it's hard" I added. "We get tired and we're a lot younger and used to it."

"I know. But you don't know what I go through, waiting here in camp. If I go with you, even once, then I'll know. Maybe then I can rest easier when you're gone…because I sure can't now. I need to know what it's like."

Both Label and I had our own misgivings. We looked intently at our father. Would we be able to protect him? Would we be putting his life in danger? Would he be able to keep up?

"Well…?" Samuel asked.

I looked to Label for the final decision.

"All right, Papa. We'll take you along," Label said.

"Besides," Samuel said, "when I was in the ghetto I gave clothes to some peasants for safekeeping and it's about time I got them back."

Now Label and I looked at each other and collapsed into laughter until tears welled up in our eyes.

"What?" Papa asked. "What?"

"I don't know if we should go out for such frivolous things, Papa," Label said, getting up from the ground and brushing the dirty snow off his coat.

"I think we have enough clothes, Papa," I said. Then both of us started laughing again. "Seems like it's warming up around here anyway."

The temperature that day was probably ten to fifteen degrees below zero. Papa couldn't see the humor.

"Well I'm going whether you like it or not," Samuel said. "I'm still the father in this family."

"It's twelve miles back to Pohost. It won't be easy," I said. Then I nodded. "But we'll go."

"When we get back, you'll look so good, you'll be able to go to a dance," Label added.

Papa was now sixty years old, and although the last months had hardened him a great deal, it was still a difficult trip. We moved much more slowly with him along.

In the village of Botow, which was very near Pohost Zagorodski, we came to the house of a farmer named Vasily. Vasily was nicknamed "Americanyetz," because he had lived in the United States for a while, and then returned to Poland. His hut was typical of a peasant's—small, only two rooms, logs covered with stucco and a straw-covered roof.

Samuel knocked on the door. Nobody answered. He knocked again. Through a side window, I could see Vasily move to the door, but make no move to open it.

As he finally let the door open a crack, a woman with bent back and gnarled legs came up and asked through the sliver of an opening, "What is your name?" It was Vasily's wife.

"Bobrow," Samuel answered.

The old, misshapen lady slammed the door shut. She screamed from inside, "It can't be! That family was all killed. You must be the devil! I don't believe it."

Through the window I could see her run to her husband and grab him by the shoulders. She screamed so loud we could hear her from outside. "It can't be Bobrow. It must be the devil that came to our door." Then she ran to the door and started screaming again. "He claims he's Bobrow, but it can't be Bobrow. So it must be the devil!"

My father patiently knocked once more. In the house Vasily tried to calm his wife. He convinced her to go to the bedroom and lock the door. Inside was her holy shrine. I could imagine her kneeling before the icon to the Mother of God and praying. She really thought we were ghosts.

Vasily came out, approaching us cautiously.

"Listen Vasily," Samuel said. "We're not devils. We escaped the Germans. We came to get some of the things we gave you to keep for us during the time we were in the ghetto."

"I don't remember," Vasily said, stalling and trying to think of a way to keep the fine clothing away from us ghosts. "I can give you some food and flour. My wife is very frightened. You cannot stay here long."

"You know," Samuel said calmly and deliberately, "if you do a good deed, it stays a good deed. If you commit a sin, it stays a sin. But no matter how many good deeds you do, they'll never cancel the sins."

"Yes," Vasily said slowly, maybe feeling guilty, "I remember something."

143

Label moved to within a foot of him to add a threat to Papa's admonishment.

"But I don't know where I put them," Vasily said.

He went back in the house and motioned for us to follow. Soon, his crone of a wife, satisfied her prayers would protect them, brought out bread, milk and honey.

We ate and patiently waited the man out. We knew we could not leave the village until night—there were too many German patrols out there. But we did not think Vasily knew this. The longer we stayed, the more frightened he became. It was obvious he thought we were going to beat him or worse. Finally, after three hours of eating and increasingly meaningless conversation, he told his wife to bring out some of the clothing, hoping that would satisfy us. The longer we stayed, the more clothing he brought out. Papa had indeed left a lot of clothes with this Americanyetz.

As soon as it was dark, we started back to the woods, taking our usual circuitous route. My father was happy to have some of his warm clothes back, but he was exhausted. He had not expected either the physical or mental toll of this kind of journey. His feet and legs were sore and it hurt him to walk.

"I can't keep up with you," he said finally. "I have to rest."

Germans or Ukranian or Byelorussian police could be anywhere. Either Vasily or his wife might decide they were unhappy giving the clothes back, or sparing the food.

I knew exactly what Label was thinking. "If we run into trouble, we'll run into it together. Right, Label?" I said.

"Of course. Can you make it to the woods, Papa?"

"No. I better rest here. You go on," Samuel said.

"Then we'll all rest here," Label said. "Abram, you go back along the path, say, a hundred yards. I'll whistle when Papa is ready to go."

"All right," I said.

"You shouldn't do this," our father protested. "I'm old. I've lived my life. It wouldn't be so bad if it just ended right here. I don't want to be the cause of you being in danger."

"Don't talk nonsense, Papa," Label said.

I think it was the most serious tone of voice I'd ever heard from Label. And this from a man who was always serious.

"You are our glue, Papa," I said, my voice cracking. "You keep our family alive. Without you…I just don't know."

I walked back toward the town. As I left, Label sat Papa down in a grassy area and started to massage his legs.

Out in the clear, treeless field, I was close enough to still see the lights of the village. All sorts of terrible situations went through my mind. I could picture fierce dogs leading soldiers out of Botow on our trail, or bandits stumbling onto us. There were also the search and destroy missions and anti-partisan units. Once we made it to the forest we would be safe, but not here in the open.

I heard a faint and familiar whistle. I breathed a sigh of relief and headed back.

We went slowly and rested often on the way back to Bagdanovka.

***

One day Label took the revolver and walked out of camp by himself, heading to the village of Borki.

We were well known in the area, and many of the peasants over a twenty mile radius of Pohost Zagorodski considered us friends.

Label had been seen talking to two such men from Borki the night before.

He told me later that it was a long walk and it did nothing to soothe his nerves. In fact, the longer he walked the more enraged he became.

The peasants from Borki had told him a strange story. There was this fellow, Nicolaichik who lived in their village. A very boastful fellow, they said. A group of Jews were hiding near his property in a bunker, some adults and a woman with two small children.

This Nicolaichik had gone to the SS headquarters in Pohost Zagorodski with his friend Boychik. They didn't tell their other friends because they didn't want to split the reward money. It was five hundred Marks per Jew. He was bragging that his share of the take was two thousand Marks. But the best part, he said, was when this lady's nephews came to talk to him after the Jews were killed. Nicolaichik said he put on such a performance, tears and all, that he was able to put all the blame on Boychik, and make himself out to be a hero. Now he had heard that all the Bobrows were dead, caught by the Germans and Ukrainians on some island in the marshes and slaughtered. Nicolaichik had had a good laugh about it all, the peasants told Label.

Label left camp without telling anyone. He reached the home of Nicolaichik that evening.

Label knocked hard on the wooden door of the peasant's house. Nicolaichik, somewhat taken aback, let him in. Label could see fear and surprise in Nicolaichik's eyes, but the cunning of a quick-thinking mind as well. Label did not waste time.

"Do you believe in ghosts?" he asked Nicolaichik.

"I, I...I don't know," Nicolaichik stammered.

"Well," Label asked, "you do believe I'm dead. Yes?"

145

"I was just telling some friends of my great sorrow when I heard you and your brother were killed by the Germans," Nicolaichik said, trying hard to recover. "This is wonderful to see that the rumors were false." The peasant smiled his big smile. Sweat was pouring down his ruddy cheeks. "Let me get you some food…and some wine."

Nicolaichik turned to leave the room, but Label grabbed his arm and forced him to turn around.

"The rumors were right. I died when my little cousins were killed. I have come back for you."

Label pulled the gun out and stuck the barrel up against Nicolaichik's forehead. Nicolaichik didn't bother to protest or beg. He knew his time was up.

"You are not worth the bullet," Label said. "You're not worth anything, dead or alive."

Label let him go. He had truly made up his mind to leave he was so disgusted with this scoundrel. But as Nicolaichik backed away, one last image of his cousins came into his mind. Label said, "But you don't deserve to live."

He squeezed off a single shot. The bullet caught Nicolaichik through the temple as he tried to turn away. He fell to the ground, dead.

THE FIFTH DAY

CHAPTER 14

DAVID

Papa took up his usual position in the chair in front of the picture window as Bill and I sat down to listen. Quietly, Mama came into the room and sat down across from my father. Papa gave her the most curious look. I've never seen him so surprised.

"You know what we're going to talk about," he said to her.

"I know."

"Are you sure you want to listen?"

"I'll see," she said.

"Well," Papa said, "if you want to contribute, or add anything, feel free."

"Oh," Mama said, "this is your story. I have my own story. You just go ahead."

But as soon as Papa started to speak, Mama interrupted him with a story of her own. And more surprisingly, considering the subject matter, she laughed. I think she felt she needed to soften the story my father was telling us.

"One day, two of the scouts returned to our new Mishkin campsite with great smiles on their faces."

"'Julia! Sonya!' the two men shouted to me and my friend. Their hands were full with a dozen pairs of soft rubber boots they had acquired from some farmers. Many of us had been going barefoot through the whole winter, and we all rushed over. The scouts tossed pairs of boots to our eager, grabbing hands, and joyous shouting voices."

"But as soon as I put on the warm boots and tried to walk in them, I realized that the hollow heel, designed to fit over ladies' high-heeled dress-shoes, made hiking not only awkward, but impossible. The boots were warm but useless."

"Sonya took off her pair and threw them angrily to the ground. I took my pair off and sat down. I knew there was a way if I could just figure it out. I wasn't going to let those warm boots sit there and rot."

Papa interjected, "Your mother was always pretty smart, you know."

Mama smiled.

"'Come with me,' I said to Sonya and the others. I led them over to the commissary tent to a pile of raw potatoes."

"'I'm tired of eating potatoes and it's about time we found another use for them,' I told the others. I reached down and picked up a potato and stuffed it in the heel of one of the boots, did the same with my other boot, and then pulled them on. My companions were all giggling and laughing."

Then Mama got up to demonstrate as she continued. "Sashaying around as though I was an actress in the theater, I said, "'It works. Go ahead and try it.'"

"Even your brother David gave one of his rare smiles as the others followed my example," she said to Papa.

Bill and I were still laughing at our mother's performance, when she stopped suddenly and smiled at our father.

"Oh," Mama said to him. "You should continue your story."

From then on, Mama joined us, sometimes contributing, sometimes correcting Papa, and sometimes just listening intently.

***

One day, David was summoned to the commander's tent for a meeting.

The commander was sitting on a log outside the tent when he arrived. There was a rifle and a half-filled box of ammunition near his feet.

"Yes, sir," David Bobrow said in a crisp military voice.

The commander nodded and motioned for him to sit down.

"David. I don't have to tell you how important you have been to this organization."

"Thank you," David said. But immediately he knew that this was the preface to a nice speech about how he had to cut them loose. David tried to think of what he could say to change his mind.

"Don't thank me. It is you who deserves our thanks," the commander said. "This is not easy for me. But it is a purely military decision."

"Why…?"

The commander looked at the ground, then found his focus on David's brow. "Your son. I've had complaints, concerns…"

"But he is a good boy."

"The Germans are being pushed back, retreating. Soon we might be caught between the regular army and the anti-resistance groups. Field Marshall Paulus' Sixth Army surrendered to the Russians in January, '43. All of Stalingrad two days later.

"Now the front is moving closer to us. We are going to be in closer proximity to the Germans, one way or another, but even an unfriendly farmer could give us away. My men are worried. What if the baby cries out

149

at the wrong time? It could be up for all of us. I can't take the responsibility. I'm sorry."

David looked hard at this man he had grown to admire. He could see there was no argument, no reasoning he could use. The commander's mind was made up. David felt helpless for the first time since he had joined the partisans.

The commander stood up. He pointed at the rifle. "Bobrow, take this. You are a good man and a competent leader. You can form your own group and be successful."

He kissed him on both cheeks, said goodbye and walked away.

***

That same January of 1943, some peasants visited my group, bringing potatoes and cabbage.

"You should know that many partisans are pulling back from the east to the Mizelyshchatz Forest near Bagdanovka," one man said.

"This means the whole front is getting closer," added another. "This war may end one of these days."

When the men left, I ran to find Label and my father. "If the front's moving closer, David might be among the partisans coming this way," I said excitedly.

Label caught my eye with a stern glance. Though no one wanted to say it, I understood. *If he's still alive.*

More calmly, I said, "Shaindel and the baby might be with him as well, and a few of the survivors from Pohost."

Papa turned his back and walked away. He sat down near a thin birch tree and leaned against it. He did not want to get his hopes up just yet.

As the days passed, more information filtered in. I heard that a group of partisans had been spotted in the locality. There were people in this group that either voluntarily separated from a larger group or were asked to leave.

Two days later, David found a sentry from my camp and asked to be taken in.

He was grinning with expectation as he and the others were escorted through the forest and led to a small clearing. Three bunkers, invisible to the eye if you did not know their exact location, were spread over half an acre.

The first person David saw on the grounds of the compound was me. Even though I had anticipated this reunion, I was completely surprised. Out of the blue, it seemed to me, here was my older brother walking up and embracing me.

"You smell, little brother," he said jokingly, and pushed me away.

We both started laughing. Then we hugged each other again as our father and Label ran up. Samuel took his grandson in his hands and tossed him into the air, catching him gently in his arms. Label hugged Shaindel and his older brother.

Your mother and a young boy from Pohost Zagorodski had come with them. There were three other Jewish men, all with rifles.

"What happened?" Papa asked.

David explained, then wryly noted, "I did notice that all the partisans they sent away were Jewish."

Your mother walked up to me. She smiled shyly. "Here is your jacket just as I promised." She held out the coat. "Of course, it's a bit shabby now."

I took the coat, swung it over Julia's shoulders and pulled her closer. I kissed her on the cheek.

Within days, seven more Jewish men from Pohost Zagorodski came in to the group. These men also had weapons. Ruven Sosnick was among them.

"Ruven," I cried, grabbing him by the shoulders. "I thought you were dead!"

"When we got separated that night, I was hopelessly lost," Ruven told me. "I wondered around in the forest for hours, heard some voices, and joined two others. We headed north and ended up near Baranovich."

"What of Akiba?"

"I don't know. I haven't seen him or anyone else from town since that night, but I heard of your brother. All of us...we heard of this Jewish man who was one of the leaders of the *Mishkin Atrad* or group. I knew it had to be David."

In the next few weeks, other small groups of Jews started to filter in, wanting to join David's band. To add to this core, David sent emissaries out to friendly peasants to see if they knew of other Jewish groups hiding in the forest. Then, he personally visited their camps to convince them to join the larger group. Soon, there were over sixty men and women in the Mizelyshchatz Forest under his command. David Bobrow vowed he would take in every Jewish man, woman or child that came to him.

Weapons were still scarce, and there were others who sought to command a Jewish *atrad*.

Julia was visiting a friend at Avremel Feldman's camp when David came to meet them. This was the same Feldman, now a bit more slender, who had earlier insisted on splitting up into small groups. The friend had invited Julia to see how they were living in their part of the forest.

Feldman said to your mother, "Why don't you get a bucket of water for David Bobrow to wash his hands? Help him, honor him, he's the commander."

Julia looked over at my brother, but he shrugged his shoulders, so she went and fetched some water from a stream while they continued to speak. Returning, she brought the pail to David. My brother put down his rifle and started washing his hands, and, with a signal from Feldman, one of his men grabbed the rifle. This was not good.

Feldman's group, after all this time, still had no weapons, and I guess Feldman himself still coveted command of the partisans.

David slowly dried his hands. He looked at Feldman, not with anger, but with sadness.

"Give the rifle back. It doesn't belong to you," David said calmly. "If we can't even stop fighting among ourselves, how are we going to unite to fight the Nazis?"

No one on Feldman's side moved. No one spoke.

David waved goodbye to your mother and left them. He went to the next small camp.

A few days later, Feldman walked into David's camp, leading twenty-five more partisans into the unit. Finding David, he returned the rifle and said, "Please forgive me. I accept your command."

David smiled and took his hand.

That night, David gathered the entire company around an evening bonfire. They were deep enough in the Mizelyshchatz, to not worry about Germans or peasants.

For the first time in a year, I thought, the smell of a wood-burning fire is good, and the warmth is like paradise. For the first time in a year, I could take pleasure in such a simple sight as the sparks flying upward against the backdrop of the tall pines. Feelings of pride surged in my chest as I watched my brother.

"Friends," David said to the large assembly, "it's time the Jewish people started to even the score. Until now we have mostly worked at survival, due to lack of numbers and lack of weapons and ammunition. We are now hardened to the ways of the forest and we should start practicing classic underground warfare. We will ambush the enemy and take his weapons and bullets. This necessitates moving closer to where the Germans are. We will hit the Germans whenever and however possible. We'll still be on the defensive, we obviously cannot fight it out toe to toe with the Nazis, but we'll give them a little something to think about."

A murmur of approval swelled up in the ragged audience. Then a cheer. Soon, David had to hold up his hands for silence.

"From now on," David said, his grim face glistening in the light from the campfire, "we should leave the peasants alone and go closer to the towns to get food and supplies from the bigger landowners. We'll go into areas under German control."

Everyone listened intently as David spoke.

"We've exhausted the peasants in the small hamlets and we can't afford to have them turn against us," he continued. "We'll concentrate on getting livestock and food and be less concerned about clothing and other things that aren't necessities."

"Hoorah for Bobrow! Hoorah for Bobrow!" the crowd shouted.

"I don't think they believe that Jews can fight back. What do you think?" His eyes swept over the crowd.

Everyone roared in defiance. It was deafening.

"I thought so," David said proudly. "I think we should call ourselves the Kaganovich *Atrad*, after the Jewish Transport Commissar in Stalin's government. Is this all right?"

Again the crowd shouted its approval.

Within weeks, David organized all the people in the woods. He assigned people to scout groups. He assigned others as spies. As far as possible, every move of the Germans would be observed. Some people were chosen to replenish food and ammunition supplies, others to be combat soldiers assigned to ambush Germans, and still others were taught how to blow up bridges and railway tracks, and cut telephone lines.

The camp was organized as a regular army bivouac, with sentries placed at all the approaches and intermediaries to keep in regular contact with other partisan groups that were in the vicinity.

But we still didn't have enough weapons.

***

German patrols often moved through the forest northeast of Bagdanovka, making sweeps of the area, looking for partisans and Jews.

One afternoon, I was walking with your mother near the *Polanka,* an open section in the woods. She was telling me stories from her time with the *Mishkins.*

"Some of the Russians wear German uniforms, because they're better, and warmer." Julia told me. "My friend Sonya shot one of these Russians by accident."

"Oh my God," I said.

"She was standing guard in a trench and saw the uniform. He was a long way off and she thought he was a German. He was a nice young, blond Russian. Luckily, he was only wounded in the leg; Sonya's a dead shot. She was lucky too. The partisans might have shot her for shooting one of their men, even more so because she was Jewish.

"When a Russian soldier makes a mistake and people are killed as a result, only he's blamed. When a Jewish partisan makes the same mistake, all Jews are suspect. It's not a big honor to be a Jew these days," I said wryly.

Suddenly, Julia burst into tears. She could no longer keep her overwhelming sorrow inside. For months, she had managed to put it aside, ignore it, and had worked so hard in every capacity for the *Mishkins* that she was always too exhausted to think. She liked to think she had been strong. But now, here with me, someone with whom she had felt so close, who knew all her lost ones so intimately, whose families were so intertwined...after all, even as children, we had played together. And, remember, I had saved her life when she fell through the ice. Well, now she completely broke down, her tears flowing like rain as she clung to my shoulder.

"I'm all alone," she sobbed. "My family is gone."

Abruptly, Mama got up and left the room. Papa got up and followed her. Papa came back alone ten minutes later and said, "This is good that your mother listened in and talked about her experiences. It's too much to expect her to listen to everything...But she is all right."

"Only my Uncle Akiva is still alive," Julia said to me. "And he disappears into the forest for days and sits and cries over his lost wife and children. He ignores me and he is all I have. I love him. That is why I left the *Mishkins* to come here. He was my favorite uncle. But when I went over and tried to talk to him, and say, `Kiva, Kiva,' that was what we called him when we were kids, and he'd say, `Leave me alone, leave me alone.' And I said, `Kiva, please. Am I not here?'" By now, Julia's tears were running down her sunburned cheeks. "`I'm alone. I have only you. Please, Kiva, don't turn me away. I beg you.' But Akiva still turns me away."

"Yes, I know," I said, trying to comfort her, but feeling helpless. I squeezed her shoulder and held her tightly. What pact with the Devil wouldn't I gladly sign to turn back the clock to those earlier days before the horror began. I remember taking the sleeve of my shirt and gently drying Julia's tears. Her crying stopped, but something else was wrong. After living so long on the edge, my senses had become very attuned to the forest. "Come," I whispered to Julia. "Something is moving beyond the clearing. Shh. Walk behind me, quietly."

I stepped forward to get a better look. Soon enough, I heard a noise, but just barely.

"Lie down, Julia," I whispered. "Stay here. I'll see what's going on."

Julia lay down in the grass behind a tree, while I stealthily crept forward, halting from time to time behind trees to take a look. I was behind a thin birch tree when I first saw them, the gray uniforms spread out over a hundred yards of grassland, and heading straight for me. I wasn't as sneaky as I thought. They saw me.

Immediately, they opened fire. Bullets whizzed by my head, but I wasn't hit. Quickly, I backtracked to where I left Julia. I jerked her to her feet and pulled her along as I sprinted back toward the camp.

The firing had stopped when we were halfway back. Ruven and Hennik Solowsky were coming toward us. Hennik was a boxer from Warsaw, and my brother David's aide. They had heard the gunfire.

"Where are you going?" Julia asked Hennik, breathlessly.

"I want to make sure if there are Germans in the area," he replied.

"You didn't hear the gunshots?" I asked incredulously.

"Of course we did. That's why we're here," Hennik replied.

I grabbed Hennik by the arm. "Don't go. I know they're Germans. They just shot at us. I saw them. Don't be an idiot. We were lucky to get away."

"We need to find out for certain," Hennik insisted.

"Don't go, Ruven," I begged.

Ruven looked at me and shrugged his shoulders. "Orders," he said.

"I'm telling you, I saw the gray uniforms," I said. "The bullets whistled by my ears, hitting the tree I was standing behind. What more proof do you need?"

Ruven shrugged again and followed after Hennik.

"I have a bad feeling about this," Julia said as we started running again.

"Hennik's an idiot," I said angrily. "I just hope Ruven's okay."

We had not gone far when we heard more gunshots.

Back at camp, we reported the direction of the shots to David. The camp hurriedly began packing. Within ten minutes, our whole camp was moving off in the opposite direction of the gunfire.

David asked me to stay in the abandoned camp as a lookout. If the Germans came, I was supposed to retreat. If not, I was to wait as long as possible to see if Ruven and Hennik returned.

I sat in the deserted camp until nightfall. As it got darker, I headed to the *Polanka*. I spent half the night scouring over the *Polanka* looking for Ruven. I felt especially bad that I had not been able to convince Ruven to go back to camp. I never found him.

A few days later, Hennik wandered into our new camp. He was limping. He said he had been wounded in the leg, but had somehow managed to escape. Ruven was shot in the head and died instantly.

Hennik was taken to the *Sanchast* where his leg was bandaged, but it took a long time to heal and it was quite painful for him to walk. He never admitted to me that he had been wrong. He was too proud.

Ruven's body was never found. There were a lot of partisans who were killed in the woods and never found.

The forest stretched on forever, from Pinsk all the way to Moscow. If our scouts and spies could give us enough information to keep us from being cut off or surrounded by the enemy, there was always a new location to move to. The new camp was only three miles away from the place where Ruven was shot.

***

"Julia," David said, holding open the flap to her tent. "Come with me. I have a problem."

David led her to an open bunker, where young Sander Zipperstein lay uncomfortably, his right foot bandaged with dirty cotton strips. Label was kneeling beside him. Sander's toes had become frostbitten during the cold winter.

Many of the Jewish partisans had no shoes, gloves or hats, and the winters in Byelorussia were extremely cold, with blizzards, sleet, and tall drifts of bright white snow.

I rushed up, carrying a pot of boiling water and set it on the edge of the trench. I jumped down into the hole, then lifted the water and set it next to the boy.

"You know he has frostbite. Our good doctor cannot bring himself to perform the operation," David paused. "You've been trained with the *Mishkins*...please don't refuse."

Julia had never done anything of this sort, and her training was less than basic.

"The doctor will guide you step by step," David promised. "He'll be here in a minute."

Your mother eased herself into the trench. Rolling up her sleeves, she washed her hands in the hot water and crouched next to her cousin. Carefully, she lifted Sander's leg and unwrapped the bandages. Three of Sander's toes were black. The smell was foul. Almost more than Julia could bear.

I have to tell you, this is one of the bravest things I ever saw anybody do. And it was your mother that did it.

Sander looked at Julia. "I have to lose them, don't I?"

156

"Yes," Julia said. "I'm sorry."

David retrieved a butcher's knife from the fire as the doctor eased down into the trench. The blade was bright red from the heat.

"I'll stand behind you and give directions," the doctor said.

"Do we have anything to give him?" Label asked.

I handed Sander a bottle of vodka.

"Saving it for a special occasion, no?" Sander joked.

The doctor told him to drink as much as he could.

Sander raised the bottle and drank. After the first swig, he coughed. It burned his throat. But then, as it took effect, he drank more and settled into a semi-coherent state.

"Rinse the knife with the vodka, Julia," the doctor instructed.

Julia did so.

"Are you ready?" he asked.

"Yes," she answered, but her hand was shaking.

"Take a small drink," the doctor said.

"No, I'll be ok," she said. She knew vodka was too precious to waste.

The doctor took a short, thick branch out of his pocket. "Put this in his mouth."

Label put the branch in Sander's mouth and then held his right arm. I held down his left, while David held the boy's legs. Julia, her nerves settled, began to cut the rotted flesh. Sander fought and groaned and tried to wrestle away, but he was held down too tightly. It was over in five minutes. Julia washed the wound with hot water, doused it with alcohol and bandaged it.

We never found out why that doctor wouldn't do the operation himself.

***

David sent me with four others to some local landowners to try to steal livestock so we could have meat in our meager diet. We hiked to a village called Plotnitza, about two miles west of the new camp.

In Plotnitza, there was a mansion owned by a Polish baron before the war. Since the Soviet invasion, it had been operated by the peasants as a cooperative.

At night, we sneaked over a wooden fence into the estate pasture. Selecting three cows, we cut them from the herd, and led them quietly out the gate to the woods. When we were far enough away from the mansion for safety, we drove them to a peasant road that eventually ran near the camp. The peasant roads through the forest were little more than two ruts running side by side. The advantage was there were so many cows driven along these roads, that no one could trace the tracks back to the partisans.

Back at camp, a butcher slaughtered one of the animals and divided the meat among all the people. The other two cows were tied to trees near the camp. David assigned me to care for and feed them.

Taking the cows out to graze the next day, my friend, Asher Goldman, and I sat down on the snow near the pasture. Before the war, Goldman's family had the concession to carry the mail from Parachunsck. Asher had helped his father and brothers with the work since he was little. Now, he was the only one of his family still alive.

Asher and I would often get carried away reminiscing about our recent past, which seemed like a hundred years ago.

"You know," I said as I playfully kicked at the wet snow with the heel of my boot. "There was a synagogue in our town. I remember when I was a kid, it was such a wonderful thing to go to the synagogue. The whole family got dressed up on Saturday and we went together. It was such a warm, peaceful feeling."

"I remember," replied Asher, easing his back down against an oak stripling.

"Remember in those days most of the houses had roofs covered with tar paper?"

"Uh-huh," Asher replied.

"Somehow a small spark struck the tar paper," I said. "It was the middle of the night. The flames rose like bright orange giants. My house was very close to where it started."

"That night we were at Parachunsck," Asher said. "There was a big shipment of mail that day and it took us all day to load it. My father decided we'd stay the night and go back in the morning."

"So you missed it," I said.

"Yes."

"My mother, Yentl, saw the fire and woke us all up. She chased us from the house. It looked like the fire would consume the whole house in minutes, like it was chasing us with clouds of flames. I was so hot I felt I was being cooked on a spit.

"We ran down to the Bobric River because we were sure the flames couldn't cross the river.

"It was so big, it consumed everything, including the synagogue, and Talmud Torah. And plenty of businesses as well.

"But you know the really horrible thing that I couldn't get out of my mind?"

"What?" asked Asher.

"The Torah. I kept thinking about the Torah scrolls. How they were burned. I was happy that my whole family was saved. Even our house was all right. But I felt a great sorrow over the Torah.

158

"We sat up all night, watching the fire. It never crossed the river. The next morning, there were only a few pieces of wood standing upright where the synagogue had been. The rest was dying embers.

"We all fell asleep. Later that day, the Rabbi came to our home and woke us up.

"'It's a miracle,' he said. 'I thought the Torahs were destroyed. At the last moment, people ran into the synagogue and rescued the Torahs. They took the scrolls home with them. Tell Samuel. We will have daily *minyans* in the homes where they are kept.'"

"I remember my father and older brothers going to the *minyans*," Asher said wistfully.

"You can imagine how I felt. Of course, the synagogue was rebuilt and was very modern. You know Julia Zipperstein?"

"Of course."

"Did you know her grandfather, Shlomo Krugley, was the architect? He was one of the leading citizens in Pohost Zagorodski, and specialized in building synagogues. It was the best in the whole region. It compared to the big synagogue in Pinsk."

"I remember it was beautiful inside," Asher said. "The carved wooden *Bima* was in the center. The ark was on the east side of the synagogue. The curtains covering the ark were dark maroon velvet, with embroidered borders depicting the twelve tribes of Israel. There were thirty Torahs sitting inside the ark. It was the biggest synagogue I'd ever seen. Fifteen hundred people could attend services."

"And there was the new Talmud Torah, with two floors and enough room for the Tarbut," I reminded him.

"Do you remember the ceremony when they brought the Torahs back to the new synagogue?" Asher asked.

"I smiled at the memory. It was like a wedding. People carried the scrolls under the Chupah. The whole town came to the synagogue to witness."

"And what about when the Chasidic Rebbi from Stolin came by train to Parachunsck and then had to ride the seven miles to Pohost in Krugley's wagon?"

"Wasn't he accompanied by ten horsemen? People were dancing in the streets for joy that he had picked our town to visit," I said.

The Rebbi would go from town to town, setting up a court where he solved arguments between businessmen and personal problems for others. People waited for years for the Rebbi to come and advise them.

Asher started laughing. "All the old people got drunk and danced in the streets. Some of them were dancing in their underwear."

159

Asher abruptly turned serious. "Abram," he asked. "How long have we been here? In the forest, I mean."

"I don't know. Perhaps a year, probably more. Why?"

"I was just wondering…where is God?"

I stared at him. "God? You still think there is a God? After they kill my mother, my brother, my sister, all those that were so close to me…so many of your loved ones?" This was something I had not thought about in a long time.

At the time of the fire, I was still religious.

"Do you still believe?" I asked him.

Asher shook his head sadly. "I don't know, Abram," he answered. "I don't know. I was brought up to believe. My parents taught me God was there, that this happened to Jews through history…a test of faith, like Job, or Abraham."

"If God was there, they couldn't have done what they did. Maybe we were sinners. That I could accept," I said. "But what about the children, the babies? They never sinned." I exhaled deeply. "I don't care about Torah anymore."

Both of us sat back in silence. Sometimes, there was too much time to think.

A half hour went by. Asher got up to stretch, and then turned around.

"Where are the cows, Abram?" he asked.

"Oh no!" I said, jumping to my feet and looking in every direction.

The cattle had disappeared. There was no sign of them except for the tracks leading away; an easily read map right to the camp. We had certainly got carried away this time.

We followed the tracks as far as we dared, then returned to the camp. I immediately found David and told him.

David could only shake his head.

"What's done is done. We have to be very careful right now."

He assigned extra guards to the three approaches to the camp to watch for Germans, police, or peasants. I took shifts with a cousin of mine. I stood a two-hour shift, then took a nap while my cousin relieved me. We constructed a little tent out of branches and used it for our break.

It did not take very long for someone to report the cows' tracks to the Germans.

At daybreak, my cousin saw Germans no more than a hundred feet in front of him. He didn't have time to get me, so he fired his rifle at the soldiers.

I was awakened by the gunshot, and rushed out of the tent. The Germans were right in front of me. We sprinted for the safety of the thick woods. By the time we got to the camp, most of the people were already packing up. Julia and Sonya were so exhausted that they slept right through the gunshots and commotion. Nobody thought to wake them. After I grabbed Shlameleh, I realized I hadn't seen your mother. I asked a few people if they'd seen her. One said no, the other said she probably left already.

I ran over to her tent, and yelled her name. No one answered, so I opened the flap, rushed in and shook her awake. Within minutes, she and Sonya were running along with the other refugees.

There was one man who could not move with the rest.

Sander's foot was bandaged and healing, but he could not run. Somehow, in all the tumult, he was also left behind. When he heard the approaching soldiers, he crawled outside the camp perimeter and hid in some bushes.

The Germans came in and torched everything, all the food and clothing that had been left behind. Then they left. Sander witnessed the whole devastation.

I also got separated from the group. When I noticed that Sander was missing, I went back to the camp. Night was falling and as I drew near, I could smell the smoke. I waited and listened. I was pretty certain the Germans were gone.

Getting closer, I heard some movement. I took a risk and said in a low voice, "Who's there?"

"It's me, Sander," he answered from the bushes.

Sometimes the Germans would hold someone hostage and lure other partisans to their deaths, so I was cautious. "Are you alone?" I asked in Russian.

"Yes, Abram. I'm alone."

I looked over the ruins of the camp and found some burned pieces of meat to share with him.

"Will we ever find the rest of the group?" Sander asked. "You know I can't walk."

"Don't worry about it," I said, trying to calm the boy. "We should sit for awhile and see what happens. I don't think the Germans will be back. I think we're safer here."

Four hours later, Label and Mulia Kozushnik came back to the camp. When I heard their footsteps, I whistled the group's signal, and they returned the correct response.

Label moved closer to the origin of the signal. It was too dark for him to see me or make out much of the surroundings. He asked in Russian, "Could it be that you're surrounded by Germans and they're holding you as hostages?"

"No Germans here." I laughed out loud with relief.

When we left the burned-out encampment, we rejoined the others in a new camp some six miles away, in the direction of Malkovich, which was much more difficult to approach. It was a spot of dry land in the middle of mud and swampland, almost like an island.

***

For the same reasons the new camp was more secure, it was also harder to supply. We could not use wagons or animals after a certain point—they would simply bog down in the mud. From that point, everything from bags of wheat to potatoes had to be packed in on our shoulders, some two miles through the swamp. There were times when the men sank waist deep in the mud while they transported the supplies. Everyone readily accepted the trade-off.

Even in this remote marshy area, rumors abounded that the Germans would eventually come and clean it out. Guard duty was still necessary. Someone always had to guard the horses and wagons at the place where the swamp began and we had to start hauling provisions on our backs.

After we had been in the camp for two weeks, the Germans found the area and killed one of the guards. But the soldiers would not follow the partisans into the swamps. It was too dangerous. By now, the Germans and their auxiliaries had a healthy fear of the partisan groups. And it was lucky for us that they did not know how few weapons we actually had.

They set an ambush in the clearing before the swamps, but David's spies found out about it and advised the group on alternate routes into the marsh.

During that same period, I heard footsteps one night while I stood watch. The standing orders were to not fire, if at all possible, since that could bring on more trouble, as well as cause much alarm in the camp. Dawn was finally breaking, and as I moved quietly in the direction of the sound, I discovered the footprints of a wolf. I chuckled to think how, in my childhood, I would have been terrified.

When I was a boy, and my grandfather came to visit from Pinsk, my sister Esther, Shlomo and I would go across the street to our uncle's house, and pass the cold winter nights listening to grandfather's stories. My grandfather was a very knowledgeable man. To me, it seemed as though he had read every book ever written. If I brought him a book, he would look at it and say, "Oh, I've read this book, but I should read it one more time to refresh my memory." He told us stories of the Bible and of the region between the Baltic and the Black Sea known as the Pale. But our favorite stories were of our own family, and how our father and uncle had always got into mischief. Entranced, we listened until two or three in the morning, until I would dutifully say, "We should be getting home." Partly, we stayed so late because we were afraid of the short walk across the street in the dark.

During the winter months, when food was scarce in the forest, the hungry wolves would sometimes come into the *shtetl* to scavenge. One wolf had somehow crawled into one of the teacher's bathrooms, and had to be shot.

So, we were scared, especially if we had heard the howl of a wolf that particular night. When we left, we bolted out the door, sprinted across the street, and jumped the fence surrounding our yard. We dashed madly to the door, threw it open, and when everyone was inside, slammed it shut, and collectively breathed a sigh of relief.

Now, I much preferred the company of a wolf. If a wolf was howling, it usually meant there were not any other human beings around, so I knew I was safe.

***

By the spring, David's intelligence agents were gleaning a lot of information, and had a knack for staying one step ahead of the Germans, but only one step. No sooner had they reported that the Germans were going to attack the area, than Papa and I would hear the first gunshots. They sounded like little firecrackers going off. The shots seemed very far away, ample warning thanks to the distance between the first line of sentries and the camp.

The sentries were among the fastest men in the *atrad* and they knew where the ground was solid, unlike the Germans. They fired a few shots to let the Germans know this would be no walkover, and then pulled back hastily.

But this time, the Germans had a local man as a guide and they came on quickly.

"Abram!" David yelled at me. "Grab little Shlameleh and carry him with you."

"Get to the river!" David yelled to others in the camp. "Weapons, ammunition and food only. Leave everything else. Let's go!"

It seemed as though he was everywhere at once, prodding, yelling, encouraging.

People started wading into the tributary of the Cna River, to the east of the camp. We could make a stand there if need be. Foxholes had already been prepared.

The Germans emerged from the forest just as the last of the partisans were wading into the river. I plunged into the Cna, wading as I carried the baby. As it got deeper, I dove in and began to swim on my back with the baby on my chest.

The Germans fired at us, but for some unknown reason, they stayed on their side, refusing to follow us into the water.

Shlameleh put his head low on my shoulder as if he knew that if he raised his head, he might be hit by a bullet. It was incredible, this two year old seemed to know the danger of the situation. He did not whine or cry. He had complete confidence in me.

As the first men reached the other side, they dove into the foxholes and put up a covering fire, driving the German pursuers away from the bank, and making the German's own firepower ineffective.

As the enemy faded back into the forest, Samuel peered after them, his rifle at the ready, only shouldering it when the last partisan crawled out of the river. "How many close escapes will God allow us?" he asked no one in particular.

***

By now, I had been with David's group for some time and I was getting more frustrated by the day. I heard that there was a proposed mission to blow up the rail lines near Malkovich.

"I want to go to Malkovich with the others," I said angrily to David. "You're always leaving me behind to stay with Shlameleh…"

"No, Abram," David interrupted. "You have to stay here. You're the only one I can trust with him. And you can see he trusts you. If we have to retreat, I want you here. If he's with you he won't cry out…Don't you see I have enough things to worry about? Don't give me something else."

"That's not fair," I told him. I have to admit, I was seething. I was tired of being a shepherd or a babysitter. "You seem to forget something, David. I lost a mother as well as you. And I lost a brother and countless others. I want to take revenge personally. Myself." I tried to control my anger and speak more deliberately. "I have this hatred for the Germans. I wish I didn't, but I do. The only way to satisfy it is with my own two hands."

"I don't like it," David said as he looked piercingly into my eyes. I'll never forget that look. But I would not give an inch. I stared right back at him.

"I'm going on this mission, David. Have someone else stay with him for this one, then I'll stay the one after that. I'm going to fight," I insisted. "I'll fight by myself if I have to."

"Not this mission, but I'll think on it. Remember, I'm still the leader of this *atrad*, and this is a military organization. Brother or not…"

I turned and walked away.

***

That day I found your mother lying on a cushion she fashioned from pine needles and branches. I sat down across from her. I was so mad I had to talk to someone. The needles were still damp from an early morning rain.

"Abram," she said, "what's the matter? You look so angry." She knew me pretty well. Before I opened my mouth she could tell I was very upset.

"I want to fight," I said.

I had always been a leader among my friends, but in this group, I was just the baby brother.

"I know my older brothers want to protect me—they want me to survive. But I also think David makes me stay here because of Shlameleh. He says Shaindel is too frail and she can't look after the baby by herself, at least not in these circumstances. I think he really thinks the baby will die without my help."

"I know how you feel," your mother said to me. "I saw how brave you were at home. I'll never forget the night at the lumberyard when you and your brothers fought off forty Polish draftees. Never. It was the bravest thing ever done by the Jews of Pohost."

I had completely forgotten about that night—it seemed so distant and unreal. Now I remembered the early fear, then events moving so fast I could only act, then the exhilaration.

***

In the summer of 1938, as the Polish government prepared for war, commissions were set up in various towns to register young men for the draft. One such commission was in Pohost Zagorodski. After some forty, roughly-hewn peasant boys had registered, they made their way to a tavern owned by a red-headed, heavy-set Polish man known to be crude and illiterate. His favorite joke was to invite a person to his butcher shop, which adjoined the tavern, stick a pig with his knife, and then lick the blood off the blade. He was also an anti-Semite.

Plying the White Russian boys with liquor, he goaded them into attacking Jewish businesses and people.

Some of my friends and I were in the marketplace when the peasant mob surged out of the inn and marched up Dworska Street. The recruits picked up stones off the street and hurled them at the windows of every house they passed that exhibited a *mezuzah* high on the right hand side of the door frame, and every Jewish shop. Some unlucky children were also targeted. At first, the police stood by, leaning on their bicycles and doing nothing. They were caught by surprise and had no idea what to do with so many drunken young men. Some looked frightened.

We ran to our homes and closed the wooden shutters, protecting the windows before the mob arrived. Then we ran to other friends' houses and warned them, the whole time trying to stay out of the way of the peasants. I recognized many of them because they had come to the lumberyard from time to time to do business.

As the police finally managed to stop the trouble in town, I realized that a large group of them were heading over the Bobric River bridge, straight for the mill. I knew I could not get through the mob, so I ran back to my house, pushed my canoe into the river and started paddling as hard as I could toward the lumberyard to warn Papa.

At the mill, Shlomo, Label, Samuel and David quickly joined me in grabbing long metal pipes that were generally used to lever logs up to the lumberyard's saws. Four Gentiles and two other Jewish men, who were working that day, also armed themselves. We could hear the drunken peasants shouting, "Kill the Jews! Kill the Jews!" as they trudged up the road.

Three men ran out to close the gate to the mill, and slotted two wooden rails in place to lock it just in time.

The peasants surged forward, shouting and screaming their threats. They tried to pry open the wooden fence, but when this failed, they jumped up, grabbed the top and climbed over.

For two hours, we held them off in hand-to-hand fighting, the peasants armed with knifes and we with our metal rods.

By the time the police arrived, there were fifteen peasant boys lying on the ground, bleeding from their injuries. Only one of the workers, an older Jewish man, was wounded, stabbed in the side.

The police waited for the farm boys to rouse themselves, then merely shooed them down the road.

"There's no point in jailing them," the police chief chuckled. "Look at them. I think they've suffered enough."

I had always looked up to my older brothers. They seemed so big and strong, and Shlomo had the reputation of being the fastest runner in the whole area. But I don't think I ever looked up to them as much as I did that day.

And Papa, so tough and almost fifty, fighting right alongside us. He collapsed in a heap after the fighting, but heard the policeman's words and started to laugh. David started laughing too. He said, "Abram and Shlomo beat them so bad they didn't know what world they were in," and "Label knocked the Pole with the pole to the North Pole."

At this, the rest of us laughed so hard we doubled up and finally had to beg him to stop.

***

Julia looked at me sympathetically. "Yes," she said, "I know what you can do."

"I just want to fight," I said. "I want to pay them back." I could feel my face flush with anger.

The next day word came that Chvador, one of the peasants from the village of Bagdanovka was working with the Germans. This was unexpected. The man was a cripple and could barely walk, but it was said that he gave a lot of information to the Germans about the location of the new camp.

David had his aide call Mulia Kozushnik, Sholom Lan and me.

Pointedly looking away from me as though he knew he had been wrong, but had trouble admitting it, David explained the situation. "I want the three of you to go to Bagdanovka, grab this man and bring him back to camp. We'll ask him point blank if the charges are true."

I was elated.

We left at dusk. This journey was more treacherous than most. Slogging through the swamps at night was incredibly difficult. One could drown or land in quicksand. The very smell of the swamp was dank and unpleasant, and Bagdanovka was over twelve miles away.

Around three in the morning, we walked up a narrow path leading to a broken-down peasant's hut. I knocked on the door for ten minutes, before a hunched-over old man in a dark nightgown limped to the door and opened it. He did not look happy with what he saw.

"We want you to come with us," I said menacingly. I admit I was relishing this new role.

Chvador was a cantankerous man. He turned around, limped to a rocking chair and forcefully sat down, as if the act itself proved he had no intention of leaving.

"You'll come to the camp," Kozushnik said, "answer some questions, and if we like your answers, we'll bring you home none the worse."

The peasant shook his head. "I'm not going. It's too far and I'm in no physical condition to walk that distance."

"You won't have to walk," Kozushnik quickly lied. He walked up to the man and pulled him to his feet. "We have a wagon and a horse to take you."

Chvador squirmed in Kozushnik's grip. "I said I'm not going," and he slipped out of Kozushnik's hands. He moved very quickly for a man with a bad leg, but we had him cornered.

Noting his quickness, I pulled a pistol from my belt. "Perhaps this will tell you who is in control here. If you don't want to go, we can shoot you right now."

167

Chvador understood. We waited for him to dress and he took his time. Then, with Kozushnik holding one arm, Sholom holding the other, and me holding the pistol on him, we escorted him out the door.

I was never certain if Chvador was really crippled or if it was only a pretense, but regardless, he was in for a rough night. Even a healthy man would have trouble crossing the swamps in the dark, and we were in a hurry to beat the daylight.

For a good part of the way to his hut, we had been up to our thighs in water and mud. It would be the same going back.

Kozushnik asked him questions over and over again during the trek back to the camp. Chvador protested that he did not know anything.

He had to stop and rest every few miles. He had an especially hard time crossing the muddy bogs, complaining bitterly.

Finally, Kozushnik could take no more of Chvador's evasions or objections. It had been a long, difficult trip and we were all dead tired. "Let's finish him off right now and be done with it," he said angrily.

"No," I said. "If he's a spy, we need to get information from him."

"Abram's right," Sholom said. "Besides, you can't use a gun on him. Too many peasants around here. They'll hear it."

"Well. I have a bayonet that wants to taste its first blood," Kozushnik replied. "He's slowing us down. I'm not going to fool with him. Who knows who's behind us, following us."

Then before either Sholom or I could stop him, he unsheathed the bayonet and stuck Chvador in the belly.

"God, Mulia!" Sholom exclaimed.

"There. It's done." Kozushnik pulled the blade out, off leaving Chvador to fall in the mud. Kozushnik rubbed the blade on some moss to clean it. Then he turned and trudged back to the camp, leaving us gaping at the dying man.

"All right, Mulia," I shouted. "You did it. You can tell my brother."

Kozushnik walked into the camp and found David Bobrow.

"I killed Chvador. I didn't want to bother with him. That's it." Then Kozushnik turned and walked away.

"Mulia—" David called after him. But Mulia Kozushnik kept walking.

David sighed in exasperation. Even for him, it was not easy to control such a mixture of individualists and headstrong men.

CHAPTER 15

FELDMAN

Even though Avremel Feldman had agreed to join the larger Kaganovich *Atrad*, he preferred to keep his camp separate, only joining our group for missions. It gave him the sense that he was still somewhat autonomous and definitely more mobile, having few women and no children or elders to worry about.

Occasionally, he would have missions of his own, and this is what brought him to our larger camp on one overcast and chilly fall day.

"I need five men," he told David. "There's a peasant who has flour and other food stuffs. She's a friend."

David hesitated. He remembered Feldman from before and was not sure of his judgment. "Wait here. Let me talk it over with some people...sit down." He gestured to a log stump. "I'll see what I can do."

Papa was helping me refill used shell casings when David came up to us and explained the problem.

Samuel was dead set against it. He looked at David angrily. It was a rare sight to see my father angry. "Don't have anything to do with this man."

I was more practical. "We need the food," I said. Obviously Papa still blamed Feldman for splitting up the groups.

"I'd rather starve," Samuel responded, freezing his expression and crossing his arms in front of him.

"It's tempting, father," David said.

"I cannot forbid it, but you know how I feel." Papa got up and walked away. The discussion had brought back too many painful memories.

"Let me go," I said. "I'll keep an eye on him. We need the food."

There were now a lot of new people in camp. David refused to turn anyone away. As a result, we were always only a few days away from starvation.

Together, David and I selected four other men and went back to tell Feldman.

It was a cold fall. Snow already covered much of the ground and I recall seeing a trail of mist that formed from our frosty breath.

At Feldman's camp, we were joined by ten of his men. We hiked through snowdrifts and mud to a farmer's house, where surprisingly everyone was invited into a barn, and breads, cheese, and even meat were brought in and offered to us.

Well, I thought at the time, if this comes to a bad end, at least I'll die on a full stomach.

Then we headed off to see a woman Feldman called Gramatskaya.

As we left the trees to enter a small clearing, we were surrounded by a group of partisans who were bandits, called *Batinzes*. We were heavily outnumbered and had to surrender our rifles.

The *Batinzes* came from the jails. When the Germans attacked Russia in 1941, they had opened the prisons and freed all the criminals. These people fled to the woods and started killing anyone they stumbled upon. They killed Germans, other partisans, but especially Jews who had escaped from the ghettos. They killed them, robbed them and left their bodies to rot in the woods.

We Jewish partisans did not have the luxury of only looking out for the Germans. We also had to worry about the peasants, the bandits, and the fascist partisan groups.

The *Batinzes* group—there were about seventy of them, had much better weapons than us, even automatic weapons that they had gotten from ambushing and killing Soviet soldiers.

A big brute of a man, with a scar across his forehead, and a nose that started out straight, then took an abrupt turn downward—obviously broken at least once I guessed—walked up in front of us. In his hands was a submachine gun, which he held, leveled at Feldman.

"We're taking you to a court where charges will be brought against you. Follow us. I warn you," he said threateningly, "if you try to escape, we'll forget about the court." A slight grin crossed his lips as if he hoped we would.

We started walking back into the forest, surrounded by the bandits. I was silently cursing Feldman and at the same time trying to figure out how to get out of this one. I kept my head still, so as not to give myself away, as I scanned the trees looking for a place to run.

Suddenly, in another clearing, I felt a shove. The next thing I knew I was on the ground being kicked repeatedly. *What the hell was going on?* For no apparent reason, the *Batinzes* had started to beat us, using rifle butts and sticks, some with their bare fists. I curled up, trying to protect my head. It was useless to fight back. There were too many.

I felt like I was being pummeled for hours, when I heard a voice yell my name.

I tried to identify the voice, but every time I just about had it, the pain from another blow blocked it out.

"Is that you, Bobrow?" the man yelled again, moving closer. He grabbed the arm of the man who was just about to hit me again. "Stop, you idiot! Bobrow! Answer me!"

Schmirov was from Dubnovich, one of the small villages close to Pohost Zagorodski. He had worked for my father at the lumberyard.

"Yes!" I shouted, looking up through my arms, and feeling hope somehow rising with every sound of the voice, wondering, could he stop this?

"Stop!" Schmirov said to my assailant. "I know this man. He's a friend." He looked at me. "Why are they beating you?"

I slowly got to my feet. "I'll be damned if I know," I said. I squinted in the darkness. "Andrei? Andrei Schmirov? From the lumberyard?" Thank God for the lumberyard, I thought. *Thank God for Papa.*

"Yes, Abram," Schmirov said as he stepped forward and shook my hand.

"Stop the beating!" Schmirov yelled to his comrades. "Stop it! Now!" He held up his arms to get their attention. "Wait here. Guard them, but no more beating. I'm going to the leaders to find out why we're beating them in the first place."

I rubbed my arms to ease the pain. I wondered if this respite would last and prayed that my old friend would return quickly. I knew this had to have something to do with Feldman.

Sitting there in the clearing, in the dark, the bandits looked fierce and uncompromising. I have to admit, maybe this was the third time in my life I was frightened.

When Schmirov returned, he told the *Batinzes* that there had been a mistake. All our weapons were returned and we were released.

Two of the men suffered broken shoulders.

Schmirov walked with us for a few miles. He had worked for Papa up to the time of the Soviet invasion.

"Your friend Feldman," he said to me, "he insulted a peasant woman, Gramatskaya. This woman works with us. She told us about Feldman and asked us to teach him a lesson. She lured him with the offer of food. This is why you were surrounded and beaten. I'm sorry. This Feldman is very lucky it was so dark. If the others identified him, it would have been over for him."

I was speechless as I limped along the well-worn cart path.

"There is something else," the bandit whispered. "This group of bandits killed your friends, the Rabinoff brothers. They raped one of the sisters and she became pregnant. Later they killed her as well. I tell you this because I want you to know I had nothing to do with it."

When we dragged ourselves into camp that night, I reported all that had happened to David.

"If I hadn't known that man, we would have all been killed, I swear to you," I said. "We were helpless. I had not felt so helpless since making it to the forest a year ago.

David had connections with a larger group of partisans who were very well armed. This group was already aware of the beatings when David approached them. They tracked the *Batinzes* down and executed four of their leaders. The rest were forcibly disbanded and placed with different partisan groups.

***

In late November of 1942, Avremel Feldman came into camp with another scheme. This time he told me of all the things he had hidden in the ghetto of Pohost Zagorodski. He had taken jackets, shirts, and slacks from his aunt's store and hid them before being forced to go to the work camp at Honsovich.

"Our clothes are falling apart and winter will be upon us soon. We need warm clothing," Feldman said in his melodramatic fashion. "If you come with me, I'll give you whatever you want."

"I'm not sure," I said. My injuries had long been healed, but I had never forgotten the earlier episode.

"Don't worry so much," Feldman chided. "I know what you're thinking, but that was just bad luck. I heard what happened to the *Batinzes*. They won't be bothering us anymore. Come on now. Go ask your brother. And ask him if we can get some men from the partisans who have heavier weapons."

David, Samuel and Label were all against it, but the more I thought about it, the more appealing was a warm pair of pants. Mine were in tatters. I had worn the same pair of gray muslin pants since leaving for Honsovich, almost a year ago. I had patched them with burlap until there was more burlap than original fabric.

There were three other men in camp who were also in desperate need of new clothing. They were not worried about the present, but they had long memories of the previous, bitingly cold winter, when they had only threadbare garments.

I know I'm going to regret this, I thought, but I let Feldman's arguments and thoughts of the coming winter win the day over the objections of my family.

I'll say one thing for Feldman, he could sure talk a good game.

Together with eight men from the other partisan group, and four of us armed with rifles, we left the camp. The other partisans had more modern rifles and a Soviet-made machine gun. I felt confident. Never before had I been in a group so heavily armed. What could happen?

There was a peasant living near Pohost Zagorodski about a mile east of the lumberyard, who was holding the clothing for Feldman.

I found out later, that at dusk, about three hours before we left camp, a detachment of forty German soldiers marched out of Pohost Zagorodski.

Feldman did not bother to tell the rest of us that he had told the peasant exactly when he would be coming.

Earlier, after arranging the meeting with Feldman, the peasant probably took his cart into Pohost Zagorodski, walked into the garrison and informed the Germans.

By now, forty, heavily-armed German soldiers were waiting in his house to ambush us.

The Yashelda was only a narrow stream on the way to the peasant's house. During the spring and fall, the rains broadened out the river, making it impassable, but in the summer and late fall, the Yashelda thinned out. In some places, it dried up completely, leaving just a flat sandy riverbed. Now it was closing in on winter, so I knew it would be cold, but we would have no trouble crossing.

As we waded across, we heard the sound of shots in the distance.

I stopped moving forward, standing silent, motionless, straining to listen. I slowly backed up toward the far side of the Yashelda.

"I think the Germans are checking up on us," I whispered.

The others, except for Feldman, began following me back.

"It's just a coincidence," Feldman said. "Besides, the shots are coming from behind us." He stood in the middle of the shallow water facing me.

"Everything is in order. What're you worried about?" Feldman asked. "Who knows who fired anyway? We've come this far, and I've gone to a lot of trouble. When you have a mission, you finish it."

Feldman was right about that. In the forest you never knew where gunshots were coming from. You always had to pay attention, but the important thing was how far away the noise was. I had learned to judge the distance and these shots were from a good way off. The gunfire behind us stopped as suddenly as it had started. After a brief discussion, the men agreed to go forward, fording the Yashelda for the second time that night.

When we were a scant two hundred yards from the house, Feldman stopped us. We were at the edge of a field of wheat. He motioned for me to join him.

"Abram. You know I'm not for taking unnecessary risks. You're the best scout. Go closer and see if it's safe. The peasant should be expecting us."

"What? Expecting us?" I asked, completely surprised.

"I told him we'd come tonight. Don't worry. I know him. He can be trusted."

I shook my head as I crept forward toward the house. Is this man an imbecile, I wondered? You never let anyone know when you are coming. Even those you trust. Then what am I doing following him? I was sweating profusely and consciously decided to slow down. I made as little noise as possible, as if I was tracking a deer.

There was little cover between the wheat field and the house, only an open grassy plain with a few small saplings.

I can't believe I'm doing this, I thought, shaking my head once more and if possible, moving even more cautiously. What an idiot that guy is, and I'm no better for going to the house. He may as well have announced we were coming and sent out invitations. I just didn't believe it.

During my time in the woods, I had developed a keen sense of intuition. This time I barely needed it. Common sense alone should have made me turn around. I slowly crept the remaining hundred yards to the door of the house.

There was noise coming from the house. A lot of noise. Too much commotion for one peasant and his family for this time of night, I thought. And the smell of too many unwashed bodies. It must be three in the morning. Not right. Time to leave.

Quickly moving back to the others, I told Feldman, "It's a trap, too suspicious. We better forget it. I think your friend informed on us."

"Nonsense," Feldman insisted. "I told you I know him. But if you're worried, let's split up into smaller groups. We'll space ourselves and go. You all know Schwedor's *chuto* near Bagdanovka. We'll meet there if anything goes wrong." He looked to see the others nodding in agreement. Lastly, he looked contemptuously at me.

"All right, Bobrow. Now are you satisfied?"

"No."

"Well? Are you coming with us."

I stared at him for a long time. I could not make up my mind. I knew they might need the extra gun. But now looking back, I know that I let my pride get the best of my reason.

"We need you, Abram," one of the other men said.

"We do," another chimed in.

We divided ourselves into four groups of three men each, spread out over the grassy field and quietly started forward. I should have turned around right then. I guess when you're young, you have no fear. Ironically, I was the youngest of the group, and I figured I was the only one with doubts or sense. Perhaps it had something to do with knowing Feldman.

When we got to within a hundred yards, all the windows of the house opened and a hail of bullets from automatic weapons buzzed by our ears like a thousand angry wasps. My group hit the dirt fast. I didn't have time to see what the others were doing.

"Do you want to go on?" I yelled at other two men in my group. "This is ridiculous. We can't afford to return fire and get into a prolonged fight."

Then I saw Feldman, perhaps twenty yards away. He looked confused. We did not have enough ammunition and the rest of the German garrison was only half a mile away in Pohost Zagorodski. I motioned to Feldman that I was pulling back. I half expected him to shout out where to meet him so the Germans would know that as well.

Feldman signaled that he agreed. All four groups scattered in different directions.

My group was lucky. We quickly reached a field with tall reeds of wheat, and dove into it so the Germans had little to aim at. We scampered on hands and knees to get out of range, but every movement of the wheat brought forth a new fusillade of gunfire.

With me were two people from deep inside Russia, totally unfamiliar with the region. They were the machine-gun operators, and dragging the weapon soon became their greatest difficulty. The going was slow, but after a few hours, we managed to put some distance between ourselves and the house.

I led them back, taking an alternate route to the Bobric River, thinking the Germans might have put an ambush there too, for it was a well-known crossing. Taking them south for a mile, I headed to a different, safer crossing.

The Germans had thought their plan out carefully. They had also stationed men at this ford. Figuring they were now safe, the Russians had started talking. I motioned for them to be quiet. I crouched down low and started across the riverbank. Suddenly, bullets began to fly. I hit the ground. Turning, I crawled back up the slippery bank, every second expecting a bullet to tear into my flesh. The Russians had dove into the forest at the first shots. Again, our luck held.

After running back another two miles from the Bobric, we fell down, exhausted. I reached into my pocket and pulled out a stale piece of bread. I ripped off a piece and tossed the larger bit to the Russians. They split it in half and devoured both halves. I never thought a bit of bread could taste so good.

I looked at the clear, moonless sky to get my bearings. With renewed energy, I got up and headed further south. This time the Russians were keeping their thoughts to themselves, I thought gratefully.

Approaching the ford slowly, my senses alert, I viewed the river. It was clear. I motioned for the others to move forward.

After swimming the Bobric, with all three of us struggling to keep the machine gun dry, I led them through a great swampy area. By the time we reached the meeting place, we were covered with mud from head to toe.

I whistled the signal. No one responded. We fell to the ground, our legs crumbling, unable to hold us up. We could go no further.

One of the Russians started to cry. "None of them made it," he said. "I don't know how we did."

I agreed. "It's a miracle any of us got out of there."

"We have to stay here, right?" the other Russian asked.

"Someone has to stand guard," I said wearily. "I'll take the first shift." But within minutes, I fell asleep along with the others.

An hour later, I was awakened by a whistle. A second group had arrived. Rubbing my eyes, I saw the wide-eyed look of amazement on their faces.

"We thought we were the only ones left," one of them said.

A half-hour later, another group of three dazed men wandered into the field by the *chuto*. They also thought they were the only survivors. Two hours after that, Feldman's group came in. No one could believe everyone was back together.

"It's truly a miracle," Feldman proclaimed.

Back at camp, David and Samuel listened to the tale with disgust.

"I warned you not to go with Avremel Feldman. We're not playing games here," David said.

Papa was more sad than angry. I could see in his eyes that he was still thinking of Michle. "Everything this Feldman plans comes out the opposite," Samuel said.

"For the pair of slacks you wanted, you could have lost your head," David scolded. "And if they caught any of you wounded, they would've taken you into town and tortured you to death." David paused for a moment, then added harshly. "And one of you might have given away the location of the camp."

Samuel took me in his arms and held me tightly. "You have to be careful, my son. That's all I ask."

I stood back and shook my head. I had learned my lesson. "Father. If I ever say I'm going on a mission with Feldman again, I want you to save me the trouble and just shoot me right then and there."

CHAPTER 16

LABEL

Now came a complete break with the past. The Germans needed enormous supplies of lumber to fix the blown-up railway tracks and to shore up the bunkers at the front. Our mill was supplying a great deal of lumber—some timber was even shipped to Germany—and orders came down from Dabroslavka, where the central command of the *atrads* was located, to destroy it.

The job was offered to Label and of course, he accepted. Jewish partisans rarely turned down missions. They desperately wanted revenge. For Label, it was the only way to ease his endless grief. Seventy pounds of explosives were dropped at the camp by other partisans.

Helicopters, flying only at night, hauled quantities of explosives and fuses to the larger Soviet *atrads*. These were then dispersed to the smaller fighting groups according to need.

The dynamite was packed into bags and divided up between Label, Kozushnik and Hennik, David's aide.

Label knew the easiest approach was from the Yashelda River, coming into the lumberyard at the same place I used to dock my canoe. But there was no cover. It was all open ground. Near the northeast side of the lumberyard, the Yashelda starts a long loop around almost three-quarters of the yard. Label decided this was still the safest way, even though they would have to swim across fifty feet of freezing cold water.

They would be completely defenseless as they crossed the river, but luckily the guard positions were facing the land approaches, and there were trees and scattered spots of tall brush between the river and lumber mill fence.

They would approach from the direction of Kamener Way.

The three of them left at dusk and reached the Yashelda around midnight. They stripped down and swam on their backs to keep the explosives and their weapons and clothes dry.

Dressing on the opposite side of the river, they stealthily made their way to within one hundred yards of the mill.

While the others stayed low, Label climbed a tall oak tree. He had not been to the lumberyard since the massacre and was surprised to see how familiar it looked. He told me he had to forcibly stop the torrent of images that came rushing into his mind's eye.

Everything was as he'd last seen it, the four buildings, the piles of logs and railway ties, the conveyer belt stretching down to the river, even the short fence surrounding the yard. But there was barbed wire on top of the fence, plus a high barbed wire fence enclosing everything but the old wooden gate, and lights had been put up for security. He could see four guards posted at different places around the yard, but they did not look to him to be regular army. They were probably peasant militia. The only other guards near the lumberyard were regular German army sentries on both sides of the bridge over the Yashelda, less than a hundred yards northeast of the yard. The bridge was guarded day and night.

Kozushnik was impatient as always, and started crawling to the gate. The other two followed

They slipped behind the barbed wire, and quietly made their way to a part of the fence, adjacent to the main building. Label climbed over the low fence, as Kozushnik gingerly held the wire up to provide an opening. Hennik then slid the bags of explosives through to Label, who stashed them close to the fence in the shadows. As soon as Kozushnik and Hennik were through the barbed wire, they headed for the first guard, at his post near the entrance.

Label snuck up from behind and clubbed the guard with his rifle butt. Kozushnik and Hennik took the guard's weapon and tied him up and gagged him. This cleared the way for Label to take the explosives and enter the building that housed the main machinery of the mill. While Label walked down the steps to the huge basement underneath the saw, Kozushnik and Hennik knocked out the other guards.

Label placed the explosives underneath the engines and transmissions that drove the axle to run the saw and the other machines. He cut off a length of fuse he estimated would give them fifteen to twenty minutes to escape. He figured that would be enough for them to at least get to the river.

Sticking the fuse into the dynamite, he lit it and ran back upstairs.

"Damn!" Label cursed under his breath. He stopped running up the stairs. He was not sure he had attached the wire to the mine correctly. He thought he must be really getting old. Did he do it right? Not wanting to take a chance, he turned around and ran back down the stairs to double check. Everything was all right. Now he sprinted back up the stairs, taking three steps at a time, and dashed out of the building.

Mulia and Hennik were waiting at the entrance to the building. Label yelled at them as he ran, "Let's get out of here!"

The three reached the fence just as the dynamite exploded. Something had gone wrong with the fuse—it only lasted five minutes. They were thrown to the ground as the whole roof of the building shot skywards and the walls began to crumble. Flames shot up as high as thirty feet in the black sky. Burning rubble and engine parts were hurled up even higher.

As they got up to run, it seemed as though they were being chased by smoke, fire and flying shards of glass.

Immediately, searchlights and flares illuminated the skies, as the garrison in Pohost Zagorodski came alive. The town was only a half-mile from the lumberyard.

From Eviah, a nearby village, Germans also used spotlights, including one from the church steeple, where there was also a machine gun, which soon began to spew forth thousands of bullets.

As the sky brightened up like daylight, Label and the others dove down into the dirt behind a pile of railroad ties.

The Germans fired blindly into the lumberyard and the outlying area. Everything from machine guns to mortars, rained down on the fast burning wreckage. The main building of the lumberyard was utterly destroyed.

Other German troops swarmed out of both garrisons, boarding trucks which roared out of the villages heading for known escape routes to the woods.

Recovering from the shock of the blast and the ensuing chaos, Label and the others got up and scrambled to the fence, and jumped over, paying no attention to the barbed wire. They crawled as fast as possible to the river. It seemed as though mortar shell explosions and machine gun fire were following on their heels.

When they reached the Yashelda, Label led them south along the riverbank, taking them back to the Bagdanovka forests by a different route. He had anticipated the German move to the woods.

At the same time, I was on a mission in the same vicinity, close to Pohost Zagorodski. My men and I heard horrific explosions. This had to be close to the lumberyard, I thought. When I later heard the news, I felt a mixture of sadness, probably more for Papa, than for the end of our business. I had given it up long ago. But there was also an elation. Label had done great damage to the German's war supplies. I think there was also a sort of feeling that "If I can't have it, you can't either."

***

Orders were not always followed in the partisan groups. Many times, David couched his orders in terms of advice so as not to offend the fiercely independent partisans.

Many partisans felt they had to be hardened and stubborn to survive. Many only kept their own counsel, not trusting anyone but themselves, whether it was an act to make themselves feel stronger, or to give them faith that they would come through alive. Some of the men only stayed for the safety of the numbers, and when trouble arose, would go their own way. Others got in trouble for their stubbornness.

Sholom Lan, who had escaped from the bunker where my aunt and nieces were killed, decided he had to go to Borki. He was tired of having no weapon and determined to get a rifle from a peasant he knew. Sholom went to David to get permission, but his mind was already made up. Getting permission was merely a formality. My brother tried to discourage him, but Sholom was stubborn. David had to settle for telling him to be careful.

Sholom went to Borki and met a peasant who was celebrating a wedding. He was invited inside where everyone was drinking. Lan was given as much liquor and food as he wanted and soon was drunk. He lingered at the party until daylight.

One of the peasants who had left earlier informed a German patrol that there was a Jew at the wedding party. The Germans went to the party, took Sholom outside, made him kneel down, and put a bullet in the back of his head.

Some of the peasants at the wedding later told David that they tried to get Sholom to run, but he was so drunk he could not even stand. He probably did not even realize what was happening with the German patrol.

"Make no mistake about it," David told me and Label, "there are quite a few instances of partisans losing their lives because of heavy drinking. Don't you two fall into that trap."

***

Hennik, my brother David's aide, went against David's advice to go to one of the peasants to get clothing. He did not pay for the garments. He claimed it as though it was his right. Hennik's wife, Sara, was pregnant and he wanted to have clothing for the baby when it arrived.

The peasant he took the clothing from was a contact for another partisan brigade made up of Soviet soldiers who had escaped after being prisoners of war.

Different partisan groups had zones under their own control. Other partisans were not allowed to take anything except food from these areas. This particular peasant was a valuable spy for the Soviet group.

The Germans thought the peasant was working for them so he had access to important information on troop movements and strengths. It did not take long for the man to report Hennik's thievery to the Soviet partisans.

Within days, a few people from the intelligence unit of the Soviet brigade came to the camp. They wanted to put Hennik on trial. David and several others tried to intervene, but our group was much smaller than the other partisan group, and they had much better weapons.

Numbers and weapons always defined the relative strength of the different resistance groups.

Hennik's wife ran up crying and screaming. She even tried to order the other partisans out of camp. Then she pointed at her distended belly, pleading mercy for her unborn child, but they would not listen.

Sara got down on her knees to David, but in this instance he was helpless. She never forgave him. In fact, some of the partisans felt she eventually began to hate David.

The Soviet partisans took Hennik away and within an hour, they tried him, convicted him, and shot him.

Abram Bobrow, special "elite" forces
Russian army – 1943

Samuel Bobrow – 1943

Label Bobrow (right) - 1943

Russian officers (Abram Bobrow on right) - 1946

Russian soldiers at site of Warsaw Ghetto uprising
(Abram, back row, far right) – 1947

Polish and Russian Partisans (3rd row Abram first
on left, Julia third from left) – 1946

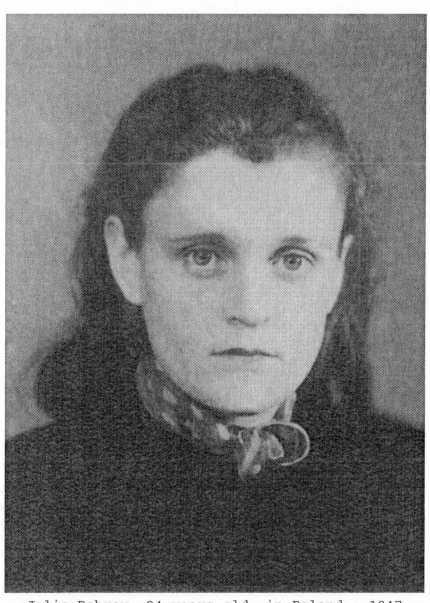

Julia Bobrow, 24 years old, in Poland - 1947

Abram Bobrow's Russian Medals of bravery, honor,
and valor (Top row: medals of honor for taking
Berlin and Warsaw; bottom row center: special
"elite forces" medal, other two medals for bravery
entitled recipient to free trip throughout Russia
each year)

Julia's Partisan Medals for bravery and honor,
veteran' s medal (center)

(TOP) Julia's Award (Medal also) for Bravery
against Nazis while in Partisans 1942-44, presented
by Head of White Russian Army

(BOTTOM) Julia's Award for Bravery - Soldier
Medical Core, Brigade Molotov

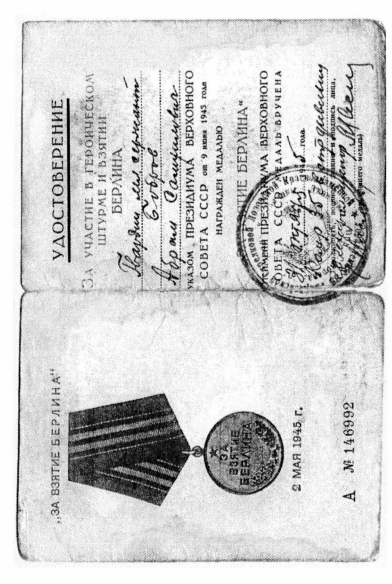

Abram's Medal of Honor and Award for taking Berlin

Julia's verification as Partisan Veteran Award
1942-45 (Byloruss)

Julia's Partisan Movement Veterans's Bravery Award
as fighter, soldier, nurse

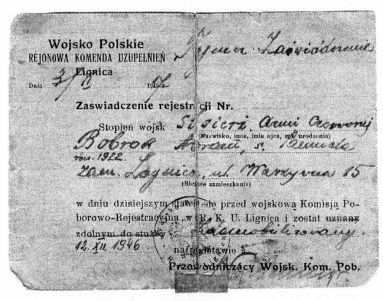

Abram's Russian Army Veteran Award (Poland)

Julia's Red Star for Bravery and Heroism and
verification of Veteran of Partisans 1941-45,
Brigade Molotov

Lignicz, Poland, soccer team (Abram fourth from left) – 1946

Label and Abram Bobrow (left to right) – 1947

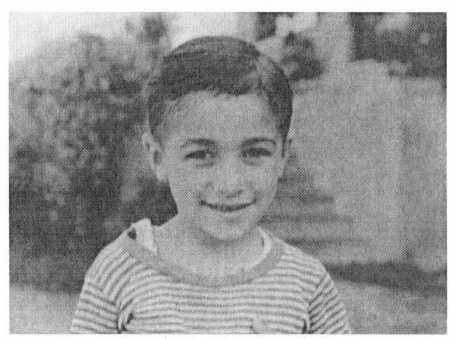

Shlomo Bobrow (David's son) Italy - 1946

Shaindel Bobrow (David's wife, center) son Shlomo
Bobrow (right) Italy - 1946

William, Abram, Julia, Samuel, Pina (Label's wife), Label, Carl (Label and Pina's son) and baby Jerry Bobrow in front. Italy – 1948

Abram visits the Bobrow lumber mill in 1993

Abram visiting monument at site of second massacre
– 1993

Julia visiting memorial in Israel in 1986 for those
killed at massacre in Pohost Zagorotsky

Jerry, Julia, Abram, William Bobrow (left to right) – 1951

Julia's Aunt Esther, William, Jerry, Abram, Julia and David - 1964

CHAPTER 17

THE *MISHKINS*

At around this time, Julia went back to the *Mishkins.* She was not happy with our group for a number of reasons, and when an old friend, Rosa Eulivich, came to visit from the *Mishkins*, and told your mother that she was still needed there, she decided to go back.

She was angry with my brother David. David was very strict and would not let her go on missions, but she wanted revenge, at least a chance at it. During Julia's darkest hours, and I guarantee you, there were many, this one compelling desire had kept her sane, had kept her from giving up and finally succumbing to her own wounds and sorrows. In the different massacres, your mother lost close to one hundred blood relatives, virtually everyone in her family.

You can see why I said how strong she was, is.

She felt David put her off as though she was still a child, when she asked to go on missions. He would tell her it was too dangerous. As I've told you, he did the same thing with me.

Julia knew he was trying to protect her, but she felt useless, like one more mouth sitting around, doing nothing, but still having to be fed. To sit and starve and wait until someone else brought her food was humiliating.

Like me, your mother did not want protection, she wanted a gun, in fact needed one, and the chance to use it for revenge.

One day she told me, "I got a potato from one of the other women who had crawled out of the pit in Pohost Zagorodski. Rivka. You know Rivka, she's ten years older than us, and so intelligent, the other partisans call her *umnitze,* 'the smart one of the forest.'

"I ate the potato but was still hungry, so I asked Rivka for another."

"'You know,' Rivka said gently, like an older sister patiently explaining a fact of life to her younger sister, 'We don't want the boys to go out and put their lives in danger so you can have another potato.'"

"It's the truth, Abram," your mother told me. "And that makes me all the more frustrated for being kept off the missions. I have to sit here and wait until Rivka offers me another potato? It's shameful, embarrassing." Angrily, she added, "I can fight for my own food."

Your mother long ago promised herself she would fight as much as she could. She felt her life was not worth anything. Everyone was gone. She was an orphan. Every day it haunted her. Why did she survive and not anyone else from her family?

"What am I accomplishing staying with David's group?" she asked me. "Either they do nothing for lack of weapons and ammunition, or they wait around to be killed by the Germans." She also remembered the trouble with Avremel Feldman. Jews scheming against Jews filled her with disgust.

Rosa reminded your mother that she was not asked to leave the *Mishkins*. Mitya, one of the leaders, had always called her the hardest working partisan. And this was true. Your mother had worked so hard because she didn't want to have time to think.

Mitya still talked about her helping with the wounded or making clothes out of parachute material. How she would always be ready for any task. Mitya expressly asked Julia not to leave their camp. They needed trained nurses desperately.

Returning to the *Mishkins* would also be safer. They had many more professional soldiers, with much better weapons.

As she visited with Rosa, Julia looked around the camp. A fresh snow blanketed the surrounding evergreens, women were doing laundry and piling firewood. Most of the men were gone on missions or gathering wood. It seemed so very unrealistically peaceful. She had mixed emotions, but one other thing stood out strongly: her family. Who would extract that measure of revenge if not for her?

Rosa had gotten Mitya's promise to let your mother go on missions.

***

Immediately upon her return, Julia was given one of the new Soviet rifles that had been dropped behind the lines by parachute. Instruction was brief: how to load, how to shoot.

With their new firepower, the *Mishkins* were about to launch their most daring raid yet. The orders were simple. They were going to the town of Kochtz Ka'Volia in force, to secure it and kill as many Germans as possible.

At midday, four groups, totaling over a hundred men and women, descended on Kochtz Ka'Volia from different directions. Julia's group approached from the east, some riding in two horse-drawn sleighs, while most of the fighters came on foot.

As soon they approached a bunker on the eastern outskirts of Kochtz Ka'Volia, they came under heavy fire. The guerilla commander thought they were in for it. He ordered his forces to get down and return the shooting.

Julia crouched behind a thick tree, lifted the heavy rifle and took her first shot.

The opening fusillade seemed to have panicked the Germans.

"Look!" Julia cried. "They're running!" She quickly fired more rounds at the retreating gray figures. "It's good to see you run, you cowards!" she yelled. She stood up and ran toward the empty bunker with the rest of the partisans as the Germans ran toward the city.

"We've forced them out of the bunker!" one of the Russians shouted triumphantly.

But now, bullets began to whiz by. The Soviets were confused. "Get in the bunker," the commander ordered.

From inside, he looked through one of the slits facing the incoming fire. There was a nearby church commanding the area with its height. From there, the Germans were shooting down on them. The Germans had used the bunker as a lure. The soldiers who ran from the bunker were soon reinforcing the soldiers already fighting from the church. Their opening salvo had forced the partisans into the evacuated bunker. It did not take long for the Russians to realize that their concrete, reinforced shelter was more like a coffin. There were slits from which they could fire out of, but these also were big enough for the Germans to fire into.

Firing upwards, the partisans were in a dangerous mismatch.

Julia and the others were reduced to firing blindly, taking a quick shot through the opening, then ducking back for cover. She prayed that she hit some Germans, but there was no way of knowing.

The casualties slowly mounted. After hours of fighting, the commander asked for volunteers. He took another shot through the slit, then quickly turned away, his back against the gray bunker wall. Breathing heavily, he shouted over the din of gunfire, "We need to evacuate the wounded! Carry them to the sleighs. We'll cover you."

The two sleighs had been left on the edge of the forest, just outside Kochtz Ka'Volia. While the fighters inside the bunker put up a fierce barrage, Julia, her heart pounding, and five others, shouldered the wounded and struggled to carry them back to the sleigh. The Germans fired down on them throughout their mad dash to the sleigh. Miraculously, no one was hit.

Piling the sleigh with the stricken fighters, the other partisans hurried back to the fight. Your mother looked at each of the wounded, did what she could to comfort them, and then spurred on the horse in the direction of Lenin. She drove the horse full out through the snow until she reached the camp *sanchast.*

At around midnight, the rest of the partisans came limping in. Many were wounded, but only three had been killed.

By now, the *Mishkins* had become experts in preparing underground bunkers that could hold as many as ten people. In the summer they stayed in tents, but in the winter, they dug huge holes in the ground and covered the tops with wood, the snow providing insulation and camouflage. They built small stoves for heating and pipes were connected to funnel the smoke outside.

The winter still was exceedingly brutal with temperatures sometimes falling to 40-50 degrees below zero, and everyone was looking forward to the spring thaw.

How many more winters will we live like this, Julia often wondered? Little better than animals in their burrows. Will there ever again be a house, heated, with the laughter of children, plenty of food on the table, good, hot food, warm clothes? Will this nightmare ever end?

Julia's new camp was in a swampy area. Early in the spring of 1943, there was a break in the cold weather and the ice on the ground was turning to slush. Suddenly the alarm went up. From peasant spies, the Germans had received information that there was a large group of partisans in the area.

The Germans could not bring tanks, trucks or artillery into the area. Heavy equipment would sink in the mud. But there were plenty of garrison troops nearby.

The soldiers alighted within four miles of the camp, having trucked in as far as the icy roads reached.

Following their spies, the Germans snuck through the mud and swamp at night, and surrounded three sides of the bivouac—the fourth side was an impassable frozen-over swamp—before giving the signal to attack.

Rifle shots were heard from the outskirts of camp.

Whether the sentries had fallen asleep or been killed, no one knew. They only knew that the alarm had been sounded too late. They would just have time to escape with their bodies and their weapons. A group tried to go to the north, but was driven back. They tried south and west with the same results. The only opening they had left was toward the frozen-over swamp.

As Julia ran first in one direction and then another, following the general panic, she thought it was hopeless. She ran to the edge of the swamp, but felt her feet sink in the slush. The Soviet-made rifle she carried was heavy. She could feel it weighing her down.

She thought she might have a better chance if she threw it away, but the memory of being so helpless in the ghetto, and for most of the time in the forest, made her determined to keep the weapon. She would rather drown in the swamp than be caught defenseless.

When she reached the river it was worse. She only ran a few feet when the thin ice began to crack. Luckily, the river was not too deep. She kept going, plunging one foot through the ice until it hit bottom, then the other. It seemed to take an eternity to pull her feet back out for each step, but she did it.

Others were running in the same direction, bullets flying all around them. A soldier in front of Julia came to an abrupt stop, as though he had run into an invisible wall. He crumpled to the ground.

Seeing Julia come up to him, he screamed, "Take my rifle!" With his remaining strength he pushed the rifle up to her. "Take it. Hurry!" It dawned on her that he felt the weapon was more important than his life.

Julia crouched down and lifted the rifle. She tried to help the soldier up, but did not have enough strength. It was hard enough to carry two rifles.

Other partisans reached them and carried the wounded man over the river. Bullets were streaking by like hail from a thunderstorm.

They ran through the icy swamp until they heard no more rifle fire, perhaps three miles. The Germans must have figured it was a rout and there was no need to pursue.

At dusk, after standing guard for hours in wet clothes, the scouts came back to the camp and reported it was clear, and they started building fires. Julia was shaking more from her cold and wet clothes than from fear. Icicles had formed on the bottoms of her sleeves and coat. She noticed others moving in slow motion, their clothes were so frozen.

As the kindling took hold and flames grew, people crowded and huddled next to the fires. Ice on their clothes began to melt and fall like clusters of rain. Tears were forming in Julia's eyes, but she was ashamed to cry.

The wounded soldier was cared for in a new *sanchast,* one of the first tents put up in the new camp. He died that night.

Julia had to do guard duty like everyone else. After warming up, she took her rifle and walked about a mile out of camp. Many times the duty was miserable, in freezing rain or thunderstorms. This night the sky lit up so brightly with lightning that Julia was certain the Germans could see her from miles away. Her stint was for two hours. Sentries were replaced every two hours so they would not fall asleep.

***

As winter was slowly ebbing away in 1943, there were many more partisans in the Bagdanovka forests. Some small areas were now controlled by the resistance, and the Germans could not enter them, even in force. The underground had blown up the bridges leading to the villages, so the Germans could only approach them with ground troops.

Stalin had reversed his earlier position that partisans behind the German lines were useless, or worse from his point of view, a training ground for counter-revolutionaries. He had now decided it was more intelligent to supply and thereby control them, especially with the German line of supply now stretched over so long a distance—an inviting target for well-organized fighters.

A unified command was set up and supplies were now sent into the forests to supply the partisans. Soviet commandos parachuted in, and explosives, weapons and other supplies were dropped in by air or landed by helicopter.

The Soviets now controlled everything from their command post in Dabroslavka. They decided who would fight, work in the kitchen, do laundry, or be nurses. Everyone had to share in the mundane tasks. Not everyone could be soldiers.

Julia received more intensive training as a nurse, and on missions, she was expected to take care of casualties, administering first aid until the wounded could be evacuated back to the *sanchast.*

***

A young girl from Brest-Litovsk was surviving by herself in the forest, almost like an animal. When a partisan patrol found her, she had no clothes, only a burlap sack. Her name was Hanka.

Your mother had two dresses; a blue polka dot dress she always wore when she worked in the kitchen, and an extra dress that one of the scouts had given her. When Julia saw the poor child, she gave her the polka dot dress.

Later, one of the Russian officers noticed Hanka in the dress and went up to your mother.

"Now don't get offended, but I want to ask you a question," the officer said. "Would you give the dress to her if she wasn't Jewish?"

"Certainly," Julia said, hiding how upset she really was. "I would give the dress to anyone who needed it. I don't have the right to have two dresses when someone else has nothing. We're not here for ourselves. We're here to take revenge for the people who gave their lives."

There were so many like this young girl who somehow made it to the forest. Hanka was lucky. Who knows how many perished there, alone, with no food or shelter? With no one to remember them.

THE SIXTH DAY

CHAPTER 18

THE *SANTIKAS*

I couldn't wait any longer. Bill had told me not to do it, but I was young and stubborn and I had to know. When we sat down, before Papa could say a word, I blurted out, "Didn't you ever shoot any Germans in the forest?"

While Bill rolled his eyes skyward, a thin smile came to Papa's lips.

"You know, son," he said patiently, "that's a good question. And it has a good, if unsatisfactory, answer. The whole time in the forest, whether it was just my small group with your grandfather and your Uncle Label, I never had much more than a pistol with six bullets, one of which I was saving for myself if ever I was in danger of getting caught. I used one of those bullets on Boychick and Label used one on Nicolaichik. That left four. Some of the men in the Jewish group that David formed had rifles, but we were always short on ammunition. We had to be very careful hoarding our bullets. They were like gold."

"So Mama shot more Nazis than you," I said.

"Well, in fact, up to this point she probably did. But be patient, we're getting to the point you want to hear."

* * *

Not long after Hennik's execution, the central command sent a new man to take command of the Kaganovich *Atrad*, our group. David was ordered to work in intelligence, while Label and our father stayed with the old group. I made contact with the Santikas, the Soviet paratroopers. I had never been satisfied with just surviving, and to my way of thinking, that was all I had done for more than a year. Certainly, our actions had siphoned off some German troops now and again, and we had done some damage to German communications and railway traffic, but it was never enough. I wanted to hit the Nazis hard. I had scores to settle. I wanted much more than an eye for an eye.

The *Santikas*, known as Igor's *Atrad*, wanted to make use of my knowledge of the woods, and I was excited to join a professional group of soldiers. It was a good trade-off. They had excellent equipment and automatic weapons, and immediately exchanged my antiquated pistol for an automatic rifle that could shoot ten bullets in one burst. Even though I was still behind enemy lines, there was a fundamental change for me with this group. I was no longer among the pursued, now I was a hunter.

***

By this time, the woods were flooded with partisans. The Soviets even built a landing strip near one of the villages, where parachutists were dropped, in addition to weapons and ammunition for the partisans. We jokingly called the field "Miniature Moscow."

When I was not leading paratroopers through the forest on missions, I was assigned to a small group whose duty was to make fires to line the airfield. When planes flew over to drop supplies, or helicopters came in to land, we would light the fires to signal the exact location to the pilots.

I remember one night when I was assigned to guard the edge of the field and make certain the fires were lit at the right time.

I heard the noise of a plane. This meant more provisions, food and ammunition. Two other men were with me. We all listened carefully.

"It's a German plane," I exclaimed.

It was a German plane tracking a Soviet helicopter.

"Put out the fires!" one of the soldiers yelled. "They might see the field."

There were six paratroopers in the helicopter. As I watched, horrified, the helicopter tried to set down too quickly. Without the guiding lights, it was impossible to see. The pilot, trying to avoid the German fighter, swerved in low. One of the rotors hit a high tree branch and got tangled up. The helicopter tumbled over and then fell straight down, exploding into flames as it crashed onto the field. Three men died instantly.

We rushed to the helicopter and pulled out the three survivors. Others rushed to the scene and managed to douse the fire before it could spread to the surrounding woods.

The survivors were shaken up but none were injured. They were led back into the woods for safety. Soon after, the dead were given a hero's service and buried next to the field.

Sentry duty was doubled. We stayed at our positions on the perimeter of the field in groups of two, one man sleeping while the other stood the two-hour watch. German patrols or farmers might have heard the explosion or seen the fire. Certainly, the German pilot would have radioed in the location.

The next morning, the commander of the *Santikas* visited the area. He decided not to abandon the field. "It's too deep in the forest," he said confidently to the paratroopers. "They'll never find it. We're still safe."

For once I hope an optimist in this war is right, I thought. It certainly hadn't happened up to now, but an army has the luxury of being a lot more confident than a guerrilla group behind enemy lines. Like I said, I was going through a psychological change. I was starting to feel that I was part of a real army.

Walking past the remains of the burnt-out helicopter, still smoldering from the heat of the fire, I still couldn't help wondering, does anyone get out of this alive?

***

Peasants from Soshna, acting as spies for the partisans, came to me one day and told me a high-ranking German officer was coming to their village in two days. I reported this to the commander of the paratroopers.

Since the beginning, I wanted to go after SS troops rather than regular army officers, but the SS never stayed in one place long enough. The SS in this region were special mounted troops used only to kill Jews. They annihilated a *shtetl* or conducted hunt and destroy missions looking for Jews all over the countryside, then moved on.

Intelligence never seemed to be able to tell us where we could find the SS. By now, toward the end of 1943, it was too late. The SS was gone—as far as they were concerned, all the *shtetls* and villages and towns in the area were *Judenfrei.* I was very frustrated and angry—I might never be able to get my hands on the SS.

That night, I led a group of eight paratroopers out to a place on the road leading from Soshna to Botow. The road went through a heavily forested area. After finding a suitable location, the Russian commandos placed themselves on both sides of the road, melting into the trees and brush.

Most of the German patrols or reconnoitering groups at the time were on horseback.

I stood watch on the Botow side, about five hundred yards ahead of the Russians. I had to be in a position where the others could see a signal.

If it was a large group of Germans, I'd give a signal to let them go. The paratroopers then waited for them to pass and headed back to camp. If it was a small group, say four or five, I'd give the signal to attack.

Experience had taught me to be careful. Sometimes the Germans would go in columns, using a small detachment as bait. If the small group was attacked, a larger formation was nearby to rush to their aid and crush the commandos. One of my jobs was to be certain we were not falling into such a trap.

I left the commandos and walked to my position. I picked a straight stretch of the road to make my job easier. It was a brisk four in the morning.

There was a cloud cover reflecting the moonlight. Visibility was good for someone watching the road. I settled in, tried to stay warm, and waited.

At about seven in the morning, I heard the dull clopping of horses' hooves. Adrenaline coursed through my veins. This was my first real action with the commandos. I'll never forget it. I waited until the riders passed, then gave the first signal, raising my rifle up and down three times. There was one German officer, a sergeant and three privates. The commandos waited for my second signal so they would know it was safe to attack. It all had to be carefully timed. The riders would take between six and seven minutes to be abreast of the commandos.

I intently watched the road to Botow. There was no movement, no sound other than the chirping of crickets and the occasional hooting of an owl. After five minutes, I knew there were no additional troops—or if there were, they had made the mistake of staying too far back. I raised my rifle up and down three more times, then started moving quietly back towards the ambush site, keeping to the cover of the forest.

The commandos waited for the Germans to reach them. As they drew parallel, the Russians jumped out of the woods. They quickly shot the three privates and pulled the other riders from their mounts. Five of the commandos grabbed the reins of the horses, quickly leading them into the forest to be shot. The dead Germans were dragged into the forest and left for the vultures.

The Russians blindfolded the others and led them back to the forests of Bagdanovka to the camp. Once there, the Germans would be interrogated by the commissars, then shot.

The paratroopers did not know where they were going to be from one day to the next, and they often had to move fast. There was simply no way to hold and transport prisoners. Besides, they rationalized, the Germans had earned very little right to compassion.

On the way back, walking in front, I held up my hand to stop the group. I had heard something.

The commandos faded into the trees, becoming invisible. The captive's mouths were covered and rifles held to their heads. To an uninformed observer, the woods looked completely empty.

A different group of partisans, unknown to me, was leading about twenty prisoners, all dressed like regular German army soldiers. Somehow, I thought, these men did not look like Germans. By now I was suspicious of everything.

The commandos stayed hidden until the other group passed.

Later, David heard about these strange prisoners as well. He was instructed to talk to them and find out their background.

They were Hungarian Jews who were compelled to work on railway tracks destroyed by the partisans. Some of the prisoners showed David they carried *tefillin*, phylacteries used for prayer.

David went to the leader of the other partisan group and appealed to them to let the Hungarians go.

"They are obviously innocent. They were forced to do the work. No Jew would work for the Germans without coercion," David argued.

"If you want them released, you're no better than they are," the leader of the partisans arrogantly replied. "After all, they were helping the Germans, so they all must die."

The men of the Igor *Atrad* refused to take part in squabbles between the other partisan units. They would not intervene. David could not turn to our old group because the Kaganovich *Atrad* had been disbanded shortly after David left, and our father and Label, along with the others, were sent to other partisan units. Central Command said simply that, "There shouldn't exist a separate *atrad* made up only of Jews."

They would not have been powerful enough to intervene anyway. All the Hungarian Jews were executed.

The man who took over for David, was not very popular and he did not last long. On a mission with his own group and some Gentile partisans, they ran into a German patrol. A long firefight ensued and the new leader was killed.

No one was absolutely certain, but rumors flew that it was not a German bullet that killed him, but a bullet from the non-Jewish partisans.

The Jewish resistance fighters always had to be suspicious of the non-Jewish combatants.

***

The commandos were always looking to find high-ranking German officers, and they made use of many spies among the peasants to find out where they could find their German prey.

Not all of the spies were peasants. There was a girl in Pohost who was actually from eastern Russia. She told the paratroopers that a high ranking general would be passing through Chuchow on a certain day.

Somehow, the Germans found out she was a spy. First, they tortured her to find out what information she had given up, then they killed her.

I was chosen to guide the eight commandos to Chuchow to capture the general. We occupied a house by the main road and sat down to wait for the general to come through.

Soon, German soldiers on horseback road up in front of the house, dismounted quickly, took cover and began to shoot, no questions asked. A boy standing right next to me was killed immediately. Strangely enough, he was the brother of the Russian girl.

I tried to revive him, but couldn't, so I moved him to the side, and hunkered down for a long fight.

Apparently, the Germans could not muster more than a few soldiers for their counter ambush, and after exchanging fire for some twenty minutes, they saddled up and left.

We did not press our luck. As soon as we were certain the Germans had gone, we evacuated the house, sprinted across the road and disappeared into the forest.

***

Now, just when I was starting to feel that I was accomplishing something, another stake was driven into my heart.

Since Central Command had moved into the village of Dabroslavka and my duties with the Igor Battalion took me there a few times a month, I always stopped by the old Prefecture of Police building that now housed the headquarters of Intelligence. David's office was in the peeling, gray, two-story building.

One day when I dropped by his office he wasn't there. A stranger was sitting at his desk.

The man told me that David was in quarantine in the *sanchast* of his old *atrad*. He had come down with typhus two days earlier.

Before he finished the sentence I was out the door. I quickly mounted my horse and galloped southeast out of Dabroslavka, raising a trail of dust.

I was scared. Many people had died of typhus in the ghettos and the labor camps, in the death camps and the forest. But if you were strong and in good health, the chances were good, and David was nothing if not strong. Not one of the survivors from Pohost Zagorodski had ever died from typhus. Your mother survived it too.

At the encampment, over a dozen were quarantined, some recuperating and others still fighting high fevers.

David was sleeping. The doctor would not allow me to come too close. He told me that David was still queasy and had an extremely bad headache, but he thought the fever had broken.

Later, I went to see my father at a local farmer's house, where Shaindel and her three-year-old were now staying.

"David is feeling better," I said as I entered the house and hugged my sister-in-law. She looked more frail than ever, but Papa was the real surprise. Ashen-faced, wrinkled, for the first time I saw him as an old man.

Shaindel started to cry. "They should move him here with his wife and father. Not leave him in the woods. I asked them to, but they wouldn't."

I didn't understand. I thought the partisans would have better medication available then my father could get. But Shaindel did not trust them.

Samuel wanted me to go to Dabroslavka to get some dried blueberries, to make tea for David. The local peasants believed that blueberry tea could help those afflicted with typhus.

I decided to go immediately, even though the market probably would not be open until the morning.

At six a.m. the next morning, I was waiting when the peasant fruit stall opened. I bought a pound of the dried berries and hurried back to the farmhouse. As I dismounted, Samuel ran out, tears streaming down his cheeks.

"Abram, you're too late. David is dead." Samuel grabbed onto the horse to keep from falling. He voice was barely audible. "David is dead." Not only had he lost his son, but he felt as though he had lost his wife Yentl for a second time. Every time he had looked at David's face, he saw Yentl—they looked so much alike.

I was so distraught and depressed I did not know what to say or do. All I could think of was little Shlameleh. How he would stay by the window whenever his father was away on a mission, and how Shlameleh would run to Shaindel and tell her his father was home as David rode up on his great charcoal horse. He would never say that again.

Every time I reached the point where I could almost endure my past losses, I lost someone else.

Throughout the war, no other people from Pohost Zagorodski died from typhus. David was the only one. Therefore, many people doubted that he actually died from the disease. Some speculated that he was poisoned. But we would never know for certain.

My brother was given a hero's burial. The head of all the *atrads* gave the eulogy, speaking for a long time about David's accomplishments, and how he contributed immensely to the organization of the partisan group.

David Bobrow's calm and rational approach to leading the *atrad* was well known for having saved many lives, both Jewish and non-Jewish, but it was never more apparent than in the month following his death.

I wanted to crawl into a hole and die. I wanted to never again have a thought in my head about my brothers. Just forget everything. But I had no choice. I had to continue my duties. Like your mother, the more I took on, the less time I had to think, but every time I had to go to Dabroslavka, my heart would become heavy. It would begin to cry.

211

As if to reinforce David's importance, several days after the funeral, I ran into a member of the old *atrad,* who told me about an upcoming mission: an ambush near Malkovich.

A day later, I learned that the ambush turned into a trap. The partisans were surrounded and only one man escaped. In the space of one month, more than ten people from the old Jewish *atrad* lost their lives. Your mother's Uncle Kiva was part of that mission, and now, with Kiva dead, Julia had not a single relative left.

CHAPTER 19

COUNTING THE ENEMY

The front was moving ever closer to the partisan areas. Poland's pre-war border was crossed by the Red Army at Volhynia on January 3rd, 1944.

The numbers in the Resistance were growing daily. Before the Germans were pushed out of Poland, there were over a million operating behind enemy lines. The danger was that they would all be trapped between the anti-partisan forces to their rear, and the retreating German regular army at their front, and annihilated. This was in fact, the intention of the Germans.

Even the Kolpak *Atrad,* which functioned some four hundred miles to the south in the Carpathian Mountains, and were blessed with the luxury of their own artillery, were forced back to the Bagdanovka forests. They fought a major battle with the Germans in the south, suffered many casualties, and then more on the retreat north. When they reached the Mizelyshcatz Forest, they still numbered upwards of five hundred men. Other *atrads* were running out of ammunition and had to pull back as well.

As the Germans drew closer, I was sent to the region northeast of Dabroslavka, to ferret out information from some sympathetic peasants, to see what they knew about the German retreat and dispositions.

These men guided six of us to a house situated along the dirt road leading to Malkovich, where we could safely view the German arrival.

We brewed some steaming hot tea, hunkered down and waited. I remember sitting at one of the windows facing the road.

Whole regiments of German soldiers soon came into my view, as they marched down the main road in neat columns.

How orderly they are, I thought as I watched. Even in retreat. Then, I was horrified to see twenty soldiers stop directly in front of the house. I ducked back, bringing my rifle across my chest. Sneaking a glance, I saw them start moving forward, as if they were going to surround the house.

Not waiting to see if I had guessed correctly, I motioned for the others to follow me. We quickly jumped through the rear windows and ran into a field of tall wheat. Without even a backwards glance, we crawled rapidly through the field, reaching the horses we had left in the woods, quickly mounted, and rode off to headquarters.

As we galloped along the road, I spotted sentries, and beyond them, work details. Some of the *atrads* were already placing mines along the roads and approaches to the woods. The roads from Malkovich, Lunenitz and Parachunsk were all mined.

We had to slow down to be guided through the new mine fields. Halfway through, I saw Label, bent over, busily placing a mine in the ground.

While the others continued on, I pulled up and dismounted.

"Label, the Germans are coming this way!" I shouted. "Not five miles from here."

Label looked up and smiled. He wiped the sweat from his forehead, then stood aright, still holding the mine. "I know."

Label turned and placed the mine in a hole. He then took a plastic igniter, squeezed it with a special pliers until it would fit in the mine, and carefully placed it inside. The mine was harmless without the igniter, but the igniter itself could blow off a hand, or rip up your mouth if you placed it in the mine like I did later, when I was in the Russian Army. I used my mouth instead of the pliers, because it was much faster.

Label covered it up with dirt and then patted the dirt smooth around the detonator. When someone stepped on the dirt, thus breaking the igniter, the mine exploded.

"Don't worry," he said casually, "they won't get through. The whole area is mined."

Label's words were apparently accurate as hundreds of partisans, perhaps a thousand in all, began moving into the woods on both sides of the road.

In the next few days, along a three mile front, thousands of Germans, including regular army units mixed with the anti-partisan auxiliaries, went shoulder-to-shoulder in a drive to end the partisan resistance once and for all. For the first time, the resistance fighters fought a major set-piece battle with the enemy. There were many casualties on both sides, but the partisans eventually had to pull back.

At least four villages were razed to the ground by the retreating Germans in reprisal.

***

With the arrival of so many German units, the *Santikas* were constantly in close proximity to the enemy.

With five other men, I was ordered to cross enemy lines between Dabroslavka and Borki to get a count on the Germans approaching for another offensive.

Even at night, I immediately recognized the area we were crossing—the minefields laid earlier by our own comrades. It would have been quite bizarre if, after everything I'd been through, I stepped on a mine laid down by my own brother.

The sun shone brightest at midday, when we came to a heavily weeded area on slightly higher ground, and sighted the Germans. Only seventy yards away, we lay down in the weeds, lifted our binoculars, and began to count.

The reconnaissance went easily at first, but soon I saw soldiers running about grabbing their weapons. The observers had been observed. We were soon being shot at.

The shooting went on and on, and we obstinately made our count even as the shooting escalated. Using my finger, I scraped a line in the dirt for every ten soldiers. Even as the Germans made signs of forming up to attack, we doggedly continued.

Finally, I saw we could do no more. Together, we had counted over three thousand infantry.

As the Germans started climbing towards us, we scrambled down the other side of the little mound, losing ourselves in the forest.

For two days, we hid with friendly peasants who were now behind enemy lines. These men were able to supply any gaps in our information.

After we went back across the minefields and the German lines, and delivered our report to headquarters, the partisans fought another nameless battle where no quarter was given.

In some places the Germans were able to break through and burn villages, sending the poor inhabitants scurrying to the woods. But this time, it was the Germans who suffered the worst casualties and had to pull back.

***

A few weeks after the battle, a thin, bearded man appeared in the camp of the *atrad.* He was looking for me.

Although he was a childhood friend, I didn't recognize him. He was so shriveled up since he had been forced to go to Honsovich.

He came up to me with a huge smile on his haggard face. He grabbed my hand and shook it fiercely. He kissed me on each cheek. Tears were forming in his eyes.

"Abram, I'm so happy I found you," he said. "I'd heard your whole family was gone. It's so good to see you."

"What is it?" I asked, too tired for amenities.

"The Germans have all run away from Pohost Zagorodski. They're gone."

I felt a tightness welling up in my chest. I had trouble breathing. Question after question entered my mind. Should I go home? Was it home anymore? Had anybody returned? Was it even Pohost anymore?

Within minutes, I decided, and went to the commander to get permission to go the *shtetl.*

With three men the commander insisted I take for safety, I rode into Pohost Zagorodski that same afternoon.

"You know," I said to the Soviet soldiers, "it's spring. The weather is beautiful. Leaves are appearing on the trees again. Everything is turning green. Look at the bright flowers, hear the bees. Smell the sweet pollen. I went out in the woods today and watched how peacefully the peasants were sowing their seeds and the children were feeding the livestock. I couldn't help thinking of my family—my brothers and my nephews, my nieces who were already lying in the ground, buried for two years already. These peasants don't act like they even know a war is on. They dance and they sing and they marry.

"Everything is normal for them. Like before the war. I'm very jealous, I admit it."

"It's not their fault," one of the Soviets said.

"I know that, but my jealousy is still great. I don't understand why we deserved to have all of this happen to us. I'll never understand." At least these simple people never turned on the Jews, I thought. I should have been thankful, not jealous, not bitter, but I couldn't help it.

When came to the bridge across the Yashelda, the bridge that forever would be burned in my memory as the place where Shlomo was caught, we dismounted. I felt goose bumps rising on my arms. My throat was dry.

The clopping of the horses' hooves sounded too loud to me as we walked the horses over the bridge. This should be a silent, reverent occasion, I thought.

The whole village was empty: no Germans, no peasants, not even a stray dog or cat. Many of the houses were torn down, some were still smoldering from fires the Germans lit as they retreated.

Every step brought its own memories, its own heartbreak. The feelings were overwhelming. And every step brought to life the horrible nightmare I had lived ever since escaping from Honsovich. If I could have only gotten here sooner, even an hour. If I hadn't taken the wrong fork in the road. If the policemen hadn't stayed so near and so long. If the peasants could have taken their cattle somewhere else to graze. If I hadn't trusted the Germans to keep their word. All the terrible "ifs." Even one less, and I might have been able to warn them, at least save a few, perhaps one life. It haunted me ever since that terrible day. It haunts me still.

Reaching Dworska Street, I was surprised to see my house still standing, just as it did before the war. Perhaps the paint needed retouching and some of the windows were broken, but all in all, it was the same as I remembered. It was all so long ago.

I could see my sister and mother. I could hear their voices, their laughter. I could feel Shlomo's hand on my shoulder as he taught me how to put the bait on my hook just so. It would *make* the fish bite he would say, and then laugh merrily.

I saw that the first house on Dworska had been torn down to its foundation. Of course, I said to myself, the Germans used my house to garrison troops. They tore down the other house so they could view the approaches. That's why my house was still standing.

Then, I first noticed the poster, stuck over one of the front windows of my own house. It read: "This City Is *Judenfrei.*"

Furiously, I grabbed the edge of the poster and tore it off the wall. I ripped it to shreds and slammed it to the ground.

Without a word, I remounted my horse and rode back down Dworska Street and out of town. I could not bear to visit the site of the massacres.

I never wanted to go back to that place again.

After returning to the encampment in the woods, I paid a visit to Label and Samuel's new *atrad.* Label was away, but I found Papa sitting on a stump, reading from the Old Testament.

"Father," I said softly, "my unit has been ordered to move to the other side of the line, to the Russian side."

Samuel put the Bible down and stood up. He put his arm on my shoulder, clasping it tightly. He drew me closer and hugged me.

"I'm already used to this place in the woods," he said. "It seems like I've spent years here. I don't want to move anymore. I'm an old man. I can't go with you. Do you understand? We have to say goodbye."

"I understand...but I can't quit now Papa," I said. "I have to do more. So far, it's not enough...nothing. Not for all the Germans have done to us."

"Can you wait to say goodbye to your brother?" he asked me.

"I have my orders," I replied with my head down.

Papa helped me mount the horse.

"Bless me, Papa," I asked him. "Like you used to do when we were children."

Both of us were in tears.

"Go, my son," Samuel said. "God bless you and keep you safe." Then, breaking down, he cried, "Promise me you'll come back to me. Promise."

Reaching down to take his hand, I said, "I promise."

Papa told me later, that as he watched me ride away, he felt an indescribable loneliness. But he also felt a strength, building in him through the strength of his sons…and pride.

He knew his sons could go on, no matter what.

***

During the German offensive, the *Mishkins* had taken over the village of Sbychovo for a week to provision. The sentries now had double duty—they had to watch for Germans and they had to keep the villagers from leaving.

On the third night, Julia and Sonya, a dark-haired girl from the village of Slonin, stood watch on the opposite ends of the village.

There was a pasture near the outskirts of the village where the peasants let the horses roam free at night to graze.

With all of the villagers effectively confined, it was very still and quiet at night, and the horses had been unattended for a few days.

Julia and Sonya heard noises coming from the pasture, but it was too dark for them to see and they were unaware of the horses. One horse must have knocked into another, causing a loud thud.

Julia, thinking it was Germans, fired her rifle into the air. Sonya heard the first shot and fired her gun as well. Pandemonium broke out in Sbychovo as everyone, partisans and peasants alike, woke up.

The sentry nearest Julia calmly walked up to her.

"Did you hear it?" she asked excitedly, pointing her rifle in the direction she had heard the noise.

"It was the horses," he said quietly. Then he started laughing, he was so relieved it was a false alarm. There were always false alarms in the partisans and they were always much better than the real thing. Pretty soon Julia joined him, doubling over in laughter. In ten minutes every partisan in Sbychovo was laughing.

Later, he went up to Julia and praised her for her alertness.

***

The next time your mother saw a horse it wasn't as funny.

"Julia!" Kolko called out. He was a tall, lean Russian who Julia thought always wore a sneaky, fearful expression. "Come over and pick out a horse to ride."

Julia walked out of a peasant's hut near Kochtz Ka' Vola. Across from the hut, there was a grassy field with horses and soldiers standing around.

218

"Would you like to ride?" Kolko asked. The partisans had just returned to camp with forty horses they had taken from local peasants. Julia was surprised to see Kolko smiling.

"Come, pick out a horse."

Julia laughed and walked up to the smallest one, not bigger than a pony. "I'll take this one. She's very cute."

"No, no, no," Kolko insisted. "You need a good horse. That one would break down after a short ride."

Kolko led Julia up to a tall, black stallion, a very proud animal. It was already saddled.

"This is the perfect horse for you. Here," he said offering his hand. I'll help you up."

Other soldiers wandered over.

Your mother had ridden before but she was no expert. "I'd rather ride the little one," she said.

"No. She is for a child," Kolko said. "Come."

The other partisans yelled: "Take the big one. Go on the big one."

Against her better judgment, Julia let the soldier help her up. No sooner had she mounted the horse and grabbed the reins, Kolko slapped its rear and the stallion took off, galloping down the road at high speed. Julia clenched the reins in her hands and hung on for her life.

Back in the field, Kolko and the other partisans were having a good laugh.

Vanya, head of this group of *Mishkins,* heard the commotion and walked up to the soldiers. "Well," he said sarcastically, "the one who was so smart better run after her. Now!"

Kolko, looking rather sheepishly at the commander, started running down the road.

By this time, the horse had already galloped a mile and showed no signs of slowing down.

Julia figured she was better off jumping than waiting for the horse to throw her. She managed to get one foot out of a stirrup, and was trying to get the other one out, while still clutching desperately to the stallion's neck.

Then abruptly the horse slowed down. He must have recognized his home and started trotting over to his familiar pasture. Julia quickly jumped down as the stallion began to graze.

"How dare you tell me to ride that horse?" Julia said to Kolko when he ran up to her. She felt like screaming at him, but she realized she was still a woman among all these men—and a Jew among all these Gentiles.

Kolko uttered a hundred apologies, but Julia knew he still thought his prank was hilarious.

***

No matter how hard she worked at exhausting herself, your mother still suffered from sleepless nights. Often she woke up in a cold sweat after a particularly gruesome nightmare of struggling to get out of the ravine near Pohost Zagorodski. Many nights she tossed and turned and thrashed about.

Her constant companion was a grenade she kept in a little burlap handbag with her meager medical supplies. For months she had slept with it as a comfort.

One day she happened to look in the bag, and found that the ring containing the pin had loosened. The grenade could have exploded at any time. She took the grenade back to the officer and he screwed it back in. She could think of only one reason why it hadn't exploded when she thrashed about during one of her violent dreams.

After all this time, she knew in her heart that her mother was still looking after her.

***

Some peasants were on the side of the Germans and some were on the side of the partisans, and some were on the side of whomever was in closest proximity at a given moment.

One could not be too careful with them. A Ukranian man took forty Russian partisans on a mission after first setting up an ambush with the Germans. All forty Russians were killed.

One of the main obsessions of the partisans was the fear and constant search for traitors within their ranks and among the peasants.

Toward the end of the partisan movement, when the Soviet lines had pushed so far west that they had overtaken many partisan units, and had made them lay down their weapons or join the Soviet Army, seven such men were brought into your mother's camp.

These men had been working for the Germans, although they had professed to be working for the *Mishkins.* They were, in effect, double agents. They had led the Germans to the forest where the partisans were hiding. Other, friendly local people told the partisans of their treachery, and the partisans' own spies gave confirmation. This was not an isolated incident. There were many stories of treachery from their kind, just as there were many stories of peasants risking their lives to help the Jewish people and the underground.

That morning, Julia was away from the camp, milking cows. She was given a sled to take the containers back to camp. As she sat milking the last cow, Ivan Vasilievich, the veterinarian ran up to her.

"Come on, come on, come on," he shouted excitedly.

"What is it?" Julia asked.

"Leave the cows. We'll come back later. Come with me. You're going to see something."

Ivan Vasilievich started running toward the main camp. Julia had no idea what he was yelling about, but she jumped up and started to run after him.

"What?" she yelled after him.

He turned and stopped for a second, catching his breath.

"Revenge. That's what it is. Come. You'll see what's going on. We're going to take revenge," he said. Then he turned around and continued running down the narrow cattle path.

When they arrived at the camp, they saw all of their comrades, men and women, standing in a large circle around a ditch. The seven peasants, all men, were sitting at the edge of the ditch.

Mitya was at the forefront of the ditch.

"You worked for the Nazis," he said simply to the trembling peasants. "And now you shall reap what you sowed."

Julia was surprised to find she could not look at the men near the ditch. She didn't want to see them executed. She looked at the doctor. He understood.

"I'm going back to finish with the cows," she said sadly. She turned around and left. As she left, one of the men got up on his knees and said, "Let me pray to my God."

One partisan sneered, "You'll need your prayers."

Sonya suddenly took up her rifle and went to the man praying on his knees. She was crying, but the wrath of God was in her eyes. "For my parents...for my sisters and brothers...for the whole Jewish community."

She ran her bayonet through the peasant's heart.

One by one, the rest of the traitors were bayoneted. Bullets were too precious to waste on them.

CHAPTER 20

THE SOVIET ARMY

After leaving my father in Bagdanovka, I led the *santikas* southwest to Luninetz, taking the better part of a week to go a mere twenty-five miles.

I remember the town. I had been there before the war. Luninetz was a lot like Pohost, only larger. If I looked carefully through the pines while we marched, I could see the lights of the city. It had been garrisoned since 1941. We had to be careful there. Lots of German patrols.

We traveled the main roads only at night, except near larger towns like Luninetz. Then we kept further into the forests. During daylight hours, we blended into the thickest part of the trees. There we would cook our meager rations and rest. I was just one of the scouts leading the one hundred and fifty men of the Igor *Atrad* through the German lines.

It now was the spring of 1944. Two long years in the forest.

Most of the snow had melted and the small rutted roads through the semi-marshy areas we would have to pass were now firm enough to support the eight supply wagons. More importantly, it was hard enough that we wouldn't leave tracks. Still, the going was slow and tedious.

Not knowing the terrain, none of the commandos rode, preferring to play it safe and walk their horses slowly and silently through the night. Behind myself and a sergeant stretched a single line—one man every fifteen yards, all the way back to the main column.

Passing a mile north of Luninetz, I then led them back to the dirt road, and east toward Lenin.

Just past the city, I stopped suddenly, craned my neck and listened. I heard the fluttering wings of an owl, disturbed from its nesting place. Pumping my rifle up and down, I signaled the man fifteen yards back of me, who stopped and did the same. So did the next, all the way to head of the column. Every commando blended into the foliage on either side of the road. We were aided by the dark night. Guns were at the ready, but it was too dangerous to start a fight unless it was critical.

A German patrol walked down the narrow dirt road, passing in between us. They came within a yard of me, but never stopped.

Either they're good actors, I thought, or they didn't see a thing.

It took the patrol a good half-hour to pass down the whole line of commandos. Then, the column waited another twenty minutes before starting forward.

The most vulnerable time was at river crossings. Wading through twenty yards of water, raging downstream as it picks up its spring runoff is difficult in itself. But what if a German patrol, or worse, a retreating company or battalion showed up when you were in the water? I led them to lesser known fords. We waited for the dead of night, then, the first crossing would be made by fifteen to twenty men, enough so they could put up a fight if need be, but not so many that their loss would destroy the integrity of the force. Commandos would cross in twos and threes after the first group was established.

At the Cna, the largest and most difficult crossing we faced, our luck held. Some of the small footbridges across the rivers were still intact.

It was dawn, three days after crossing the Cna River when we reached Radziherava. We were behind Soviet lines. Now the patrols we met were Russian.

Fires were lit, food was cooked, but most of the men fell asleep on the bare ground before eating a bite.

The next night, rested, our stomachs full, and feeling the security of Soviet territory for the first time in over a year, we were eager to continue the march. I led them towards Mikosewich, and then headed northeast in the direction of Lenin. Like I said, this Lenin was a city I knew before the war. Now it had its own story of tragedy. As we passed it, I stopped once more and gestured off to the south to the sergeant.

"What do you see now?" I asked.

"I can't see anything. Where?" the sergeant asked, straining his eyes. It was another pitch-black night.

"There," I said, pointing. "But you won't see anything. That used to be Lenin. A pre-war border town. It's empty. A year after Lenin's Jewish population had been done away with, the *Einsatzgruppen* came back, rounded up the remaining five thousand White Russian inhabitants, herded them into a large barn, then set it on fire and destroyed it with artillery."

"My God," was all the Russian could say.

That morning, local guides took over from me. I was no longer familiar with the territory. Every ten to twenty miles, a new guide would take over.

It was funny. We called it the German lines, but we must have traveled some forty miles to get through them.

For another two weeks, we marched until we reached the big city of Bobruisk, more than a hundred miles from our starting point. It was the end of June.

It was strange for me during that journey, especially after crossing to friendly lines. I had made my decision to go with the Russians, and I really wanted to fight. But at the time, I started feeling guilty about leaving my father and brother and your mother. I knew they understood, but I couldn't help it. I'm sure part of the reason was that they were still under the guns of the Nazis.

We arrived on the outskirts of a city which was in ruins from the earlier German advance, and now from the Soviet. It was a horrifying spectacle. The roads were clogged with horses and wagons bearing the dead and wounded. We could barely make progress amidst the groans and confusion.

A tremendous battle had been fought as the Soviets smashed through the Bobruisk-Mogilev-Vitebsk line. Nearly thirty German divisions were trapped, mostly around Minsk, which later fell on the third of July. But the price in casualties, as it often was for the Soviet armies, was extremely high.

The advance of the Soviets had been so swift, no one had time to bury the dead, or even move them. Most of the population had fled on the eve of the battle. Few people were left in the city to do the work.

***

Reaching the headquarters, the head of the *atrad* summoned the Jewish members of the unit.

Most of the Igor commandos were Army paratroopers and they were sent off to their original units, while the Jewish members were asked if they wanted to be in a new police force the Soviets were forming, or if they wanted to join the regular army. They told us that most of the partisans that joined the army would train for elite units because of their experience—they would get the best training.

There were also rumors that partisans who did not want to join the army or the police force could be sent to Siberia or shot, but none of this mattered to me. It was an easy choice. I was desperate to join the Soviets since the first days of the invasion. The coercion made no difference. I wanted to fight. I would have begged to be in the army if they had not offered it, and now I was going to be in the Special Forces, like the Army Rangers.

With a group of twenty-nine others, I was sent to a school to study to become a sergeant and learn how to handle mortars.

In four tough weeks of training, I became quite proficient at operating the mortars and especially at setting the distance. For once, there was no shortage of ammunition. The Soviets had captured warehouses filled with missiles as they reconquered German territory, and although German shells were 81 mm. in caliber, and the Russians shells were 82 mm., we could still use them. There was no limit on how many we could fire.

The only thing was, we had to be careful about firing too rapidly and overheating the barrel—or the missile wouldn't fire. The danger was putting another missile into the barrel before the last one fired. In combat, we would have to shoot rapidly, and if the mistake happened, it was fatal. More than a few times, an extra missile was thrown in and the mortar exploded, killing all five people around it. There was a plate on the mortar that the operators stuck their foot on. If it jerked, that meant the shell had fired. If it didn't, the operator needed to wait before putting another shell in the barrel. You learned quickly or you were dead.

The learning was not that difficult and all of us absorbed it quickly, but I did not want to waste my time training, I wanted to join the fight with a real army.

Finally, thirty of us were given orders. We reported to the Bobruisk train station and boarded a train filled with soldiers headed to the front.

By this time, the Soviets had pushed the Germans back beyond Pinsk.

I sat down by a young soldier, named Gregor, who told me he had been in uniform since retreating with the Soviets in 1941, and he was a good friend of one of my cousins from Pinsk.

I told him about my partisan experiences and that Label, Papa and Julia might have gone to Pinsk after the liberation. Unfortunately, I had no idea where they might be.

Gregor told me that the train stopped at Pinsk for an hour, and he thought he could find them. You can imagine how excited I was. Arriving at Pinsk, on a hot, muggy day, we disembarked. Gregor led me to a ghetto near the station. We headed toward a small, brick apartment near the ghetto entrance, but even on the short walk, I had a feeling of claustrophobia. The street was narrow, not much sunlight got in, everything seemed to be in shadows. It reminded me of Honsovich. All that was missing was the barbed wire.

I knocked on the door. It opened slowly. Label stood just inside, shock registering on his still youthful face. My face almost ruptured from the smile. I jumped into his arms and we hugged each other so tightly we could hardly breathe. Then we collapsed in laughter, and then we cried.

"Why aren't you in uniform?" I asked. "Why are you here? I thought they took everyone for the army."

Label had had enough of the war. He laughed. "Don't worry. I'm not hiding out from the gulags. Fortunately, the Soviets needed administrators for the cities. I was given one of the jobs of managing food distribution in Pinsk. All food supplies—salt, sugar, grains and produce—they're all controlled by the government."

"Where's father?" I asked.

"When the Russians overtook the front, he went back to Pohost Zagorodski. I don't know how he can live there," he said, shaking his head and the smile leaving his face. "I couldn't. I tried to talk him out of it."

"And Julia?" I asked anxiously.

"She's here in the ghetto, working. But how did you get here, Abram?" Label asked.

I said, "I'm going to the front." I thought Label would be pleased, and proud of his little brother.

Aghast, Label's expression completely changed. He grabbed me by the arms. He shook me as if to put some sense in my head.

"What are you doing? Do you realize how many dead and wounded pass through the Pinsk station? On a daily basis? Haven't you seen enough of people suffering and dying for a lifetime?"

I looked into Label's eyes. I was surprised. If anyone could understand, I thought it would be my brother who had gone through almost everything that I had. I remember stammering, "I—I have a mission to accomplish. I have to take revenge. To square accounts. So far, I've accomplished nothing."

"No! Abram, that's not true. You've done more than your share. Please don't go," Label pleaded. Tears again came to his eyes as he lowered his head unto my chest. He grasped my arms even tighter. "Abram. I don't think I could bear to lose another member of my family. I beg you, don't go."

"I have to. I have to repay the Russians. They saved us. And I want to kill Germans. I want to kill a lot of the S.O.B.s." Then, and I still can't believe it, but I got so angry with pent-up hatred and frustration, anger at the Germans, with the killing, with the loss of so many loved ones, with the realization that I would never get enough revenge—that it got the better of me. And I still regret to this day what I said. "Perhaps you're a traitor," I said to Label.

Then I turned my back and stormed out of the house and away from Label. By the time Gregor and I were out of the ghetto, I was angrier with myself than with my brother. How could I say such a thing?

"I have to go back and apologize," I said to Gregor. "And I need to find Julia."

"That's for sure, but we don't have time now," Gregor replied. "If we're late for that train, we'll be the ones who are considered traitors."

On the way back to the Pinsk station, I chastised myself over and over, wracked with guilt. How could I ever say that to a man as brave as Label? To a man who was my brother, and who I loved dearly? I beat myself up over that one for a long time. And your mother…I thought I'd be lucky if she ever talked to me again. But such was my thirst for revenge.

We ex-partisans cut strange figures in the Army. Having not yet been issued uniforms, we were still wearing the clothes we had worn in the forest. I had rubber boots, a rough brown woolen jacket, a white flannel shirt, and khaki pants, all of which were desperately worn out.

The train took us to Brest-Litovsk, across the Bug River, to Wlodava, where there was so much railway traffic going in every direction, that we were delayed and thus able to get off the train and walk around to stretch our legs.

On the station platform, I saw Gilek, a friend from my days with the partisans. Gilek ran toward me and hugged me.

"Where are you going?" he asked.

"To the front."

In a strange echo that reminded me of Label, Gilek said, "You're in Wlodava. You should get off the train and not go with them to the front."

I looked at him in surprise.

"What is wrong with you?" Gilek asked, raising his voice. "Didn't you see enough sorrow for a lifetime? Can't you see the trainloads of bodies coming from the front?"

My friends and I turned and went back to the sanctuary of the train. They just don't understand, I thought. I don't care if I die. I'm not afraid. I had already died ten times over, with every friend and family member that I'd lost.

I watched Gilek on the platform. As the train pulled out of the station, Gilek yelled, "Children! Don't go to the front! Don't go. Don't go to the front." His voice haunted me like some Siren wailing at sea. I can still hear that voice. Twenty five miles later, we disembarked at Chelm. As soon as we got off the train, still without uniforms, we were mustered into formation, then divided into different groups: those with machine guns went to one group, those with rifles to another—I went with the group with mortars. More training. Now I was even angrier.

I learned a stark truth. Being in the Soviet Army didn't necessarily mean you would have enough to eat. The food consisted of dried out, semi-rotten fish used for cooking soup, plus small pieces of pumpernickel bread. It almost seemed we were scrounging for food more than training. For a whole month there were never enough rations. Soviet soldiers were always hungry.

And in that month the weather started changing.

I think I was hungrier in the Soviet Army than I was in the forest with the partisans. By now it was November.

The peasants seemed smarter in these areas. They stayed away from their fields so we could not bother them for food. I convinced the others that even though it was cold and the fields were frozen, we had to dig up some potatoes to fill our stomachs.

A friend of mine from Baronovich, somehow found out there was a Russian Jewish officer in the Army. He went to the officer and told him we were starving.

"Officers get much better food than simple soldiers," the major confided. He told us to come in the evening when no one would be around. He would see what he could find."

Later, the major got us a large can of sardines, but insisted we tell no one. He could not feed everybody.

That night we feasted. I felt guilty to eat in secret when others were still starving, but we did what we had to do to survive. After eating I told my friends. "This food saved my soul."

Now, more conditioning. Shoot and drill. Shoot and drill. I'm ready, I thought, seething with anger. I hated the maneuvers. I thought we'd either starve or run out of ammunition before we fought.

In late November, several thousand soldiers were called together. Each soldier was given an injection for a wide spectrum of diseases: diphtheria, tetanus, and pertussis, plus others for typhus, smallpox, yellow fever and cholera. The shots were so massive in dosage that many soldiers fainted, some even fainted at the mere sight of the needle.

I was finally issued a new uniform, and sent back to the Chelm train station. This was another disappointment. The new uniform was not even as warm as my old clothes. I immediately regretted not having kept them, at least to wear under my uniform. I should have known better. This was typical of the Soviets.

On the station platform was a large orchestra playing classical Russian music. We entered the cars to the sound of Tchaikovsky's *1812 Overture*. The music crescendoed as the train rolled out of the station, the cannon shots supplied by real artillery. Many soldiers had tears in their eyes, as they stared proudly, if somberly from the railway cars. Some were so deeply inspired by the music that they actually wept as the train pulled out of the station. Even a non-Russian like myself felt adrenaline and patriotism coursing through his veins.

At the second and third stations down the line, there were also orchestras playing Russian martial music for us.

In the middle of these two stations, we had to get off the train to cross the Vistula River, between Deblin and Pulawy. All the bridges had been destroyed by the retreating Germans, so we crossed the river in pontoons, reboarding a different train on the other side.

At the third station, north of Radom and about fifty miles south of Warsaw, we stopped and got off the train. Lining up unit by unit, we marched past a platform holding a number of generals. Every unit yelled, "Hurrah!" as it passed the platform.

I was proud. It was a very fitting gesture for those about to fight the Nazis.

We continued marching for two hours down a dusty road until we came to a small wooded area. There we were divided once more and headed in the direction of the front.

By the time I arrived at Radom, the Russian Army had crossed the Vistula, but the offensive ground to a halt at the beginning of August while the Polish uprising in Warsaw was crushed to death by the Germans.

Many of us wondered if we had outrun our supplies. Were we indeed out of food, ammunition and fuel as some officers said? The soldiers were certainly exhausted. I had learned a great deal about the Soviet system during the two years Pohost Zagorodski was under Communist rule and this was easy to believe. The more cynical among us thought that Stalin just left the anti-Communist Poles of the uprising to their fate. I figured it was wiser to let the commissars worry about it.

***

Everything about this kind of warfare was new to me. I was surprised to see we were not forming up in the woods. This was more like what I'd heard about the First World War. There were foxholes and long lines of trenches dug in the earth. Each group was marched to a section of the line that they would defend. My group walked a mile before we were ordered down into a trench.

Again I was disappointed. I wanted to attack. I did not come this far to sit in cold earthworks. If I had known what I was letting myself in for, I probably would not have been so eager.

During the last two months of 1944, the Soviet lines on the Eastern Front were extensive—stretching from Memel on the Baltic to the mouth of the Danube in the south, a distance of over twelve hundred miles. With each major gain, trenches were dug and mines placed in "no man's land" to protect from a German counter-offensive.

"Where are our mortars?" I asked the first officer I saw.

"Mortars?" the officer said. Then he laughed. "No mortars here. We need infantry. Your group replaces the infantry that was wiped out in the last battle."

"But we were trained for mortars, sir," I replied, although after what I'd been through, I felt silly grumbling about anything in this army. This was heaven compared to that hell.

229

"Be a good fellow," the officer said, giving a solid pat to my shoulder. "No mortars for the time being. You're needed for the infantry."

We were sent down another half-mile of trenches where I was again surprised. A different officer pointed at a heavy machine gun called a *pulimiot*. I was assigned to handle the gun along with three sergeants, two Jewish and one Russian. The others in my group were sent further down the line to man bunkers built into the trench system.

I was made second in command of the weapon. Immediately, I was shooting at Germans. This was it. Now I loved the trench line. I could fire as fast as I could reload and as much as I wanted. There was no shortage of ammunition here, unlike how it was with the partisans, and most of the firing was at night, aiming at German lines only one hundred fifty to two hundred yards away.

After twelve days, I was so expert at the *pulimiot* that I was named the number one gunner. If I noticed the slightest movement from the German trenches, I would open up with a withering salvo of fire and wipe them out. It was at that instant that I was the happiest. "The moment they lift their heads above the trenches," I told the others, "they don't have a chance. I'll knock them off." The *pulimiot* became second nature to me. My commander said I was born to it. During the day, I ate and rested, during the night I fired the *pulimiot*.

The lines were so close, we had to always keep to the trenches, even to go to the kitchen to eat.

Sand from the trench walls would fall into the open containers of food when you walked back to your position. There was no choice except to brush off as much sand as possible, and eat the food.

If you walked on top during the day, the Germans would shoot your head off. The Germans had the same problem if they left their trenches.

There was one sector where criminals were taken out of jail and put in the front line as punishment.

These men would not walk in the trenches with their food. They walked on top. The reason was the Germans also punished criminals by putting them in the front line, and these two groups somehow got in contact and worked out a deal not to fire at each other.

When the Soviet command found out that nobody was shooting at the enemy in this sector, they became suspicious. When they found out about the deal, they sent the criminals to the back lines. So it still worked out in their favor.

At night, I walked back from the kitchen on top of the trenches—so at least I had my dinner sand-free. At night, we could walk out in the open, but anyone stupid enough to light a cigarette was a dead man.

Another aspect of the war that was new to me was the propaganda. The Germans broadcast Russian music across the lines. The soldiers loved the Prokoviev, Mussorgsky and pure Russian folk music until they heard the anti-Russian propaganda at the end, appealing to them to surrender and become well-treated captives with plenty of food instead of continuing to fight under such poor conditions.

A Russian sergeant told the newcomers, "Don't worry about it. Soon, we'll probably hear German music coming from our side telling the Germans how wonderful it would be for them to surrender to us and go to our luxurious gulags."

***

The night of January 2nd, 1945, the music was by Stravinsky. I looked at the enemy lines through my binoculars. I hoped the Germans would broadcast for a long time—it covered the noise of mine laying. This was the specialty of the sappers, or engineers.

Leading twenty volunteers, I crawled out of the Soviet trenches at midnight and made my way over the scarred, broken land to one hundred yards in front of my own lines. From this close I could almost read the lips of any German foolhardy enough to pop his head up over the fortifications. I remember thinking it was too bad I couldn't bring the *pulimiot* with me.

Looking from side to side, I could see the other men silently and painstakingly digging holes for the mines.

This new minefield was to be to a depth of one hundred yards. All anti-tank and anti-personnel mines had to be laid at night, with the mine-laying details within range of the enemy during the whole operation.

The nearest man to me got up on his knees and laid his mine in the hole he had dug. Moving forward on my belly, I crawled over to the man and placed a detonator in the mine. I carried the detonator capsules, while the rest of the men carried the mines.

There was a special pliers to place the capsules at the right depth inside the mine, but I never used it. I put the capsule in my mouth and placed it using my teeth, always at the right height. My lieutenant did not like it, thinking I would blow my head off, or worse according to him, the explosion would clue the Germans in to the work detail so that they could wipe out the whole unit.

It took too long with the pliers. Using my teeth it only took seconds— crucial seconds. There was no cover and we only had thirty minute intervals in which to place the mines. The Germans would rake our lines with machine gun fire every thirty minutes, so we had to lay all the mines in the

231

space between their salvos of fire. Also, we had to place the mines before daybreak.

You have to understand that sappers had the highest casualty rate of any specialization.

I reached into the worn green pack that held the detonators and pulled out a folded map. I penciled in the exact location of each mine, then, carefully refolding the map, I would put it back in the knapsack and crawl over to the next mine.

The mines had to be spaced close enough to each other to make certain nothing, neither tank nor man, could get through.

I had to precisely record every mine on the map in detail. I checked and rechecked. The faster I completed the job, the faster we could retreat back to the safety of the trenches. But I took enough time to make certain the map was correct, because this was not the most difficult part. Before an offensive, our task was to defuse and remove the anti-tank mines, thus clearing a route for the Soviet tanks to attack. I wanted to know exactly where to go. Our lives depended on it.

***

The attack on Warsaw was set for January 12th. As the jumping off point drew nearer, I was asked to lead a group of four commandos through the Russian mine field.

These were hardened combat soldiers who were specially trained and better fed than most of the Soviet soldiers. They deserved it. Their job was to reconnoiter the area of attack and capture a live German officer and bring him back. The soldiers jokingly called the mission a *jazik*, which means "tongue" in Russian. The mission was a success if the interrogators could make the officer talk. Many of these missions were ambushed by the Germans and the men never returned.

Two days before the planned offensive, I took advantage of a thick fog that had began rolling in about ten p.m. I led the commandos safely through the Soviet mine field right up to the German minefield. Now came the hard part. Not only did I not have a map of the German minefield, but the Germans had developed a new type of mine that I was unfamiliar with. This field was saturated with the new mines.

As I felt my way through the German minefield, I experienced something I thought I had left behind long ago—fear. I could feel sweat dripping down the small of my back as I carefully probed the ground in front with my knife. Progress was measured in inches.

When we reached the end of the minefield, we quietly said our goodbyes. I turned around and crawled back to my lines. I never saw any of those men again.

Other such missions on the same night succeeded in bringing back live officers. Many talked and much information was garnered for the offensive; the different formations and branches of service, the order of battle, the fortifications, the armament, and the state of morale of the enemy.

***

On the eleventh of January, I went into "no man's land" once more. Again, we went under cover of night, and with the help of the map, located and uncovered the anti-tank mines, extracted the glass capsules, and then dug up the 10x10-inch boxes of dynamite. As each mine was unearthed, I stuck a little wooden stick in the ground to mark it for the tankers.

We did not touch the smaller anti-personnel mines. It was too hazardous. The main trick was to stay away from the smaller mines which, unfortunately, had been intermixed with the larger anti-tank mines for defense. The smaller mines were removed by special tanks, also at night.

"I can defuse the small mines," one man whispered to me. I couldn't believe it. Why would he even want to? He was a grizzled veteran who had fought and survived Stalingrad, so I guess he figured he was invulnerable.

"Don't," I warned him. "It's too dangerous." No one can be that stupid, I thought. We don't even have to touch those things.

But as I finished removing the capsule from another anti-tank mine, the man crouched down near one of the smaller mines. All of the other men moved back, as he carefully brushed the dirt away with his hands. He took the pliers and reached in to extract the capsule. The mine went off in a horrific explosion.

You idiot, I thought as I ran over to the soldier. What about the offensive? Now the Germans know we're doing something here. They'll be ready for us. And we haven't cleared all the mines. Damn it!

When I reached the man's side, what I saw made me sick. Both the man's arms and legs were gone. His face was shattered, blinding him.

Immediately, the German gunners started firing in the direction of the blast, endangering the whole group.

We all hit the dirt.

Hugging the ground, we pulled the wounded man back fifty yards through the German fusillade, then lifted him up to carry him back to the trenches.

He no longer could bear living. For two days, through a morphine haze and incredible pain, he kept begging his friends to shoot him. Finally, an officer obliged.

***

Barely had I returned when barrels of schnapps and vodka were delivered to the front lines. Everybody drank the liquor as though it was water. We were so hungry, the vodka took the place of food. After all, we joked, it was made from potatoes.

Soon after the last of the liquor was consumed, a great scream of "Hooray!" echoed up and down the line and crescendoed as the Russians rose out of the trenches and ran forward. The scream was both deafening and inspiring. Explosions from mortars and artillery sent up clouds of dust all along the advance, and the ground was torn up beyond recognition, as the Germans saturated the advancing army with everything they had. When the bombardment reached overwhelming proportions, the Russian line, as if one body, hit the dirt as if trying to disappear into the ravaged soil. When the salvos slacked off, they rose again, hurtling forward toward the Germans.

I advanced in the first wave of this body of men, my adrenaline surging over my semi-liquored state. I ran, crouched, dove into the torn-up earth, then pulled myself up and ran forward again, moving forward for a mile, before I felt like someone smashed me in the face. It was shrapnel. I fell to the side of the road, dazed. There was not much pain, and I could not understand why I was lying on the ground. I should be up, attacking the hated Germans. I put my hands underneath my chest and tried to push myself up. There was no strength in my arms and I collapsed back into the dirt. This close and no closer, I thought. No closer. I thought this was the weirdest feeling I ever had. The next thing I knew, I was being nudged awake by a nurse. She bandaged my face to stop the bleeding and moved on, leaving me for the stretcher-bearers to carry back to the rear of the battalion.

The doctors stitched up the wound and kept me in a field hospital for three days until they were satisfied my face was healed. I was then sent back to the front.

Through sheer weight of numbers, the Russians broke through the German defensive line. There had been four hundred men in my battalion before the advance. Over one-half were killed or wounded.

My first day back, I entered the outskirts of Warsaw. The city looked like a smoldering ancient ruin, ravaged by the passage of centuries. Even while the Soviet Army was crashing through their defense lines, the Germans were still using dynamite, flame-throwers and bulldozers to destroy what was left of the city after the uprising. Not a house was left standing. It was a burned-out wasteland. Just rubble, debris and crumbling walls. There were very few people left in Warsaw when the Soviets arrived.

CHAPTER 21

RETRIBUTION

After the liberation of the Warsaw ruins, the German retreat quickened in pace.

My battalion headed south to join the offensive at Czestochowa. As I entered that city, I saw the bodies of German soldiers crumpled on the ground in strange, twisted positions. Some of their faces were contorted in terror. I did not understand what could have happened.

I found out later that Soviet units had reached Czestochowa before us, and although there were still many Germans in the city, the Poles had taken heart and rebelled.

I heard a scream and looked up. A German soldier was being held at the window of a tall building. He looked terrified. Suddenly the soldier was shoved out into the air. He hurtled down a full six stories, screaming all the way. As I looked around, I saw others thrown from fourth and fifth floor balconies, some shattering glass as they crashed through windows. Some were already dead, but the live ones shrieked all the way to the pavement.

More and more German soldiers' bodies littered the ground as we went further into the city. The time of retribution had begun.

We proceeded cautiously along the streets, and carefully scanned the tops of buildings, especially tall church steeples. We walked in two single-file columns, one on each side of the street.

As we first entered Czestochowa, we were actually worried about being crushed under the weight of a falling German soldier, but as we went deeper into the city, the concern was more serious. Snipers.

Soon enough, a brief "pop" was heard. A Russian in front of me fell to the ground, dead.

The men immediately dove for cover. I looked around and was not really surprised that nobody seemed frightened. We were like robots in a stupor. We just reacted. No time to be scared. I was relieved. The fear I felt in the German minefield had left me.

We examined the taller buildings to try to spot the sniper. Sometimes, a sniper was careless, and we spotted his rifle poking over a ledge or out of a window. Sometimes, we saw his body as the sniper greedily looked to see what damage he had wrought. If we spotted him, we would try to find a

236

place that would give us a good angle for a shot, or we would go into the building, up to the top floor and kill the sniper there. If we could not find a vantage point, we called in the artillery to destroy the whole building.

A few times, we were out of luck. No one could spot the sniper. On one such occasion, I took refuge in a heap of rubble and gave hand signals to the men on the other side of the street. A sergeant nodded in agreement, then pointed at two of his best sharpshooters to hold their place. I did the same.

The majority of the soldiers cautiously started forward, while these four men stayed behind to watch the possible hiding places. When the sniper revealed himself to take another shot, they would try to kill him. If they were lucky, they would get him before he was able to kill another of our company.

Another "pop," and another soldier fell dead, but this time, the sharpshooters spotted the sniper on the bell tower of a church and opened up. The German fell dead to the ground.

The main body of infantry and mechanized units had moved on to continue the chase as soon as the German lines were broken.

My unit stayed in Czestochowa to mop up stragglers, small units of Germans who had been cut off during the offensive, and snipers—mostly tough veterans who called themselves werewolves and expected no mercy. The werewolves promised to take as many Russians with them as they could before they died. My unit made sure they died.

A lot of the other soldiers were taken prisoner, but many were also shot on the spot. Generally, large groups of Germans were taken as prisoners, while small groups or snipers were summarily executed.

***

After Czestochowa, my battalion headed towards the German-Polish border near Frankfurt-on-the-Oder.

Already tired from constant marching, advancing and the inevitable mopping-up duties, we were now assigned to mechanized units, meaning we had to keep up with tanks. It was extremely cold and there was a lot of fresh snow. We passed many Germans frozen in macabre positions on the ground. They had obviously frozen to death. Many Russians also fell by the wayside, and froze where they had fallen. There wasn't time to stop and help them. Each soldier was only concerned with his own fate, and that meant keeping up with the tanks.

My unit crossed into Germany southwest of Poznan with Zhukov's 1st Byelorussian Front and bivouacked in a burned-out house with no roof. The walls barely provided shelter from the wind. It was icy cold inside.

What did it mean for me to enter Germany after all this time, all this tragedy? I can tell you this: there was no exhilaration. No sense of triumph. We were numb, our bodies and our souls.

So we were a little bit closer to the end. Right now it was too cold to worry about. My feet were burning, they were so frozen. Personally, I was only concerned with getting and staying warm.

I remember telling my comrades, "I saw a bank back there, a few blocks away." "So what?" sniffed Kamerov, a Russian soldier who had become my friend. Kamerov and I were both rubbing our hands together and stamping our feet on the ground to keep warm.

Another friend, Kovsky, approached us. His teeth were chattering uncontrollably.

"Well," I asked them, "do you want to get warm?"

"Of course," Kamerov replied. "Do you think I'm crazy?"

"Gather around," I said to the others, some ten in all. I remember somehow grinning through my thin Soviet-issue scarf. I was so cold I'm surprised I could get my mouth to turn up in a smile. "We'll go to the bank." I paused for dramatic effect at this point. Then I added, "And we'll rob it."

"All right" Kovsky said. "So you're the one that's crazy. What good would it do us? We'll probably be dead tomorrow. Frozen like those corpses we passed on the way in. Besides, it's just more to carry. And the officers would probably steal it from us anyway. Hell. Where would we spend it?"

I started laughing. "We're not going to spend it, you idiot. It's most likely worthless. But Reichsmarks are made of good quality paper, and paper burns. We'll burn it all up and stay warm for the first time since we reached Radom. Can't you just feel it?" I said, as I rubbed my arms. I was visibly shivering. I stamped my feet on the ground once more to emphasize the point, but also to warm them up. I remember it was like stamping down on a steel floor, the ground was that frozen.

"Come on! Let's go," I said, and I motioned for them to follow.

Kamerov and Kovsky nodded their heads and laughed. All the soldiers followed my lead.

At the bank, Kamerov and I slammed our rifle butts into a boarded-up window, caving the wood in.

We pried off the boards still nailed to the window. I handed the wood shards to some of the soldiers. "This'll burn as well."

The safe was empty, but lying scattered about the bank's floor, were bundle after bundle of Reichsmarks, some new and still crisp, others old and crumpled—all green. Two of the men tore open a bundle and threw it in the air, laughing.

"Don't get so excited," I told them. "You can't spend it. Gather it up. Let's go back and make a good fire."

Back at the roofless house, we cleared the middle of the room and started the fire.

"Are you sure?" Kamerov said, hesitating to send the fortune up in smoke.

"It's worthless," I said, exhausted. "If not now, it certainly will be by the time we end the war."

To the crackle of the flames, we drew lots to see who would stand guard. The winners collapsed into a deep sleep. I was one of the lucky ones. I was so tired, I fell asleep with my machine gun under my head for a pillow, and woke an hour later so dazed it took me a few minutes to get my bearings. I looked around, confused. My machine gun was gone. I walked to another house that was also occupied by soldiers from my battalion, went inside and took a machine gun from another soldier who was asleep.

On the way back, I was amazed at how many soldiers lay asleep outdoors on the snow-covered ground. They had stopped and fallen from exhaustion. I wondered how many would still be alive in the morning.

The next day, as we marched forward, I saw smoke coming from the direction of our advance. The infantry ahead of us had put many of the small villages and hamlets to the torch.

A week later, my battalion received an official order that no houses should be burned in any of the towns. If they were destroyed by artillery, that was one thing, but to intentionally burn houses was strictly forbidden.

Hatred for the Germans, whether soldiers or civilians, seemed to mount with each step closer to Berlin. As I crossed a large bridge over a dry ditch, I happened to look down. I saw one hundred to a hundred-and-fifty Russian soldiers with their heads cut off. I could tell they were officers by the insignia on their uniforms. It did not take long for the whole battalion to know what was down in the ditch. They marched by silently, each man with his own thoughts. It did not take much to see why we hated Germans.

What were these people? These Germans. I just could not fathom it. I still can't.

The Russians were getting a good idea of what we went through.

Reaching a line of abandoned German bunkers that night, twenty of the men settled down inside. There were many open cans of food and all the men were tempted, but they had been warned never to eat food from an open can—the Germans were known to poison the cans and many Soviet soldiers had died from eating the contents.

Luckily for the starving soldiers, there were enough unopened cans of preserved beef, ham, and kraut lying around the bunker. After eating, most of the soldiers found cots to sleep on, while I organized the watch with guards changing every hour and a half. From time to time, I went out of the bunker, touring the perimeter to make sure no guards fell asleep. As I got up around two a.m., I thought I heard a noise coming from below the bunks. I hurried back inside to find my lieutenant.

"Sir, there's somebody here with us," I told the lieutenant.

"Bobrow," the lieutenant replied, both exhausted and irritated at being awakened, "we're all tired here. I'm sure it's your imagination. Go back to sleep."

But I could not sleep. After checking the guard once more, I went back to my cot, lay down, and listened.

The cots were supported by wooden platforms on both ends and elevated two feet over the floor, and consisted of twenty boards laid side by side stretching to the north wall of the bunker.

I heard it again, but couldn't quite make out what I was hearing. Damn it, I decided. If for no other reason, I'm going to find out what it is just so I can get to sleep.

I got up. This time, I went up to the lieutenant, took him by the arm and literally pulled him over to the bunk.

"I think this is hollow," I whispered, pointing to the boarded-up section beneath one of the elevated bunks. "Someone could hide under there."

The lieutenant motioned for me to move quietly away. Together, we gathered six of the others, using hand signals to keep things quiet. Everyone fixed bayonets.

Two soldiers got down on their hands and knees and crowded around the open end of the long bed of cots.

I shouted, *"Raus! Raus!"*

Soon, all the others joined in, jabbing their bayonets into the dark opening. The soldiers sleeping on top of the boards woke up not knowing what was going on.

A German officer sheepishly crawled out. I scrambled under the cots and reappeared dragging a radio.

The German had been left behind to spy on our movements and report them by radio.

After interrogating the officer to our satisfaction, he was taken outside, put up against a wall and shot.

"You know, Bobrow," the lieutenant said later. "If I ever doubt your eyes and ears again, you can take me out against the same wall."

***

As the advance continued, I was struck by the barrenness of all the German towns, small or large. They were devoid of men, all of whom had either run away or been killed. Only the women and young children were left. The older children had been drafted into Hitler's war machine.

240

The Russian soldiers began to steal whatever they could find, even chairs and pillows and cheap eating utensils. Rape was commonplace.

Just short of the Oder River, southeast of Frankfurt-on-the-Oder, most of the Russian Army units stopped and gathered. A general announced that anyone caught raping women would be executed. He said that rape was not the way to take revenge on Germany.

In spite of the order, the raping continued. The only thing that changed was that after raping, the soldiers killed the women and girls so there wouldn't be any witnesses.

***

As in any army, there were ambitious officers who wanted glory and advancement without caring how many of their soldiers were sacrificed in the process. You have to understand that the Soviets felt that the state was all that mattered. Individuals were only important in that they served the state. It seemed that it did not matter to our officers how many soldiers' lives were lost, as long as the state survived.

My major asked for volunteers to blow up a factory that produced rope. Naturally, I volunteered.

Taking five men and all the mines and dynamite we could carry, we headed to the front lines where we were stopped and brought to a colonel in command of a tank unit.

Finding out the nature of our mission, the colonel blurted out: "You must be crazy!" By now, I was having a few second thoughts about volunteering again as well.

"No. We're not crazy," I replied. "Our officer, Major Rashkow asked for volunteers. He sent us on this mission. It's pretty bad, isn't it?"

"Bad," the colonel said, incredulously. "It's murder, yours. That factory is heavily fortified. You'll never make it."

"Sir," I asked politely, seeing a chance that I could avoid this obvious suicide, "is it possible for you to call Major Rashkow and tell him that you are keeping us from executing our mission?"

I was nervous as the colonel asked his aide for a phone line to Rashkow. I thought I would probably be arrested for insubordination and sent to a gulag: this, if I was not shot. Rashkow would certainly not be pleased.

"I have a better way of blowing up the factory," the colonel said, adding pointedly, "without risking any lives of our soldiers."

I could almost hear Rashkow hemming and hawing, as he stalled to come up with a better rationalization for his plan, but in the end he had to agree. Above all, he was outranked.

Immediately after hanging up the phone, the colonel directed six of his tanks, their guns loaded with missiles, to line up facing the factory. They fired in unison for over an hour. The factory was completely blown apart, and not one Russian soldier had to risk his life.

I wished that I had had this officer for the whole campaign.

Later, I could tell that Rashkow was not too happy with his volunteers, but luckily, there was not much he could do.

Several days later, an enormous infantry battle started on the outskirts of Kuestrin, just north of Frankfurt-on-the-Oder, as the Russians began a new offensive.

Now that the combat was in their own country, the Germans fought over every inch like devils.

When the army reached the Oder River, I was transferred back to the sappers and ordered to report to the engineering headquarters. As soon as I arrived, my battalion again asked for volunteers. The casualties in the ongoing battle were so high that more reinforcements were needed for the infantry.

I took the remaining twenty men from my battalion. The rest had been wounded or killed.

Reporting to an infantry captain in a roofless, bombed-out house near the banks of the Oder, we were greeted with cheerfulness. They must really need us, I thought. That had not happened before.

"Well, boys," the captain said, "you may have arrived just in time for a massive German counterattack. Make yourselves at home, but be extra careful during the day," he warned. "This ground is full of sticky clay. The tanks can't move in it, and you won't be able to dig foxholes."

It was early morning, very crisp, and it looked like the cloud cover would linger. I had long since learned it was better to find out things for myself. I sent two men to boil water from some coffee grounds they had liberated from the Germans. Two men were sent to try and dig foxholes and I took the rest of the men to the woods near the house to find cover. I regretted it immediately. There was an overwhelmingly putrid smell. German and Russian corpses were lying all over the place. The battle was still going on and once more there was no time to bury the dead. Not being able to handle the sight or the smell, I led the men back to the command house. There, I learned from my men that it was indeed impossible to dig foxholes in the clay. I drank some coffee with the men, then walked behind the roofless house and sat against the east wall, quickly dozing off for twenty minutes.

While sleeping, I had a vision of my mother, Yentl. She came to me silently and smiled. Then I awoke and she was gone. The vision was so real,

I could not believe she was really gone. Somehow, I knew I would come out of this mission all right.

As dusk approached on that first night, I walked down to the banks of the Oder to get some water to boil. I smelled something foul—my stomach began churning with nausea. There, near the water's edge, were fifteen naked German women with bayonets sticking through their bellies. They lay pinned to the ground, with the rifle stalks standing up in the air. I could not tell how long they had been lying there, but I figured they were probably raped before they were murdered.

The corpses remained there for the duration of the campaign. Every night for ten nights I saw the still, decaying bodies. Nobody came to claim them or bury them.

As hardened as I was from the never-ending death and suffering, I felt an immense sorrow for these unfortunate women, no less innocent than other victims in the war. But every time I saw them, I could not help but think of how the Germans stripped naked the Jewish men, women, and children, *my own family*, lined them up, shot them and threw them in pits like they were worthless chattel—along with all their other victims. Now our soldiers were paying them back, I decided.

As darkness fell, the firing from the German side, which had been sporadic toward our position, increased from both small arms and artillery. The counterattack was starting. Germans were advancing across the river in small boats. Their artillery fire was so intense, we could hardly look up to shoot. By the time it lessened, the German infantry was starting to beach on our side of the Oder.

The captain called us all into his headquarters and suggested we split up into groups of three, spread out and try to stop the German advance.

When I emerged from the house, there were already new casualties from machine gun fire lying on the ground.

My group fired a few rounds, but there was no good protective cover. We quickly started pulling back to the woods, and then another mile, where we remained, hugging the ground behind some pine trees and purposely mingling our bodies with the many corpses lying there.

The German counterattack was a success at first. In the darkness, two hundred infantrymen of Busse's Ninth Army advanced right around the three of us as we pretended to be part of the dead, and bypassed us.

I remember slowly turning my head to follow the movements of the Germans. I could hardly believe what I saw. The two Russians were raising their weapons as if to fire at the rear of the Germans.

"Are you crazy?" I whispered frantically. "There're over a hundred of them. We're just three."

243

By the time the Germans were two hundred yards beyond us, my comrades surprised me again.

"Then I'm going to surrender," one of the Russians said.

"I'll surrender as well," the second Russian said, sniffing, "or we'll die for sure."

As they started to stand, I nudged the first one in the ribs with my machine gun barrel. I knew that if I surrendered, I would be executed on the spot as a Jew.

"Get down," I commanded. "If either of you tries to surrender or even makes noise, I'll shoot you both."

The Russians hunkered back down, knowing by the look on my face that I meant it. All three of us remained lying in the mud by the trees, not budging for three hours.

Then, massive firepower emanated from the Russian side. After having advanced over two miles, the Germans began to retreat. Again they passed us, this time at a run, with most of the Russian Army pressing them.

Following our own army, we made it back to headquarters. Grenades had been thrown into it, further demolishing the house. By some miracle, the captain and two others only suffered wounds, but the captain was in shock. He did not even know where he was.

The Germans had left behind two artillery pieces. We did not have any grenades to blow them up with, so we dismantled the guns and threw the parts into the Oder.

When replacements arrived at the front, we volunteers were sent back to the sappers. Only eight were still able to fight from the original twenty volunteers. Of the other twelve, some had been wounded, but most were killed.

***

I want you to know, I always volunteered, no matter what the task or how dangerous the offensive. It was not because I was so brave, it was for two reasons: I still needed to pay back the Nazis, and I thought, as a Jew, I had to be better than the rest. I always felt I had to prove myself to them.

***

If I took a nap and dreamed of my mother before a mission, I knew I would not be hurt. As strange as it sounds, the only time I did not dream about her or see her in a vision, was the time I was wounded by shrapnel, outside Warsaw.

Back at engineering headquarters, twenty amphibious vehicles had been shipped up to help move across the soft clay. They were slow moving and could not move at all in the daytime.

The Germans still had plenty of fighter aircraft to attack anything that moved during the day, and the amphibious vehicles soon became known as death traps. Nevertheless, after being loaded with pontoons, they moved slowly to the banks of the Oder.

Kuestrin was the next target. It was situated where the Oder and Warta met, and had been a fortified strategic town as far back as Frederick the Great's day.

The objective of the new offensive was an impregnable citadel built on the island of Kiertz, virtually in the middle of Kuestrin at the juncture of the two rivers. Kuestrin had always been known as the gateway to Berlin, only forty miles away to the west.

Can you imagine how we felt? We were only forty miles from Berlin, and the end. I could taste it. It made me work even harder.

Russian troops already occupied a beachhead on the west side of the Oder, but were in danger of being thrown off if reinforcements did not arrive soon, and the Soviets did not want the fortress standing intact at their rear.

When the pontoons arrived, we volunteer engineers off-loaded them and dragged them down to the river. We slipped the pontoons into the icy March water one by one, and, wading waste-deep into the river with them, began to fasten the floats together, until they stretched to the beachhead. Next, we rolled out a metal track over the pontoons, until we had a bridge that was sturdy enough to hold tanks.

When I reached the beachhead with the other engineers, Major Rashkow approached me.

"Bobrow," Rashkow said in his usual serious monotone, "we need people to row the troops over and we need people to steer the pontoons."

"Yes sir," I replied, giving Rashkow a crisp salute.

"Each boat will have two men. Pick someone to take with you," Rashkow said, then he marched off to secure more volunteers.

The assault was scheduled for daybreak. The Soviets started the offensive with a massive artillery bombardment, mixed with smoke shells to cover the crossing of the troops. The wind had come up during the night and the current was known for being powerful.

A half hour before dawn, sitting at the stern of my pontoon, I watched as thirty soldiers in full gear came aboard. Other troops pushed the pontoon into the surging water of the Oder River.

I had long been experienced in rowing boats. I figured the pontoons were pretty much the same as the boats I used to row on the Yashelda. More importantly, I knew how to handle boats in strong currents. Giving orders to the soldiers to coordinate the rowing, I steered the boat upstream so the current would take us to the right position on Kiertz. My pontoon was the first of thirty to reach the island.

We were ordered to stay with the boats on the Kiertz beach in case there had to be a sudden evacuation, but soon, forty German soldiers who had surrendered were marched down to the beach.

I remember looking at them. Not one of them was over sixteen. What looked like stubble on their faces was actually dirt and all of their uniforms were too big. They should have been in school. But there was no time for sympathy. They were still Germans.

"Get in the boat," I ordered in German.

The prisoners crowded into the pontoon. I sat on one side and the Russian soldier I had picked was on the other. We both trained our automatic weapons on the prisoners.

The Russian soldiers who had escorted the prisoners to the shore pushed the pontoon out into the Oder.

"You people pick up the oars and row," I ordered the prisoners, again speaking in German.

"We don't know how," one of the Germans replied.

I knew what they were thinking. If they did not help row against the current, the pontoon would drift down the river to the other side and German territory.

"If you don't help," I said threateningly as I patted my gun, "I will shoot each and every one of you and toss you over the side. You are less than nothing to me. I'm ready to start now."

The young soldiers stared at me, trying to decide whether it was a bluff, or even if they should rush us and try to take over the boat.

Sensing their indecision, I fired a short burst over their heads. Immediately, they picked up the oars and started to row against the current and the boat headed further up the river.

At this point, the Oder-Warta was over half a mile wide. When I judged we were far enough out into the river, I maneuvered the boat so the current would carry us back to the Russian lines.

We were the first to bring our pontoon back with prisoners, and were greeted by a tall, slim, handsome man in a full-length brown leather jacket, General Vojenkov, who ceremoniously kissed both of us on our cheeks in the Russian manner.

"For this accomplishment you'll receive one of the Russian Army's highest decorations," Vojenkov said, appreciatively patting both of us on the back.

"Please follow me to the field kitchen. Heroes deserve a hero's meal."

We smiled broadly and followed our benefactor. A real meal was better than any medal.

Later, Vojenkov went to the third floor of an apartment building that was the tallest structure in the sector. It was the same lookout that the Germans used when they controlled the area.

As I sat in the general's quarters eating the finest meal I'd had in years, I heard a single shot. Somehow I knew. We stopped eating and ran out of the general's cabin. Soldiers were running up to the tower. We followed them and found the general slumped over, his binoculars still cradled in his hands. A German sniper had shot him through the head. Vojenkov was one of the most popular Soviet generals. I realized what had happened. The Germans had used that same tower for observation, so when they evacuated, a German sniper must have sighted in the same observation window they had previously used, and waited until he saw a high-ranking officer appear.

The Russian soldier and I no longer had any appetite for our "heroes meal."

CHAPTER 22

ON TO BERLIN

The island of Kiertz was mostly flat with only meager rolling hills. One lone tree, a giant pine, still stood as if in defiance of the merciless, endless bombardment. All others had been knocked down, severed, smashed.

The object of the offensive was to take the heavily fortified citadel that commanded the center of the island. This battle for Kiertz raged on for ten days.

At night, we engineers ferried pontoons of replacements to the battle zone through shellfire that dogged us the whole way. Coming back, we brought prisoners, wounded Soviet soldiers, or boatloads of dead.

This went on for eight never-ending nights.

Most of the reinforcements came from Moldavia, and although I found them to be good, warm-hearted people, I learned they were not the best fighters. They suffered tremendous casualties. When one of the Moldavians was wounded or killed, many of them would literally gather in a group to lament. This gave the Germans the opportunity to rake the whole group with machine gun fire.

I saw ever-increasing numbers of wounded and dead Moldavians transported back to the beachhead. It was terrible. But I had become hardened. I felt bad for the poor devils, but we were here to win a war.

On the ninth day, the Russians brought in replacements from Siberia. The Siberians were young and strong and spoiling for a fight. They kept advancing no matter what happened. Two days after their arrival, the fortress was taken and occupied.

***

Once Kiertz had fallen, an offensive was prepared to finish Kuestrin. At midnight, I was sent with a detachment to clear a passage through the minefield protecting the Russian lines.

Before Frankfort-on the-Oder could be attacked, the right flank on the road to Berlin had to be secured. Kiertz was the start of the operation; Kuestrin would finish it.

Two hours before dawn, a massive artillery barrage began to pound the German positions.

Barely back from the minefield, I sat for a few moments in a deep trench, drinking a rancid cup of coffee. When the bombardment stopped, it would be time for us to attack.

While I waited, I watched my friends, the veterans, and the mostly new, unknown replacements. They talked about many things: women, food, sleep, the end of the war. Some of the replacements worried about being crippled or blinded. Some of them still thought that war was glorious. They would learn soon enough.

Many of us smoked, vodka was doled out by the officers. I drank my portion. It soothed the nerves.

Virtually no one worried about death. People die like flies, we veterans thought. No one cared. No one worried. At least no one admitted it.

There is an old Yiddish expression: "Everybody knows what happened yesterday, we know what is going on today, but nobody knows what will happen tomorrow."

Death would be a relief, I thought—an end to all this struggle and sorrow. But I knew this would not yet be my fate. While I waited in the trench, the vision of my mother returned. It seems so strange now, but I swear it. Once more I knew I wouldn't be harmed.

The Germans returned the bombardment with salvos of their own, but they were very weak in our sector. So inured were the soldiers to the bombardment that no one even felt the need to cringe or duck.

A horrific thumping seemed to echo in my chest as the very ground shook from the Russian shells.

How could anybody survive this, I wondered? Hardened as I was, and with good reason to hate the Germans, I felt pity for the enemy involuntarily arising. No one, not even those barbarians, should have been made to go through that hell.

The barrage lasted until the break of day. Then the infantry started forward, climbing the dirt steps built into the trenches.

I moved forward, crawling from crater to crater, scrambling from wall to wall, never exposing myself too long to enemy fire. There were many bombed-out buildings and rubble. We used them for protection from the German artillery, which grew in intensity as we advanced.

No matter how well the Soviets took cover, or how carefully they advanced, many fell during the push forward. I knew that thousands of soldiers were dying on both sides. In front of me, to my left and right, I saw them fall. I'd never seen so many of our men go down. Just keep going, I told myself.

When we got to the western suburbs of Kuestrin, German artillery fire rained down on us. A radioman called for help from the mobile *Katyusha* multiple rocket launchers to respond.

I recognized the sound of our own artillery shells coming over and cheered. Hundreds of Russians cheered. Then we realized the mistake. The missiles were dropping too soon. They hit our own positions. Many Russian soldiers were killed by our own *Katyushas.*

This was too much—being shelled from both sides. I ran into a house and jumped down the stairs to the basement. Five other Russians followed me to get out of the worst of the bombardment.

We sat and listened. There was nothing else to do. The ceiling and walls above us shook, sending debris and plaster down on our heads. It didn't take long for us to get used to it. If you were still alive by this time, you could get used to anything. And it was certainly safer than being out in the open.

One of the Russian soldiers, named Soniev, started exploring the house. He collected some trophies and ladies' clothing he found lying on the floor in what appeared to be a storeroom, and made a little package.

"What's that for?" I asked him.

"My sister and I are orphans," Soniev said. "We can't get things like this at home. If I survive, I want to take these things to her."

We stayed for several hours until the clamor and shaking diminished in force. It was time to go out and search for our unit.

I had no idea if anyone else had survived. It seemed as if there could not be anyone else alive in the world. There was a hole high up in the cellar wall, close to the ceiling. I placed a wooden chair next to the wall and used it as a ladder. From there, I pulled myself up a heating pipe to the hole to look out.

One of the Russians cautiously walked up the steps. He crawled through the debris, and was just clear of the building, when a German sniper shot him between the eyes. I saw him fall.

"What now?" another Russian asked. Before anyone could answer, Soniev put down his package and started to walk up the steps.

I slid back down the pipe. "Where are you going?" I asked excitedly.

"I'm going to pull him in."

"Don't do it," I said. "There's a sniper."

"He might still be alive."

I grabbed him by the arm, trying to restrain him. "Just give me five minutes. I'll try to figure out where the sniper is. I've done it before," I pleaded.

Soniev wouldn't listen. As soon as he poked his head out of a window on the first floor, the sniper shot him through the head. The package never left the basement.

Now the artillery fire began again, from both sides. Even without the sniper, it would have been impossible to leave the basement safely. There were now only four of us left, and we were all hungry.

With nothing to do but wait, I started to look around the cellar. After a few minutes, I found a wounded goose hiding in a corner. There was also some coal, and one of the men found some liquor that no one could identify.

Butchering the goose, I started cooking it over a fire that the others built.

I warned them not to drink the liquor because it could have been poisoned, but the others did not care. They mixed it with water, boiled it over the fire, and let it cool.

Everyone took a small drink and immediately fell into a deep slumber.

When we woke up, it was daybreak and the goose was burned to a crisp.

My stomach growling with hunger, I climbed up to look through the hole in the wall. I was concerned that the sniper, if he had survived the barrage, still had the door upstairs sighted in. I strained to see any movement, or shadow, or rifle barrel. All I could see were shell craters. There were virtually no buildings left standing. It was strangely quiet, eerie, as if both armies had packed up and gone home.

"I think the sniper left, or was killed," I whispered back to the others.

We cautiously left the building and looked around the rubble for twenty minutes. There was nothing to see. Then we headed in the direction of Kuestrin. After an hour's walk, we saw a large trench filled with soldiers from our battalion. With huge smiles on our faces, we ran over and hugged every soldier we knew.

***

There had been seven major defensive lines stretching from the Vistula back to the Oder. Now there was only Frankfort-on-the-Oder, and my battalion was mercifully excused from that operation.

Instead, Major Rashkow came in front of the soldiers and announced a well-deserved and long overdue rest as we waited for replacements.

***

Two days later, on April 15th, Rashkow once again came before our troop of engineers. Some long rest.

"Tomorrow, we head to Berlin," the major said. There was a solemnity and pride in his voice that we had never heard before.

A hush fell over the gathered soldiers. Each one knew that the end was in sight. The hush became a murmur. The murmur grew louder and louder, and finally exploded into an ear-splitting "Hurrah!"

The sappers would accompany the new Soviet tanks, the T-34s, nicknamed "white bears," because they were huge and fast, like the Siberian polar bear.

Two sappers would ride on every tank as mine sweepers, and two other soldiers would ride as machine gunners. If there were evidence of mines, such as a blown-up jeep or horse-drawn cart, the sappers would jump off the tank and run their sweepers over the ground like vacuum cleaners. When they came upon anti-tank ditches, their job was to pile logs into the ditch so the tanks could ride over them. The lead tanks carted the logs. The soldiers with the machine guns were there to guard against infantry attacking with hand grenades.

On my tank, the other minesweeper was a forty-year-old man from White Russia. His face was sunburnt even this early in the spring, and his hair had turned white long ago.

When we started forward on the 16th, the artillery from both sides was so devastating, I thought it was greater than the bombardments from all my previous battles. The air rolled like thunder, and *Katyushas* screamed overhead leaving long trails of smoke.

"Heaven and earth are turning," I shouted at the other minesweeper, but he could not hear me.

There was such a tremendous, thick dust; we could not see an inch ahead of us. The White Russian ripped his shirtsleeve off to make a scarf to cover his nose. I did the same.

Opposing tanks got mixed up with each other, sometimes firing on their own comrades.

After advancing about a mile, both machine gunners on our tank were hit by small arms fire and fell dead off the tank. The other man and I moved behind the turret.

Suddenly, the T-34 stopped. We jumped off and hurriedly started to dig a foxhole. The tank was too big a target.

The colonel in command opened the hatch and jumped down as well. As soon as we had our hole deep enough to provide a reasonable amount of safety, the colonel crawled over on his belly and ordered, "You crawl out and let me get in there."

I was so used to orders that I did not give it a second thought. I rolled out and started to dig another. It was only when I was safely in my new foxhole that I thought, if I ever see this guy in civilian life, I'll teach him a thing about courtesy and digging.

We stayed hunkered down in the foxholes for over a half-hour, and then the tremendous barrage started to ease up. The colonel climbed out of his hole and started to board the tank.

"Get up," he said imperiously. "Get on the tank. We're moving forward."

We brushed the dirt off our clothes and followed his orders, again crouching behind the turret to avoid enemy fire.

By now it was dark. I could see the tracers from the enemy fire heading straight for the tank. Most of the shooting was from small arms and bounced harmlessly off the armor. The White Russian could not follow the tracers as well as me, so I spent most of the night moving the man from side to side to avoid the machine gun fire.

"If it wasn't for you, Bobrow," the man said over and over, "I wouldn't be alive."

In two more days, the Soviet Army approached the outskirts of Berlin. The fighting had been cruel and vicious the whole way in, and was expected to worsen as we closed on the city. The small streets of the suburb were clogged with refugees running from Berlin, which was being bombed incessantly by allied planes.

The tank stopped and the colonel opened the hatch and emerged. He talked into his radio. "Sir, there are women and children everywhere, wagons, bicycles, horses and motorcycles, all blocking our way. They're fleeing the city."

I could hear the voice coming through the radio. I was amazed. "Don't pay any attention," the voice of the commander rang through. "Push them aside. We must get into Berlin. Keep going until you reach Berlin."

The colonel went back down into the T-34, closing the hatch behind him. The White Russian and I, still on top and exposed to sniper fire, were both astonished. As the tank started plowing forward through the ill-fated refugees, we both edged to the front of the tank. Shouting and waving frantically, we tried to warn them to get out of the way. So clogged was the road, that there was little room for them to move.

We knocked on the turret. I screamed, "What are you doing! We're not Nazis! We're not butchers like them."

I felt my guts churning inside, my heart hammering in my throat.

The hatch remained closed and the tank moved on.

I edged back to the front of the tank. "Get out of the way!" I screamed at the terrified people in German.

For three miles, the tank drove over horses and wagons, people walking, people on bicycles; blood spurting all over.

Finally I sat, head down, sobbing hoarsely, not caring if I was killed or not.

At the boundary of Berlin, an enormous tank battle erupted. As my T-34 reached the second street inside the city line, I felt a jolt as the tank was hit by a shell from an anti-tank weapon, called a "Panzer Faust."

The tank immediately caught fire. The acrid smell of expended munitions filled my nostrils as the White Russian and I grabbed our weapons and jumped. The colonel and the driver and gunner were incinerated as the tank went up in flames.

I was only sorry I had left a bag inside that had pictures from home. Still, I felt pity for the colonel and others.

Following behind the other tanks, we helped clean out the snipers that were firing down from windows of the few remaining tall buildings.

Later, running into some soldiers from the 38th Battalion, we were pointed in the direction of headquarters, two blocks further down the street. There, we were reunited with others from the battalion at the field kitchen.

At dawn, a captain came up and pointed toward the Reichstag. There was a heavy mist on the ground, in some places reaching as high as the men's waists.

Even though the Reichstag was only a few blocks away, it took two hours of desperate fighting to get there. We went forward from building ruins to heaps of rubble. There were mines and snipers. We had to climb over vast amounts of rubble, and barbed wire. Allied planes were still dropping bombs. Halfway to the Reichstag, the screech of a falling bomb scattered everybody into the ruins, but the captain and a woman captain standing nearby were too slow to react and were killed. As in so many instances in this war, the bodies were left where they fell.

Now, before us was the Reichstag. To a man, all the Soviet soldiers stopped advancing. They stopped scrambling from building to building. They stood upright and stopped hiding from snipers. They stopped their slow, cautious movement forward. This hated building symbolized to them all the suffering of the past five years, all the loved ones who had been killed, all their deprivations, the devastation of their beloved country.

Now we rose with one determination and rushed across the Konigsplatz through a murderous fire, directed at us not only from the Reichstag itself, but also from the Tiergarten and Opera House. At first, we were beaten back by the heavy machine gun fire and artillery.

At one p.m., a fierce artillery barrage from Soviet tanks, artillery and *Katyushas* smashed down on the Reichstag, throwing up clouds of smoke. Three battalions of infantry charged across the Konigsplatz, over a deep, water-filled anti-tank ditch and into the ruined building, hurling aside or mowing down the defenders. Using knives, rifle butts and bayonets, savage hand-to-hand fighting broke out.

German banners with the eagle and the swastika were torn down, spat upon and set on fire. The red flag of the Soviet Army was hoisted to the top of the devastated Reichstag.

The Reichstag was taken, but the intense fighting for Berlin continued. By now, I thought it would never end.

Hours passed, as we painstakingly advanced beyond the Reichstag. Suddenly, loudspeakers began a loud drone. Everything fell silent, as though everyone, defenders and attackers alike, hoped for some kind of reprieve from the horrific toil of battle.

The artillery ceased, small arms fire stopped. Looking up through the clouds of smoke, I saw wisps of blue sky. Planes were doing victory rolls instead of dropping bombs.

The whole time we were advancing through the outskirts of Berlin up to the time we reached the Reichstag, the ground was shaking from the bombs and artillery, continually vibrating like a constant earthquake. Then suddenly, voices blared on loudspeakers all over the city, announcing it was over. Berlin had surrendered. The shaking stopped. It was May 2nd, 1945.

We had taken Berlin, I thought. It's over. Now the hardest part begins. I sat down and cried.

For four years I'd tried to keep everything back, deep within my being, by never thinking, never stopping, by volunteering for everything, even the most dangerous, suicidal missions. Now I had time to think, to remember. We all did. We had to put our lives back together. But how many pieces were missing, I wondered—never to be recovered? *How was I going to do that?* First, I must find my father and Julia, and apologize to Label.

While the soldiers ate, people started emerging from what was left of the houses. The field kitchen was about half a mile from the Riechstag, east of the Brandenburg Gate, on the Unter den Linden.

A haggard, frightened looking man walked directly up to me and waited patiently until I finished and stood up.

"I am Jewish," he said in a weak, sad voice. "So are you. Correct? I've been hiding in a cellar for a very long time. Could I have some food for myself and the others?" The man kept his eyes downcast.

"There are Jews still left in Berlin?" I asked wearily, handing the man some bread.

"I know of, perhaps, three hundred. I'm not sure. Most of them are in mixed marriages," he added, greedily tearing at the bread with his mouth.

I gave him enough food to take back to the cellar to share with his friends. I was too tired to be amazed that Jews had survived the entire war hiding in Berlin.

Now, all was quiet except for a few shots fired from windows. The snipers took the last shots for Germany. The Soviets found them and put an end to the shooting.

The day after the surrender, Major Rashkow marched up to our makeshift camp, summoned the troops and commanded us to follow him. I looked at him closely. It was the first time I saw Rashkow even come close to a smile.

The major led us to a subway on Wilhelmstrasse, near many SS warehouses and close to the underground bunkers where Hitler and Goebbels committed suicide. As we went closer, I couldn't help but notice a sickening putrid smell.

"A lot of Germans are hiding down there," Rashkow said, pointing to the subway where many soldiers, especially SS, were hiding like rats.

At the surface, near the entrance were hundreds of dead bodies of Germans piled high like mountains in the middle of the ruins. They had been doused with gasoline and set on fire.

Forcing ourselves to ignore the ghastly sight and smell, we lined up in two columns while Rashkow and the other officers yelled through loudspeakers for the Nazis to come out.

It was not long before I heard the slow, muffled tramping of feet. As the Germans emerged from the darkness in twos and threes, they were made to take off their shirts.

We looked under their right arms to see if they had numbers or insignias tattooed. Those having numbers belonged to the SS. They were told to go in one line, to be dealt with in accordance with their deeds; the others, without tattoos, were sent to another line.

This was the greatest moment of my life. How tall and powerful the Nazis had looked four years ago when they had so arrogantly marched into Pohost Zagorodzki. Even the smallest of them had looked six feet tall. Now I was the one they were looking up at. Now I was a witness to the destruction of this horrendous evil, of a world turned upside down. I will never forget.

***

Papa let out a loud sound like "whoosh." His whole body slumped in his chair. The sun had long ago departed and we had missed dinner. Mama had gone to bed hours earlier.

I don't think I ever saw Papa so exhausted. Bill ran into the kitchen to grab some biscuits, cookies and milk, but I guess I was the relentless one.

"What about—?" I started, but Papa cut me off before I could even finish the question.

"Tomorrow, Jerry, tomorrow."

THE SEVENTH DAY

CHAPTER 23

REUNION

The engineers were billeted in the Russian sector of Berlin. Our post-war tasks were to stockpile and inventory mines, mine capsules, mine sweepers, automatic weapons, uniforms; anything left over from the engineering battalion.

After two weeks, I was demobilized and sent back to Pinsk. In the meantime, my father and Label had gone to Poland and found smugglers to take them over the border to Czechoslovakia.

I went back to the Pinsk ghetto I had visited on my way to the front. Pinsk was once more part of Russia. I had had enough of the Soviet Union and of Poland—there were enough unbearable memories in those countries to last me many lifetimes. I wanted only to reunite with Samuel and Label, and perhaps journey with them to Palestine as I had dreamed in my more innocent youth. But there was one person I did not want to leave behind.

I sought out your mother in the ghetto, but found she was living in a large house with four other families close to Poniatowski Plaza, across from Pilsudski's statue.

Still in my sergeant's uniform, I went to the door, walked in and called out, "Julia—"

When your mother appeared, I walked up to her, put my arms around her and kissed her on the cheek. For the first time in many years, I thought, a reunion is a happy occasion, and not filled with tears.

The war had made me a no-nonsense, matter-of-fact man. I remember thinking, if she says yes, I would be eternally grateful, and if she said no…well, I would be sad, but I would wish her the best and be on my way. My hands still on her slender waist, I searched deeply into her eyes as if to see the answer, and asked, "Well, are you ready to leave for Poland?"

This was a day Julia later told me she had dreamed of, ever since I had pulled her from the ice that night so long ago when little Avremel had clung to her hand to keep her from vanishing in the water.

So many images flashed through Julia's mind. She remembered how her sister Esther, Shlomo's wife, had kidded her about me. She remembered weddings where they danced, family gatherings, seders celebrated together, canoeing, the owl, the lumberyard; so many ways our families were intertwined. Then, she thought of all the loved ones taken from her. How the year before I had disappeared into the vast Soviet Army and she had been certain that I, along with most of the soldiers, would never return. This was a day she never thought would come to pass. If the truth be told, Julia was still afraid to get close to anyone.

"With whom?" she replied, her heart beating in her ears, apprehension rising so rapidly, she could not even guess how she would reply.

"With me," I said.

"Yes," Julia said.

Then I hugged her tightly. Tears welled up in our eyes and we stayed, silently holding each other for a long time. Then we kissed. I know that both of us were wishing that our families could have been there to see this moment.

***

Two days later, we went to the local Soviet magistrate. I borrowed a ring from a friend. I was in my uniform and Julia was in her best dress, one of the only two she owned. There was no ceremony. We were pronounced man and wife.

Even though we were Polish citizens, we had to go to the government offices at Baranovich to get the correct papers to allow us to leave. It was impossible to emigrate from the Soviet Union. In Poland, it was also illegal to depart, but I knew we could pay smugglers to take us out.

The officer at the passport desk could not believe we wanted to go back to Poland. There were still anti-Semites there and pogroms had been recently reported. He thought we should stay in the Soviet Union for both safety and gratitude. After all he said, without the Russians, how would we have survived?

Julia answered, "We are grateful, but the only living relatives we have are in Poland."

I pointed proudly to my uniform. "I know how to fight."

The officer looked at us. Both of us felt he was studying us, trying to divine our true intentions. Then he smiled, nodded his head and stamped our papers in triplicate. Permission to leave was granted.

Outside, the sun was shining brightly on a crisp spring day. People were outside, walking about. We could hear the sounds of hammers and engines as people were starting to rebuild their lives and their homes.

The papers firmly in our hands, Julia looked solemnly into my eyes. "There is one place we have to go before we leave. I know you don't want to go, but I have to."

I could not deny her this request. So, early the next morning, we boarded the train to Parachunsk. Arriving in an hour, we walked down the old familiar road to Pohost Zagorodski.

Julia did not want to see the *shtetl*. She was only interested in a ravine on the outskirts of the city. It was six miles to the town, a little less to the ravine.

Our wedding had not been the joyous occasion she had dreamed of as a little girl. No relatives had been present, no father to give away the bride, no blonde little Aviva to be the prettiest flower girl. Tears of remembrance had poured down her cheeks during our brief marriage ceremony. So much had been missing.

Now, Julia felt the need to be in the presence of her loved ones' last resting place. She needed to share the happiness of her marriage with her family. She needed to be near them one more time. Julia prayed they would hear her.

At the top of the ravine we said the Kaddish.

"This is my worst place, and my dearest place," Julia said softly. "Sarah and Rachel, Esther, Leah and Avremele, Papa...you will always be in my heart and in my thoughts. Always."

I led her away, my arm around her shoulder.

We took the train back to Pinsk, and the next day, boarded a train for Lignicia in Poland.

***

It gets rather complicated from here on in.

Julia's Aunt Fradl and her family had been sent to Siberia because their son was a Zionist. Ironically, the punishment saved them from the Holocaust. Fradl moved back to Lignicia, less than forty miles from the Czech border, immediately after the war's end.

She was in contact with a sister, Esther, living in Brazil. Because they were all from the same *shtetl*, the Brazilian aunt had received a letter from my father, Samuel saying he and Label were in Ostia, eighteen miles southwest of Rome, and Esther relayed the information to Fradl.

The *Brichut,* a Zionist organization, sent young Israelis over to Europe to coordinate the Jewish survivors and bring them to Palestine any way possible. These people were not allowed into the Soviet Union. Zionism was illegal in the communist state.

Upon arriving in Lignicia and locating Julia's Aunt Fradl, my energy went into contacting these Israelis to find your mother and I a suitable smuggler.

Lignicia had been a German city before the war. Now it was occupied by the Poles.

It took almost a year before we could leave. By that time, we had been able to contact my father and brother in Italy. At first, we thought we might be able to leave legally, but as time passed, this hope began to fade.

Both Samuel and Julia's aunt from Brazil sent money through the mail to help us. It would cost fifty dollars for the smuggler to take us out. Then more money to leave Czechoslovakia.

For the time being, I worked as a guard at a Jewish orphanage. All these young children had lost their parents to the Germans. I had to carry a loaded rifle to protect them. One of my friends, a fellow partisan, had been killed while on guard duty at a Jewish refugee camp.

The Poles were not any less anti-Semitic due to the end of the war. The Soviet passport officer was right. It was still dangerous for Jews in Poland. Poles had often moved into Jewish houses and now refused to leave when the owners came back to claim them. Many Jews were killed trying to repossess the property they had lost during the war. Some Jews were killed by bandits and others were killed by ordinary Polish anti-Semites.

Once we had the money and had settled on a smuggler we thought we could trust, we took the bus southeast to Klestko, then east through the Jesenik Mountains to Peczkow, which was close to the border. You will never know how eager we were to get out of that place forever.

Leaving Peczkow that same night, we stopped a few miles out of town. Getting down from the bus, the smuggler guided us and four others across the last two miles of Polish territory, around the border checkpoints to the Czech side.

To my surprise, as soon as we got to the other side and so close to freedom, the smuggler handed us over to the Czechoslovakian police. Quickly, I formulated a plan in my head for both of us to run at the first opportunity, but your mother was much smarter and calmer than I was.

"These police will not send us back," she said. "I know it for a fact."

She was right. Instead, the police took us to their station in Javornik and made us the best coffee we ever had. It tasted like freedom.

Had the police been bribed I wondered? No. They felt compassion for refugees, born of their own experience under the Nazis. It must have been a "there, but for the grace of God," feeling I decided.

Making our way to Prague, we waited for the *Brichut* to arrange the next step to Austria. This turned out to be the simplest part of the journey. All we had to do was board a train to Vienna.

As soon as we arrived, we again made contact with the *Brichut*. Austria was a much more difficult proposition. Vienna's Displaced Persons camps were so crowded with refugees, on one night the only bed Julia could find was a bathtub.

We were then sent to Salzburg, where there were Jewish refugee camps, some holding as many as five to six hundred people, mostly concentration camp survivors. In the Salzburg camps, we had to sleep on rough, gnarled boards, and your mother swore that these beds were worse than any place she had slept during her whole time in the forest.

We ended up staying in the camp in Salzburg for almost a year, living on donations from the U.N. and packages from relatives. Everybody in the camp told us that we would be able to cross over to Italy legally, so once more we waited. During that year, Bill, you were born.

But my patience had finally reached its limits. No matter how many times we tried to get government approval, it was not forthcoming. Julia was now pregnant with you, Jerry, and I was determined to not have two children born in refugee camps.

From our first days in the Salzburg camp, some unsavory characters would wander in from time to time and casually make mention of smugglers who could take refugees over the border. I went to these people and asked them to introduce me to a smuggler I could trust.

Another fifty dollars was needed, and that took time to collect. A smuggler was found, not too suitable, but as far as I was concerned, he was better than nothing. The time had come to move. Soon, the smuggler had us on the road to Innsbruck, near the Italian border.

The smuggler was as disagreeable as the man who recommended him. The more I saw of the man, the more I distrusted him. I knew I would have to keep an eye on this fellow, but I kept telling myself he was better than nothing.

It was September. A dark clear night. We had never seen so many stars.

Luckily, there was no snow on the ground as yet, and it was quite warm for the Alps in early fall. The smuggler ushered us along with three other refugees aboard a bus. Getting to Italy was easy. The Austrians were not concerned with people leaving their country.

The bus followed the road right up to within a half mile of the frontier. Walking close to the border, we saw that the road ahead was strangely illuminated. The border checkpoint.

The Austrian smuggler now asked for his money. The other refugees handed the man his due. I hesitated.

"You either give it now or I take them," he said, indicating the other people, and then pausing for emphasis. "And leave you behind. This is the deal. The only deal."

Can I trust him, I wondered? I had planned to pay when we were safely on the other side of the border. Another surprise.

"You don't pay. Finish!" the smuggler said contemptuously.

Searchlights from the Italian border guard covered the road we were on. I could see we would have to go straight up through the mountains, probably over them. There was no way we could make it ourselves. I handed over the money. This left me with only a few dollars. The smuggler nodded and turned. He started up the mountain. I followed, carrying you, Bill, in a brown army blanket I'd tied around my chest like a backpack. Your mother joked that she carried one of the children as well, so I shouldn't think I was too important.

Not long after we reached the first crest, I noticed that the smuggler was hanging back, moving slowly, so I did the same. I handed you to your mother.

The smuggler slowed down to a crawl, then suddenly he turned to run. I sprinted after him. Closing in, I jumped and tackled the man. We rolled over the rough ground before hitting up against a ridge that broke our fall. I grabbed the smuggler firmly by the neck.

"If you try to run away again, I won't just catch you, I'll kill you," I said matter-of-factly. "This I promise. I could strangle you right here on the spot. Understood?" He knew I meant it.

We climbed for three days. Inching upwards to the tops of mountains, and sliding down over rocks on our backsides. We had only crackers and rye bread for food.

On top of one of the mountains was a little cabin that served soup and hot food to climbers and tourists.

We reached the cabin on the second day. The proprietor warned us that patrols often stopped at the cabin to eat. That night, the warning turned out to be true as four Italians from the border patrol stopped by around six in the evening. The landlord and his wife hid us all in the attic while the soldiers ate. Julia's biggest fear was keeping you quiet, Bill. But she knew the worst thing that could happen was we would be returned to Austria—a far cry from what would have happened if David's baby had cried out in the forest at the wrong time.

She nuzzled you and rocked you in her arms. You were a good boy. You never made a sound.

On the third day, we came down from the Alps, evading any customs posts. At the first town, there were a few people with cars waiting on the outskirts. They made their living transporting refugees.

I hired one of the drivers to take us through the infamous Brenner Pass to the Marano train station, where we took a train to Milan.

At the Milan Displaced Persons camp, the director placed a phone call to Ostia to a number I gave him. Immediately, my father and Label dumped some fresh vegetables and fruit into a bag, took a car to the Ostia train station and boarded a train to Milan.

Early the next morning, we thanked the director of the camp. One of the staff drove us to the Milan train station, and there we waited for an hour, Bill cradled in the same makeshift backpack in which I carried him through the mountains.

Tears, this time of joy, welled up in our eyes.

Julia sat down on one of the rough benches facing the tracks, but I could not sit still. I started pacing up and down the boarding area. Every time I reached the far end, I craned my neck to listen for the sound of the train, and tried to peer over the trees to the southeast for a column of smoke.

Finally, there it was. A thin wisp of dirty white smoke drawing nearer by the second. Soon, I could hear the clackity-clack of the train.

A whistle blew. It was the sweetest sound we had heard in years.

I ran back to your mother, grabbed her by the hand and pulled her from her seat.

"Abram," she cautioned, holding her swelling belly. "Remember the baby."

"Come. The baby will be fine," I said as I half-ran, half-towed Julia to the end of the platform.

As the train slowed its way into the station, we moved backward along with it, now your mother was jumping up and down with me. We were like two children trying to peer into the passing compartments.

"There they are!" I shouted as I spotted Label and my father through the compartment window.

We skipped along, waving and shouting until the train drew to a stop.

Before the conductor had managed to put the wooden step in place, Label leaped down onto the platform. He ran to me, enveloping me in his arms. Samuel followed, carefully walking down the steps, and hugged Julia.

Samuel took you from me, Bill, and rocked you to and fro. We were all crying, all except Bill. You gurgled and laughed as if, in your innocence, you could see a happier future.

Samuel walked over to the station ticket counter and purchased four tickets to Ostia. The stationmaster said the baby would ride his first train for free.

As we boarded the train, I could not stop smiling. I looked at my father and brother, my wife and baby and thought, I have a family again.

EPILOGUE

Some forty years have passed since the night my father finished his story. I have my own family now, and Julia and Abram have three grandchildren. Papa still has his nightmares and frequently sleeps on the couch, his arms flailing and his tormented voice crying out. Mama sometimes adds details, but for the most part, still remains silent, finding the past too painful to examine.

As soon as my parents reached the United States, they became more and more involved in the Jewish community. At first, after hearing the story, I couldn't understand why. Finally, on the day after my Bar Mitzvah I asked him. Mama overheard and before Papa could say a word, she said, "We already paid so high a price for being Jewish, how could we now give it up?" To this day they still go to Temple.

Papa continues to astound me. I remember Bill and I, and our younger brother David, who was born in the States, being amazed around the time our father sold the chicken farm and bought a furniture store across from a lumberyard. Papa, friendly to a fault, and of course, quite knowledgeable about the lumber business, began visiting the lumberyard and making friends. The biggest of the workers were fond of having arm-wrestling contests and constantly bugged him to take part. Of course Abram was much older, shorter, and more slender than the brawny lumbermen. He usually turned them down. But one day, after a lot of nagging, he agreed to arm-wrestle the biggest man at the yard. Our mouths dropped when our father took him down in a minute. The man was so embarrassed he wouldn't speak to Papa for a couple of months even though Pop tried to make amends by saying it was just luck. I guess he was awfully strong, just like his brothers.

But one episode, much more recently, had me gaping in wonder once more.

Not too long ago, my daughter came up to me, very excited, and asked, "Why did Grandpa do that?"

"Slow down." I said. "Do what?"

"You didn't hear? Grandma told me. Last week, Grandpa was driving down the street and he stopped at a stop sign and this man jumped in the car with a gun."

"What?"

"Yes and he pointed the gun at Grandpa and told him to keep driving. Grandpa didn't listen. He drove into the parking lot of a busy gas station where there were lots of people, stopped the engine and said in a very calm

265

voice, 'Get out of here before I break your neck.' The man was so startled he opened the door and ran away. How did Grandpa have the courage to do that?"

I thought for a while and wondered if Abram would categorize that under the heading "short-sighted," rather than courage.

I had no answer. "I think you better ask him," I suggested.

She came back to me a few days later with his reply. It was not courage or foolishness he told her with his usual candor.

"What was he going to do to me?" Abram asked. "I already died a long time ago, every time one of my loved ones was killed in the forest."

During World War II, tens of thousands of Jews escaped to the forests and fought in partisan units in Poland, Yugoslavia, Byelorussia, France, Italy, Lithuania, Slovakia, Greece and Russia. Many, like my father, fought and survived, but many more fought and died in the forests and had to be left where they fell.

THE END

Family Tree

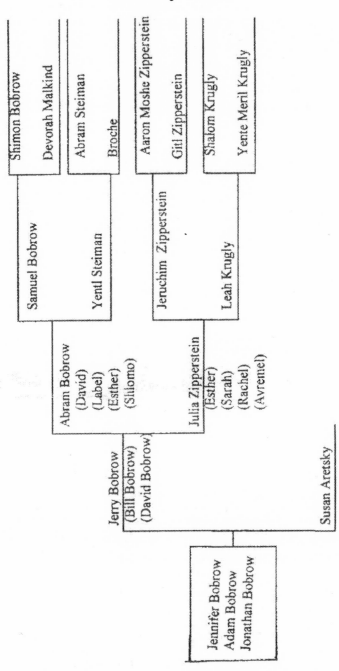

Descendant Report

David Bobrow
 Shlomo Bobrow (m. Shoshke)
  Shimon Bobrow (d. 1934, m. Devora Malkind)
   Label Bobrow (d. 1930)
   Moshe Aaron Bobrow
   David Bobrow
   Pesach Bobrow
   Hanna Leah Bobrow (Fialcov)
   Bashka Bobrow (Goodman)
   Menasha Bobrow
   Yankel (Jacob) Bobrow
   Unknown Bobrow
   Samuel Bobrow (b. 1889, d.1972, m. Yentl Steiman)
    David Bobrow (b. 1911, d. 1944, m. Shaindel)
     Shlomo Bobrow (m. Claudia Carlson)
      David Bobrow
      Alissa Bobrow
      Karen Bobrow
    Label Bobrow (b. 1913, d.2002, m.Pina Sokol)
     Helen Bobrow (m. Jeff Resnick)
      Elyse Resnick
      Hallie Resnick
     Carl Bobrow (b. 1945, m. Ruth)
      Howard Bobrow
      Renee Bobrow
      Sandy Bobrow
    Esther Bobrow (b. 1916, d. 1942)
    Shlomo Bobrow (b. 1918, d. 1941, m. Esther
     Zipperstein)
    Abram Bobrow (b. 1922, m. Julia Zipperstein)
     William Bobrow (b. 1945)
     Jerry Bobrow (b. 1947, m. Susan Aretsky)
      Jennifer Bobrow (b. 1978)
      Adam Bobrow (b. 1981)
      Jonathan Bobrow (b. 1985)
     David Bobrow (b. 1964)

Descendant Report

Aaron Moshe Zipperstein (m. Gitl)
  Lazer Zipperstein (m. Hanna Greenblatt)
    Yitzchakclabe Zipperstein
    Albert Zipperstein
    Eddie Zipperstein (m. Sarah)
      Esther, Leo Zipperstein
    Max Zipperstein (m. Molly)
      David, Lynne Zipperstein
    Jake Zipperstein
    Larry Zipperstein (Supperstein)(m. Leah)
      Jaime, Barbara Supperstein
    Sam Zipperstein
    Stanley Zipperstein (m. Yette)
      Faye Zipperstein
      Mike Zipperstein
      Marianne Zipperstein
      Milton Zipperstein
    David Zipperstein (Stone) (m. Juli (Ethel))
      Greta (Gitl) Stone
    Esther Leah Zipperstein   (m. Zedel Riterman)
      Yakov Riterman
      Bashke Riterman
      Boruch Riterman
      Sholom Riterman
      Ita Riterman
      Mayer Riterman
    Tzipe Zipperstein
    Sheih Zipperstein
    Freidel Zipperstein
      Dorothy Zipperstein (m John Boruchin)
        Isaac, Faye Boruchin
      Mula (Sam) Zipperstein (m. Ryea)
        Irenne, David Zipperstein
      Hannah Zipperstein (m. Leon Sturmwind)
        Jack, Gita, Harry Sturmwind
      Mayer Zipperstein (m. Anna)
        Ralph, Victor, Evelyn Zipperstein (m. Russ Albert)
      Rochel Zipperstein
    Blume Zipperstein (m. Motti Garbus)
      Yasha Garbus
      Fishl Garbus
      Unknown Garbus (female)
    Jeruchim Zipperstein (b. 1894, d. 1941, m. Leah
      Krugly)

Esther Fredel Zipperstein   (b. 1919, m. Shlomo
    Bobrow)
Julia Zipperstein (b. 1923, m. Abram Bobrow)
    William Bobrow (b. 1945)
    Jerry Bobrow (b. 1947, m. Susan Aretsky)
        Jennifer Bobrow (b. 1978)
        Adam Bobrow (b. 1981)
        Jonathan Bobrow (b. 1985)
    David Bobrow (b. 1964)
Sarah Zipperstein (b. 1925)
Rachel Zipperstein (b. 1925)
Avremel (Abraham) Zipperstein (b. 1929)

About the Author

Voices from the Forest — The story of Abram and Julia Bobrow is a story that had to be written. It is about the indomitability of the human spirit. As an experienced author, I wanted to write it myself, but couldn't. It was too draining, too difficult. I was too close. My good friend Stephen Paper came to the rescue. He was the perfect author to research and write this story. He had been searching for a story of not only survivors, but also fighters. His interest and knowledge of history in general, and the Holocaust in particular, gave him tremendous insight into not only the time period, but also the hearts and minds of those who resisted. His writing is strong, touching, sincere. I watched Steve labor for almost five years over every detail and careful revision to get the information and the story just right.

Thank you, Steve, and my parents thank you!

— Jerry Bobrow
April 20, 2002

WITHDRAWN

Printed in the United States
1475400007B/79-96

9 781403 355607